4-14

D1246775

D.W. Griffith's *Intolerance*

D.W. Griffith's *Intolerance*
Its Genesis and Its Vision

by
William M. Drew

McFarland & Company, Inc., Publishers
Jefferson, North Carolina, and London

Photos have been reproduced by permission of the following:

Kevin Brownlow and the National Film Archive:
 pages 13 (bottom), 24, 29, 38, 60

The Museum of Modern Art Film Stills Archive:
 pages 2, 21, 23, 26, 39, 40, 46, 56, 58, 66, 70, 72, 79,
 82, 92, 150, 156, 160, 162, 164

Marc Wanamaker and Bison Archives:
 Title page and page 13 (top)

Other illustrations are from the author's private collection. The advertisement on page 130 is reproduced by
permission of *The San Jose Mercury-News*.

Library of Congress Cataloguing-in-Publication Data

Drew, William M.
 D.W. Griffith's Intolerance.

 Bibliography: p.
 Includes index.
 1. Intolerance (Motion picture) 2. Griffith, D.W.
(David Wark), 1875–1948 — Criticism and interpretation.
I. Title.
PN1997.I5173D74 1986   791.43′72   84-43200

ISBN 0-89950-171-0 (acid-free natural paper) ∞

Printed in the United States of America.

McFarland   Box 611   Jefferson NC 28640

To Abel Gance, Frank Capra and Kevin Brownlow
whose encouragement enabled me
to pursue the study of film history.

Contents

Introduction

On a night in late summer, 1916, under the approaching shadow of war, D.W. Griffith first presented his epic motion picture, *Intolerance*, to the public at the Liberty Theatre in New York City. Prodigious in its dimensions, Griffith's masterpiece was the most spectacular achievement of the new medium of the cinema, perfecting every existing film technique into a dynamic, innovative structure.

A milestone in the history of the arts, *Intolerance* is a culmination of Griffith's cinematic genius which transformed the motion picture from an inventor's toy into a new art form. Unlike many of his other major works such as *The Birth of a Nation*, *Intolerance* is an original conception which does not derive from any direct literary source. Because of its advanced cinematic techniques, it became a paradigm for filmmakers throughout the world. At the same time, its power in projecting a social-historical vision provided a precedent for world epic cinema. Griffith's vision evolved not only from the facts of history and his previous works, but also from his knowledge of the arts. Thus, *Intolerance* climaxes a century of artistic activity in music, painting, theater, poetry and fiction even as it points the way toward the new experimental artistic language of the twentieth century.

In its interpretation of human events, the 1916 epic vividly reflects the social and political thought of its day. The film is imbued with the spirit of the Progressive movement which sought to fulfill the democratic promise of America set forth in Jeffersonianism. Indeed, the film's subsequent fate in the United States and in foreign nations provides a barometer of the social and political currents of the early twentieth century.

Upon the film's release, Archibald Henry Sayce, a distinguished scholar of ancient civilization, wrote the director:

> I had the pleasure of seeing *Intolerance* last night. It is an astounding piece, and it is not wonderful that it should have been so successful. I do not think that anything comparable to it has ever been staged before; it appeals equally to the historian, the poet and the student of modern sociology. Indeed, its appeal to the feelings is one of the most remarkable things about it.[1]

Years later, noted film historian Theodore Huff was equally enthusiastic, describing *Intolerance* as

> the greatest motion picture ever produced. In its original form and properly presented, it is a masterpiece of creative conception and execution which ranks with such works of art as Beethoven's Ninth Symphony, Rembrandt's *Descent from the Cross*, Da Vinci's *Mona Lisa*, the sculptures of the Parthenon, or with works of literature such as Tolstoy's *War and Peace*, the poetry of Walt Whitman or Shakespeare's *Hamlet*.[2]

Despite these accolades, some writers over the years have tended to disparage the film, acknowledging its technical importance but viewing its structure as unwieldy and its theme as confused. What has been lacking is a more extensive study of the film's meaning and intellectual lineage. Although there are innumerable accounts of the facts surrounding the production of *Intolerance*, facts which have become legendary in the annals of the cinema, there has been no detailed study of Griffith's treatment of historic events, the artistic and political influences that formed his vision, or the thematic relationship of the 1916 epic to his other works. Since this film is the key to Griffith's entire work, crystallizing themes featured in his other films, and a landmark in man's efforts at self-expression, it is the purpose of this study to discover, through a comprehensive analysis of its background, the true significance of *Intolerance* in the history of the arts.

William M. Drew
June 1983

1. The Man and the Art

When D.W. Griffith reached manhood, motion pictures were in their infancy. Largely self-educated, Griffith drifted into the film industry, transforming the medium into an art form that became a means to express a personal view of life. His vision was shaped, in part, by his experiences as a youth of the post–Civil War South and an aspiring actor traveling the United States with turn-of-the-century stock companies.

Early Life

David Wark Griffith was born January 22, 1875, near La Grange, Kentucky. His middle-aged parents, Jacob Wark Griffith and Mary Perkins Oglesby, instilled in him the heritage of a glorious Southern past that had long given way to the bitter contemporary realities of defeat and devastation. From his father, a Confederate Civil War veteran, western adventurer, and Kentucky legislator who created his own legend, David derived his taste for the romantic and dramatic. A farmer and an adherent of Jeffersonian and Jacksonian Democracy, Jacob Griffith also bequeathed to his son the spirit of individualism and self-reliance that characterized his own colorful career. From his mother, a devout evangelical Methodist, David gained his spiritual and ethical values.[1] His older sister, Mattie, a school teacher, kindled his passion for literature, engendered by his father's habit of reading classics aloud to his family.[2]

When David was ten, his father died, leaving the family poverty-stricken. Creditors confiscated the family's mortgaged farm, forcing the Griffiths to move to a farm owned by a relative. David attended a small country school at this time, a painful and unhappy experience for him, as he remembered years later:

> Here my first real battles with life began. In retrospect, it seems to have been a constant war in miniature....
>
> ... Looking back over my youth ... I am inclined to believe that the chance for a permanent peace in this crazed world is slight, indeed. There seems to be inherent in all of us the liking for a good fight. For example, when I first started to this little country school in Shelby

1

David Wark Griffith

County, the other boys made it pretty hot for me. Whether it was because I was a stranger in the community or whether it was just the general cussedness of my own disposition, I am unable to say. Anyhow, the boys went after me pretty strong....

These boys all came from what is termed "good, clean American stock." They came from families of allegedly high moral principles and, of course, church-going people....

This talk of war to end all wars and bring about a lasting condition of peace is so much hokum. The boyhood experiences recounted above and added to many other ... force me to the conclusion that the majority of people prefer most anything to peace.[3]

When the attempt to work the worn-out soil of the Shelby County farm was unsuccessful, the Griffith family moved again, this time to Louisville where David's mother opened a boarding house, a venture that soon failed. David sold newspapers to help the family finances, and later dropped out of high school to take a better-paying job as an elevator operator in a dry goods store. He left this position to work in a bookstore, which, as he described later, became his "university," exposing him to the world of ideas.[4] In his leisure time, he familiarized himself with vital political and social issues by attending public discussions.[5]

It was also in Louisville that David developed a fascination for the theater. Fired with an ambition to become a great playwright, he began his twelve-year career as a stage actor in 1895, appearing in a play in Louisville under the name of Lawrence Griffith. The following year, at a time when parts of the nation were still affected by the Depression of 1893, Griffith joined a touring stock company. Although prosperity had returned by the end of the century, these were lean years for Griffith. In his travels across the country between theatrical engagements, he "rode the rails," begged for food, lived with hoboes, stayed in flophouses and worked as a manual laborer shoveling ore, picking hops and earning his passage on a lumber ship, all of which gave him added insight into the plight of the underprivileged and the working class.[6]

During play rehearsals when he was not on stage, he was "forever writing or reading from a manuscript which he carried with him."[7] His aspiration to become a playwright was given a boost in 1907 when James K. Hackett produced a play he had written entitled *A Fool and a Girl*; it was a failure, however, closing after five performances in Washington, D.C., and a week in Baltimore.[8]

Griffith temporarily abandoned his dream of being a playwright when his marriage to the young actress, Linda Arvidson, made him look for a new way to earn a living. Turning to the fledgling motion picture industry out of sheer necessity, he initially worked as an actor and scenarist in New York. Near the end of 1907, he played the lead role in the one-reel film *Rescued from an Eagle's Nest* produced by the Edison Company. He soon moved to the Biograph Company's New York studio where he continued to act in films and supply stories. Several months after he started with Biograph, Griffith was hired as a replacement when the chief director became ill. In 1908, Griffith directed his first film, *The Adventures of Dollie*, beginning a new, decisive chapter in motion picture history.[9]

Early Film Industry

By the time Griffith entered the field, the cinema had become a significant source of entertainment around the world, emerging first as a public amusement in 1894 with Thomas Edison's new peep-show machine, the Kinetoscope. The following year, Thomas Armat in the United States and the Lumière brothers in France created an immediate sensation when they projected motion pictures on the screen for the first time. Since the earliest films were limited to brief scenic views and stage skits, they soon lost their appeal and within a few years motion pictures were relegated to "chasers" between vaudeville acts.

Public interest in the new medium revived with the introduction of the one-reel story film, five to fifteen minutes in length. Georges Méliès, the French director and first important artist in the cinema, discovered that the screen was an ideal medium for creating magic effects with "trick" photography. He employed these techniques in his most famous work, *A Trip to the Moon*, a 1902 release that established the popularity of the story film and demonstrated the potential of the cinema as a vehicle for expression of individual imagination.

Simultaneously, in England, pioneer filmmakers G. Albert Smith, James Williamson and Cecil Hepworth experimented with camera tricks, close-ups and editing in such early contributions to the cinematic narrative form as Hepworth's 1905 *Rescued by Rover.* Meanwhile, in the United States, Edwin S. Porter, working for the Edison Company, in 1903 directed *The Life of an American Fireman* and *The Great Train Robbery*, the first American narrative films that used editing techniques. *The Great Train Robbery* was such a success with American audiences that in the next few years small theaters devoted to motion pictures, known as nickelodeons, sprang up across the United States. J. Stuart Blackton of the Vitagraph Company, Porter's equal in the early days of the industry, brought prestige to the primitive cinema when he introduced literary and historical subjects in his films.[10]

Prestige was badly needed in the nickelodeon period, when established stage stars refused to appear in films, and middle-class Progressive reform leaders considered the motion pictures immoral and a corrupting influence on the working class and immigrants who were the mainstay of the audience. The sensational melodramas and risqué comedies appearing on the early screen reinforced the reform leaders' assessment of the new amusement, which they believed belonged "in the same class as brothels, gambling dens, and the hangouts of criminals."[11] With the foreign imports and the sophisticated work of Blackton and Griffith gaining more respectability for the films, the character of the audience changed as the middle class began to frequent the nickelodeons in larger numbers. By the time the first full-length features appeared in 1912–14, motion pictures were attracting a solidly middle-class audience.[12]

From 1895 to 1908 the United States, England and France were predominant in the international film industry, producing the overwhelming majority of films shown across the world. French and English films were shown in America as often as American productions. By 1908, the film industries of Italy and Germany rivaled England, France and the United States. Simultaneously, the embryonic form of film production in Russia, Japan, Denmark and Sweden presaged the rapid development of the industry into significant national cinemas within the next decade.

During this period the American film industry was dominated by seven companies: Edison, Biograph, Lubin, Vitagraph, Selig, Essanay and Kalem. Attempting to maintain his initial control of the field, Edison charged his competitors with infringing on his patents' rights, generating a lawsuit that was resolved only when these companies banded together to form the Motion Pictures Patents Company. The new trust was promptly challenged by a group of independents, including Carl Laemmle, the founder of Universal Pictures, resulting in government antitrust action against the Patents Company which ultimately solved the infringement controversy.[13]

Prior to 1910, production in the United States centered in the East, with Edison, Biograph, Vitagraph and Kalem located in New York City, and Lubin in Philadelphia. The exceptions were Selig and Essanay, which were headquartered in Chicago. Location shooting caused companies to seek a more amenable winter climate; Lubin and Kalem set up branch studios in Jacksonville, Florida, while Selig pioneered production in California, establishing a branch near Los Angeles in late 1907 to film *The Count of Monte Cristo*. In 1909, the New York Motion Picture Company, an independent attempting to avoid legal harassment by the Patents Company, became the second film company to move to California. Biograph, at Griffith's urging, opened a winter studio in Los Angeles in early 1910, setting a precedent followed by most of the major American film companies within the next few years.[14]

Griffith at Biograph

During the five years that Griffith was with Biograph, he made hundreds of films, mostly one-reel in length, bringing the motion pictures from a crude novelty to an expressive art form. When he entered the field, narrative film still tended to be unimaginative, consisting primarily of theatrical long-shots recording stagy performances, despite the achievements of the French, British and American pioneers. It was Griffith's singular genius to blend previous experiments with camera tricks and effects, close-ups and editing into a coordinated cinematic technique, giving motion pictures their basic grammar, which became the foundation for film art throughout the world. His use of close-ups and medium shots enabled the spectator to empathize with the emotions expressed by the characters. His editing style created a sense of excitement and suspense, intensifying the drama. His vistas or panoramic long-shots communicated an impression of epic grandeur. At the same time, his innovations in lighting, aided by his cameraman G.W. "Billy" Bitzer, added mood and an aesthetic quality to the images.[15]

Griffith built a stock company of fresh young actors and actresses, including Mary Pickford, Blanche Sweet, Mae Marsh, Lillian and Dorothy

Gish, Robert Harron, Henry B. Walthall and Lionel Barrymore. Under his direction, his players developed a naturalistic, intimate style of acting suited to the screen, breaking with the exaggerated gesticulations of the earlier dramatic films.[16]

In his prolific period at Biograph, Griffith created compact models of cinematic art in many of his short films which are precursors technically, thematically and stylistically of his later work in features, including *Intolerance*. At the height of his career, he commented on the opportunities his work at Biograph provided to master his craft: "I interested myself in short story pictures in much the same way as a painter interests himself in smaller works in order to earn the wherewithal to devote his time to a more ambitious effort."[17]

His dramatic chase and rescue films exemplify his mastery of rhythmic editing "to increase the tempo and build the tension."[18] *The Lonely Villa* (1909), *The Lonedale Operator* (1911), *The Girl and Her Trust* (1912) and *A Beast at Bay* (1912) are outstanding prototypes of Griffith's ability to intercut action between the chaser and the pursued in climactic rescue sequences, alternating shorter and shorter shots to add to the suspense. In *The Girl and Her Trust*, he used the tracking shot with a camera mounted on a moving car to photograph a speeding locomotive gaining on a railroad hand car. Again, in *A Beast at Bay*, he employed the technique to film a thrilling race between the heroine's touring car and a train commandeered by her rescuing boyfriend. His most sophisticated use of this method is incorporated in the complex climax of *Intolerance*, which cuts between four stories. In these fast-moving sequences, tracking shots film hundreds of Persian chariots sweeping toward Babylon in the Babylonian Story, intercut with a breathtaking race between a car and a train in the Modern Story that is reminiscent of the pursuit in *A Beast at Bay*.[19]

Griffith's social vision began to take shape in much of his Biograph work. His realistic depictions of poverty and injustice in contemporary American life contain themes and plot elements that are forerunners of the Modern Story in *Intolerance*. In the 1908 film *The Song of the Shirt* he depicts the sufferings of a girl employed in a sweatshop; in *A Convict's Sacrifice*, made in 1909, he denounces prison brutality; he condemns the corrosive effects of stock-exchange manipulation on the public welfare in the 1909 release *A Corner in Wheat*; he makes a scathing indictment of society's neglect of the aged in the 1911 film *What Shall We Do With Our Old?*; in *One is Business, The Other Crime*, made in 1912, he attacks political corruption; and in *The Musketeers of Pig Alley*, another 1912 production, Griffith exposes the underworld in a semi-documentary shot on location in the slums of New York. Caught up in the reforming mood of the Progressive Era, Biograph, under his influence, began in 1912 to solicit "plots contrasting the rich and the poor."[20]

While at Biograph, Griffith proved he was equally adept at projecting his social vision into films about past eras. In dramatizing the expansion and settlement of the United States in such films as *Comata, the Sioux* (1909), *The Redman's View* (1909), *Ramona* (1910) and *A Mohawk's Way* (1910), he assails the white man's cruelty to the American Indian. His portrayal of white settlers forcing Indians off their land in *The Redman's View* and *Ramona* symbolizes the attempted genocide of native Americans, while his poignant portraits of unscrupulous white men exploiting the Indian's naivete in *Comata, the Sioux* and *A Mohawk's Way* also reveal his sensitivity to past injustices. This gift for social comment appears again in his European period films, including *The Death Disc* (1909), adapted from a Mark Twain story of religious persecution in the time of Cromwell resembling the French Story in *Intolerance*.[21]

He demonstrated his flair for historical spectacle at Biograph, departing from the stiff, costumed tableaux of his predecessors to present past epochs on an animated canvas. In several western and Civil War films, including *The Last Drop of Water* (1911), *The Battle* (1911), *The Massacre* (1912) and *The Battle of Elderbush Gulch* (1913), he intercuts between mass action battle scenes to close-ups of the emotional reactions of his characters, thereby infusing his historical recreations with a kinetic passion and spirit of humanity. In *Judith of Bethulia* (1913), his final Biograph film and first full-length feature, Griffith adopts the spectacle form to project an ancient Middle Eastern setting that foreshadows the Judean and Babylonian Stories in *Intolerance*. His depiction of the assault on Bethulia, prefiguring his recreation of the siege of Babylon, displays his ability to "relate the bigness of spectacle to a small personal story" as he cuts from "the visual excitement of the battle scenes to the calm, closed-in, isolated room where Judith watches from her window."[22]

Reviewing Griffith's Biograph films, it is evident that the social and historical vision in *Intolerance* is not solely a response to the time in which it was made, but evolved, in part, as an outgrowth of his earlier work. As *The Boston Transcript* noted when *Intolerance* was released in 1916, the form of the new film represents "a stunning departure from the customary moving pictures" but "it is not so much of a departure from Mr. Griffith's past as many may think.... You may find 'studies' for the various parts of *Intolerance* in other films" made for Biograph.[23]

Fame and Controversy

Griffith's success in motion pictures, like so much in his life, was marked by a succession of ironies. Forced by economic necessity to leave the "legitimate" theater to enter films, he found the means for artistic expression in a medium he had once held in contempt. In the initial phase of his film career he was grateful that he worked anonymously, a practice of American studios before 1910, when they withheld the names of their technicians and players from the public. With his development as an artist, his respect for the new medium grew until, by the end of 1912, he took pride in seeing his name featured in trade-press accounts of the film industry. In 1913 Biograph began publicizing his name along with the players' in the company's advertisements.[24]

Griffith left Biograph to join the ranks of the emerging independents. Chafing at the restrictions imposed on him at his old studio and seeking autonomy to produce feature-length films, he entered into a partnership with Harry Aitken of Mutual. In a display of flamboyance, he announced his new status in a full-page advertisement in *The New York Dramatic Mirror* in the fall of 1913, listing his technical innovations and many of his Biograph successes.[25] By this time he was recognized throughout the film industry as its foremost creative figure. How radically he had changed in his attitudes toward the art he had once disdained and the venerable art that inspired his youthful dreams is illustrated in a 1914 interview appearing in *The Theatre*:

> Moving pictures can get nothing from the so-called legitimate stage because American directors and playwrights have nothing to offer.... For range and delicacy, the development of character, the quick transition from one mood to another, I don't know an actress on the American stage, I don't care how great her reputation, who can begin to touch the work of some of the motion picture actresses.... [26]

1914 was a banner year for Griffith, with the establishment of his studio in Hollywood and his release of four independently-produced features. His prestige within the industry and among the filmgoing public soared as his work received extensive coverage in the motion picture magazines and the trade press. It was in 1914 also that he began production on a film about the Civil War and Reconstruction, an idea fostered, in part, by the Southern ascendancy with the inauguration of the Wilson administration. Not only did he believe a historical epic of this scale would bring him wider recognition as a director, but he also hoped it would reveal the tremendous possibilities of the new art and respond to the competition from the spectacular Italian films receiving acclaim in the United States.

Griffith derived the material for his epic from Thomas Dixon's novel and play *The Clansman*, from the authoritative historians of the day and from his own Southern heritage. He tackled his immense project with great enthusiasm in the summer and fall of 1914, certain that it would instruct his audiences in the horror and futility of war. In early 1915, the spectacle, *The Birth of a Nation*, was ready for release. It premiered in Los Angeles on February 8, in New York on March 3 and was screened at the White House for President Wilson in late February. It proved to be yet another irony in Griffith's career. As it took the country by storm, it was rapturously acclaimed for its artistry and, at the same time, bitterly condemned for its portrayal of the blacks and the original Ku Klux Klan in the postbellum South.

The debate ignited by *The Birth of a Nation* brought Progressives into the fray, with leaders either praising the film or calling for its suppression. The controversy was accentuated by the allegation and subsequent denial that President Wilson, after seeing the film, declared, "It's like writing history with lightning and my only regret is that it is all too true." Novelist Booth Tarkington, clergyman-reformer Dr. Charles Parkhurst, Hiram Johnson, the reform governor of California, and Bryan Democrats Senators James Martine of New Jersey, Duncan Fletcher of Florida, Henry Lee Myers and Thomas Walsh of Montana and Representative Claude Kitchen of North Carolina were among the prominent Progressives who gave their endorsements, which were frequently included in newspaper advertisements for the film.[27] Leading the attack on the film were the influential Progressives Jane Addams, Oswald Garrison Villard, publisher of *The New York Evening Post*, Dr. Charles Eliot, president of Harvard University, and Rabbi Stephen Wise, who joined with the NAACP in its attempt to have the film banned.[28]

While opposed by a minority, the interpretation of history in *The Birth of a Nation* was within the mainstream of Progressive thought. In an era in which the Dunning School dominated Reconstruction historiography, Progressives like Roosevelt and Wilson and noted Socialist Victor Berger espoused doctrines of racial inequality, while Jack London, the outstanding radical novelist, asserted, "I am first of all a white man and only then a Socialist."[29] Author Thomas Dixon and Southern politicians Benjamin Tillman and Tom Watson, regarded as troublemakers by many Progressives who otherwise supported the status quo on the race issue, exemplified the minority of racist extremists that became part of the Progressive movement. Despite opposition to Dixon's best-selling racist tracts, *The Clansman* and *The Leopard's Spots*, among many Progressives, even in the South, the author counted Roosevelt, Wilson and novelist Frank Norris as his friends. Indeed, *The Clansman* was praised by several prominent Americans, including Secretary of State John Hay and Mark Twain's friend and biographer, Albert Bigelow Paine.[30]

Griffith's attraction to *The Clansman* was based as much on the dramatic possibilities he saw in the melodrama as on its Southern viewpoint. More importantly to him, however, Dixon's portrayal of the Reconstruction period as a reign of terror in which the people of the South were saved from marauding blacks by the original Ku Klux Klan was in accordance with the eminent historians of the time, including William Dunning, Walter L. Fleming, James Ford Rhodes and Woodrow Wilson. In fact, as drama critic Montrose J. Moses observed in 1921, the "sensational aspects" of Dixon's racist writings were "wisely softened ... in *The Birth of a Nation*," an effect reinforced by Griffith's conscious effort to authenticate his presentation through historical research.[31]

Nevertheless, in an age of segregation and lynchings, the emotional depiction of the Civil War and Reconstruction adapted even in part from the racist pen of Thomas Dixon antagonized the black leadership and the Progressive minority sympathetic to their cause. Oswald Garrison Villard described *The Birth of a Nation* as a "deliberate attempt to humiliate ten million American citizens and portray them as nothing but beasts" and Eliot "charged it with a tendency toward perversion of white ideals" and a "misrepresentation" of the birth of the American nation.[32] Joining in the attack were conservative Republican politicians, who used the controversy to help maintain their black constituency. *The Indianapolis Freeman*, a black newspaper, reported that Negro voters supported Calvin Coolidge in his successful 1915 campaign for Lieutenant Governor of Massachusetts partially because of his opposition to *The Birth of a Nation*.[33] Opponents of the film, fearing that its showing could result in racial violence, called for its suppression as a public nuisance. In clamoring for censorship, Villard declared that the film "should not be tolerated in any American city"; but he and his supporters managed to have it banned only temporarily in a few cities and two years in the state of Ohio.[34] Their concern that the film would incite riots proved exaggerated, since protest demonstrations, limited to Northeastern and Midwestern cities, consisted mostly of a few skirmishes and scattered vandalism.

Believing he had presented an accurate picture of the Civil War and Reconstruction, Griffith was both shocked at the charges of racism and angered at the attempts to suppress his film. In his polemic article, "The Motion Pictures and Witch Burners," Griffith decried the censors:

> The witch burners, who burn through the censorship of the motion picture today, when they have nothing left but the charred and blackened embers of that which promised once to be a beautiful art, when this grisly work is finished, where will they turn their attention next?[35]

He maintained in his pamphlet, *The Rise and Fall of Free Speech in America*, that "The pictorial press claims the same constitutional freedom as the printed press."[36]*

The attempt to ban The Birth of a Nation, *an effort opposed by a number of newspapers, proved the tenuousness of the liberal consensus on yet another issue — censorship. Like the earlier attempts to censor motion pictures, the suppression of dissent during World War I and the Red scare, the enactment of Prohibition, and Bryan's prosecution of Scopes to thwart the teaching of evolution in public schools, the unsuccessful efforts to prevent screenings of* The Birth of a Nation *revealed the Achilles' heel of the reform era. For all of their faith in the limitless capacity of mankind, Progressive leaders were often quick to shield the public from ideas and influences that they considered harmful, a dichotomy that Griffith attacks in* Intolerance.

Smarting from the attacks on *The Birth of a Nation*, Griffith made plans for another great film that would not only outdo the Civil War epic in scale and popular appeal, but would also respond to his critics while expressing his personal view of history and life. For his new project, he turned to *The Mother and the Law*, a film about social injustice in contemporary American life he had commenced in late 1914. He decided to expand the film to form part of a great historical epic that would comprise four stories, tracing injustice through the ages, a historical conception inspired when he saw "a billboard advertisement from a train window ... bearing the words 'the same today as yesterday.' "[37] In a trenchant observation capsulizing the cyclical nature of history, those words appear on a sign in the background of a scene in the Modern Story in which strikers are shot by the state militia.

Griffith and the Film Industry

Despite their importance in establishing the Hollywood film industry, *The Birth of a Nation* and *Intolerance* were produced and distributed outside the major American motion picture corporate structure. Harry Aitken, a principal backer and coproducer of Griffith's two epic films, was the founder and president of the Mutual Film Corporation, an alliance of independent companies, including Thanhouser, American, Reliance, Majestic, Ince's New York Motion Picture Company, and Sennett's Keystone Company, founded in 1912 to resist the control of the industry by the Motion Picture Patents Company. When Griffith joined Mutual in 1913, Aitken placed him in charge of the Reliance-Majestic merger, which produced his first four independent features and many other films made under his supervision.

Griffith and Aitken initially elicited backing from Mutual for *The Birth of a Nation* in early 1914. With escalating costs of the forthcoming spectacle causing investors to perceive it as a risky venture, members of the board opposed Aitken's support for it, charging that he had given financial backing without their authorization or knowledge. After Aitken relieved Mutual of its investment in the film, Griffith and his partner were forced to obtain financing from individual investors, including W.H. Clune, proprietor of the auditorium in Los Angeles where *The Birth of a Nation* had its world premiere. Griffith and Aitken also approached the prestigious Adolph Zukor's Famous Players Company, hoping it would take charge of the distribution of the film. When they were turned down, they formed the Epoch Producing Corporation to present *The Birth of a Nation* in cities throughout the country.[38]

The success of *The Birth of a Nation* allowed Griffith and Aitken to reassert their independence. They left Mutual, taking Ince and Sennett with them to form the new corporation, Triangle. Aitken gave managerial control to Griffith, Ince and Sennett, who all had their own studios and released films under separate trademarks. While he was associated with Triangle from 1915 to 1917, Griffith was so absorbed with his work on *Intolerance* that he had little time to devote to his supervisorial responsibilities. His main involvement was apparently to provide scenarios for some of the releases, which, like the Mutual productions, were made by filmmakers and stars he had trained.[39]

In contrast to his struggle to raise money for *The Birth of a Nation*, Griffith had no difficulty in obtaining backing for his new epic. With profits pouring in from *The Birth of a Nation*, investors were convinced they would reap similar returns from *Intolerance*. Using his own profits from his Civil War film, along with the capital put up by investors, Griffith was able to cover the production costs of *Intolerance*, estimated in the range of $386,000 to $2,000,000.

Intolerance was an independent production, distributed by the Wark Producing Corporation, a separate company set up solely for that purpose by Griffith and Aitken in December, 1915. By the latter part of 1917, the company was in financial trouble, with *Intolerance* failing commercially. Griffith bought back the property from its disgruntled investors, and by 1921, the Wark Producing Corporation was bankrupt, leaving debts that took Griffith several years to repay.[40]

Although *The Birth of a Nation* and *Intolerance* were both made outside the corporate structure, they strengthened the nascent Hollywood system, which evolved from 1910–1920 and lasted until the 1950s. A bittersweet triumph, *The Birth of a Nation* grossed more than any other American silent, in spite of its controversial aspects, verifying that motion pictures had a mass-marketing potential in the United States. *Intolerance*, a "succes d'estime" but a commercial failure in the United States, enhanced the artistic and technical standards of the American film, extending its influence thoughout the world. This added prestige, coupled with the profit-making possibilities of the American film, both domestically and internationally, as demonstrated by *The Birth of a Nation*, helped solidify the corporate base that dominated the industry in the ensuing thirty years and secured Hollywood as the motion picture capital of the world.

Through its evolutionary period, the Hollywood-based film industry owed its expansion to a large degree to its most significant creative artists of the 1910s. Among these, in addition to D.W. Griffith, were Thomas Ince, Mack Sennett, Cecil B. DeMille, Mary Pickford, Charlie Chaplin and Douglas Fairbanks, all of whom elaborated the scope and style of the American cinema, giving it universal appeal. Although each made unique contributions, Griffith's work, as the earliest and most innovative, spawned the achievements of the other six, who were either trained by him or looked to him for inspiration. Ironically, his commitment to social idealism and his lack of business acumen made him less of a commercial success than those who were indebted to him for their success.

Top: "Intolerance" set in background of this view of Griffith's Fine Arts Studio in Hollywood. Bottom: Babylonian set abandoned and disintegrating after filming completed.

Besides providing the example in cinematic techniques and dramatic construction, Griffith initiated the "one-man, one-film" concept in which the producer-director infuses his work with his own personality and world view.[41] Ince, Sennett and DeMille, who were among the earliest filmmakers to set up their own companies, following Griffith's lead, created distinctive film genres, stamped with their individualistic styles that expressed their particular tastes and values. Ince decisively shaped the western in films ranging from epic spectacles to the star vehicles of William S. Hart, capturing the romance and excitement of the Old West as well as its starkness and grueling hardships. Sennett, mirroring his working-class background, founded the genre of slapstick comedy, which allowed him to satirize the authority and values of the establishment. DeMille, who was from a cultured Eastern family, pioneered in society comedies and dramas distinguished by an unusual blend of the ornate and the sophisticated.

All three capitalized upon Griffith's film grammar, modifying it or embellishing it to suit their own styles. Departing from Griffith's improvisational approach to dramatic construction, Ince evolved the detailed written screenplay or shooting script which became the model for the industry. Sennett's contribution lay in adapting the editing techniques of Griffith's serious chase films to the frenetic pacing of his short comedies. DeMille's most notable early elaborations of the Griffithian pattern were his experimental use of lighting effects to project mood and his assiduousness in visual composition.[42]

As he moved his camera closer to capture the facial expressions of his players, Griffith introduced a naturalistic, intimate style of acting that made possible the star system, in which the film is used as a vehicle to exploit the popular appeal of the film personality. While he himself did not use the star system, his innovations in screen acting started the trend, which soon became an integral part of the film industry, for fashioning identifiable screen personae.

Mary Pickford, Charlie Chaplin and Douglas Fairbanks rose to stardom as they benefited from Griffith's method of presenting screen characters. Working under Griffith's direction, Pickford evolved her persona as a spirited waif, a characterization she amplified in the feature-length films she made for her own company after leaving Biograph. To ensure a credible portrayal, she supervised her films from start to finish, including the choice of stories and directors. Griffith's emphasis on believable characters also had an impact on the work of Chaplin, who began his film career as a member of the Sennett troupe. Breaking with the frenzied Sennett mode, Chaplin began directing his own films, setting the stage for the development of the Little Tramp, the universal character who mingled humor with pathos. Douglas Fairbanks, recruited to the cinema by Griffith for the Triangle Company, adapted the director's model of credible characterization and spirited action to fashion his light-hearted screen personality. With his series of action comedies quickly rivaling the films of Pickford and Chaplin in popularity, Fairbanks retained control over his work by setting up his own company.[43]

The vast profits earned by the film's creators brought a new breed of producers into the industry. The new "movie moguls" raised motion pictures from the cottage industry of the nickelodeon days to a mammoth enterprise housed in spacious studios and employing thousands. Mostly Jewish immigrants, they entered the field, in most cases, as proprietors of nickelodeons, remaining to build the huge corporations which still dominate the industry.

Their entrepreneurial control was aided by the industrial wars of the 1910s, which saw the demise of many of the original companies. Wedded to the dramatic short film and targeted by the government antitrust action, the companies comprising the Motion Pictures Patents Company were beset with financial difficulties that ultimately forced all but Vitagraph, which lasted until 1925, to cease production by 1918. Mutual and Triangle also collapsed around 1919, leaving Aitken, their founder, dependent on reissues of *The Birth of a Nation* for his principal source of income. Equally transitory were World Films Corporation, Selznick Pictures and Select Pictures, corporations started by Lewis J. Selznick.[44]

With business flourishing, the rapidly rising magnates, who had survived the upheavals of the 1910s, extended their monolithic grip on the industry, controlling not only the distribution but also the exhibition of their films as they constructed chains of lavish theaters across the United States. These entrepreneurs included Carl Laemmle of Universal Pictures, William Fox, Samuel Goldwyn, Louis B. Mayer, the Warner Brothers and Adolph Zukor and Jesse Lasky of Paramount. Demonstrating their keen business sense as well as their ability to judge the public's taste, they exploited the star system and the vogue for feature films. Their power was also attributable to the reorganization of their corporate structures, resulting in significant mergers which enabled them either to absorb their competition or to eliminate it completely.

A group of independent artist-producers, too individualistic to adjust to the mass-production methods of the Hollywood conglomerates, formed a new company. Included in this group were Griffith, Chaplin, Pickford and Fairbanks, who, in 1919, joined together to initiate the pioneering corporation, United Artists, in order to preserve their artistic integrity and independence in the face of the dominance of the gigantic studios. They also hoped to benefit from a greater share of the box-office gross since they were managing the distribution as well as the production of their films.[45]

Griffith's attempts to elude the Hollywood system ultimately failed. In another of the many ironies that studded his life, he was overwhelmed by the monolith that his genius had created. After he left Triangle in 1917 and prior to the formation of United Artists, he released his films through Paramount and First National, still maintaining creative autonomy. With the establishment of United Artists, Griffith, attempting to distance himself from the Hollywood system, closed his California studio, transferring his operations in late 1919 to his new studio in Mamaroneck, New York. (This was a reversal of his assertion of independence from studio control when he brought Biograph to California at the beginning of the decade.) He was headquartered at Mamaroneck for five years, alternating artistic personal works with more commercial ventures, all of which he released through United Artists. Heavily in debt from bank loans he incurred to finance his films and lacking any ability as a businessman, he experienced a series of commercial failures that came about with changing public tastes and the expense of managing an independent studio on a lavish scale.[46]

He was finally submerged by his financial woes and was forced to shut down his Mamaroneck studio in 1925 to work for Paramount's Long Island studio as a contract director. Unhappy with his loss of independence at Paramount, he returned in 1927 to United Artists and Hollywood, where he soon found himself again thwarted in his desire for autonomy. He came into conflict with Joseph Schenck, a production executive who sought to exercise control over Griffith, who was increasingly regarded as a commercial liability. Their dispute reached a climax with Griffith's first talkie, *Abraham Lincoln* (1930), when Schenck interfered with the director's creative conception of the scenario and the editing of the completed film. Griffith then sundered his ties with Schenck, returning to New York, where he was able to obtain financing for *The Struggle* (1931), his first independent production since the closing of the Mamaroneck studio. The film, distributed by United Artists, was a commercial and critical disaster, and ended his career as a director.

Griffith spent the remaining years of his life in enforced retirement, endeavoring to fulfill his literary ambitions. Much of this period was marked by frustration and alcoholism, with his announced plans for new films never coming to fruition, and his second marriage (to Evelyn Baldwin) ending in divorce. The highlights of his later years were a special Oscar presented to him by the Motion Picture Academy in 1936 for his contributions to film art and a retrospective of his work in 1940 by the Museum of Modern Art. On July 23, 1948, at the age of 73, he died in Hollywood of a cerebral hemorrhage and was buried in Kentucky near his birthplace.

It is apparent that Griffith's creative career constituted a search for independence, a desire to express his vision of life in a new form. In this quest, although he revolutionized the cinema, metamorphosing it into an art, he found himself increasingly at odds with the standardized production methods of the rapidly-growing industry. *Intolerance* represented not only a mature summing-up of his art and ideas, but also a break with the commercial and artistic trends of the new monolith. His desire to stake out his creative independence is evident in the unusual structure of *Intolerance*, in which he departed from his own narrative precedent. His most radical experiment, the 1916 epic became to Griffith the centerpiece of his work. Looking back on his career in later years, he told interviewers that he regarded *Intolerance* as his greatest single achievement, both technically and artistically, and that it was his personal favorite of all his works. [47]

2. Narrative Structure of *Intolerance*

With *Intolerance*, Griffith created a complex work, interweaving four stories widely separated in time and space, marking a radical departure from the narrative structure of previous films. Shooting without a script and using only notes to guide him, he alternated between the Babylonian Story, dramatizing the fall of Babylon to Persian invaders in 539 B.C.; the Judean Story, centering on the Crucifixion of Christ in A.D. 29; the French Story, dealing with the massacre of the Huguenots in 1572; and the Modern Story, depicting the capital-labor struggle and related social injustice in the United States at the time of the film's production. The unusual structure, reflecting modernist conceptions of time in art, philosophy and science, is linked by a recurrent image of a woman rocking a cradle, a symbol for the continuity of the history of the human race through all its joys and vicissitudes. To buttress his didacticism and achieve unity in his work, Griffith utilizes both intrinsic parallelism and contrast throughout the film.

Griffith chose not to present his narrative in chronological order, explaining in his program notes, "events are not set forth in their historical sequence or according to accepted forms of dramatic construction, but as they might flash across a mind seeking to parallel the life of the different ages."[1] It is this intrinsic parallelism that establishes a thematic unity in the otherwise apparent disparity in the recreation of four epochs, and allows Griffith to comment on man's inhumanity to man brought about by the intolerance of entrenched political, social and religious systems. As Pierre Baudry observes in *Cahiers du Cinema*:

> DWG's film is the scene of a *tension* between the heterogeneity of its fictional material and the rationality which fuses and unifies it. That is why the unity of the work is not to be found in the four episodes by themselves, but in that which presides over their union: one may say that *Intolerance* is a film *on* history; the principal effect of the intertwining is to attribute to each of the episodes a partial stamp of which the totality of the film is none other than the commentary. Recounting side by side several stories, *Intolerance* thus comments on their historical character.[2]

18

The Conception of Time

In addition to serving his didactic purpose, Griffith's novel arrangement of the historical epochs in *Intolerance* grew out of the late nineteenth and early twentieth century milieu, when writers, philosophers, scientists and filmmakers simultaneously began to speculate on time in ways that represented a dramatic break with traditional linear views of temporal reality as flowing "like a steady stream, independent of our activities."[3] Griffith's contemporary, the philosopher Henri Bergson, conceived time as "duration," "the continuous progress of the past which gnaws into the future and which swells as it advances."[4] The poet T.S. Eliot, who began his career in the early twentieth century, conveyed his impression of time in the following lines: "Time present and time past/ Are both perhaps present in time future,/ And time future contained in time past."[5] Albert Einstein, in his theory of relativity which revolutionized physics in the twentieth century, argued that "space and time are intimately related. One cannot exist without the other." Instead of representing "absolute constituents of reality," space and time "are flexible and dependent on the state of motion of the observer."[6]

Einstein's perception of time as the fourth dimension was anticipated by British novelist H.G. Wells in *The Time Machine* (1894) in which he theorizes on time travel, describing a machine that is capable of going into the past and the future. Wells' perception, intrinsic to the nature of the film medium, inspired Robert W. Paul, the British film pioneer, to develop in 1895 a method of motion picture projection and to conjure up an elaborate device that was never built consisting of "revolving stages, combined stereopticons, projection machines, scenic settings, masked seating sections and platform rocking devices to simulate travel motion."[7] Film historian Terry Ramsaye, commenting on Paul's project, states that it sought to "materialize the human wish to live in the Past, Present and Future all at once," but was not constructed because it required "a clumsy collection of mechanical expedients."[8]

Ramsaye points out that Paul's concept was realized not with the aid of mechanical devices, but through Griffith's innovations in cinematic techniques. Thanks to Griffith, "The photoplay of today moves backward and forward through Time with facile miracle from the Present into the Past and Future by the cut-back, flashback and vision scenes."[9]

The construction of *Intolerance*, resembling a time machine presentation, is the mature fulfillment of early cinematic experiments in the juggling of time and space. Paul had envisioned "a novel form of exhibition whereby the spectators have presented to their view scenes which are supposed to occur in the future or past, while they are given the sensation of voyaging upon a machine through time." He planned that his device would allow the audience to journey "backwards from the last epoch to the present."[10] A cinematic approach by Griffith in *Intolerance* produced an effect similar to Paul's proposed invention: the film begins in the present, travels to the past, depicting Judea in the time of Christ, then jumps forward to sixteenth century France, returns to the present, and then reverts further back in the past to Babylon in sixth century B.C. After some fifty transitions in all, the film concludes in the present with a vision of the future, a millenium of universal peace. Representing the eternal present is the contemplative image of the woman rocking the cradle, the "uniter of here and hereafter." In the final reels, the rapid intercutting between the four epochs produces a climax of "near hysteria" in which "history itself seems to pour like a cataract across the screen."[11] The effect resembles Wells' account of time travel as a feeling "of a helpless headlong motion," sensations which merge "at last into a kind of hysterical exhilaration ... faster and faster still."[12]

The Modern Story

Intolerance begins and ends with the Modern Story, giving it a necessary spatial and temporal point of reference from which Griffith proceeds to draw his historical analogies. The plot, based upon current news accounts, involves a strike by millworkers, protesting a cut in wages which Jenkins, owner of the mill, justifies as a means of financing his alleged charitable activities. To suppress the strike, Jenkins calls on the state militia, ordering them to fire upon the strikers. The father of the hero is among those who are killed, forcing the young man to turn to a life of crime when he is unable to find work.

A fateful series of events leads to the hero's conviction for a crime he did not commit. While the Boy, as the hero is named in the subtitles, is imprisoned for petty theft, his young wife, called the Dear One, bears his child. The members of the Jenkins Foundation, dubbed the Vestal Virgins of Uplift by Griffith, seize the Dear One's child on the pretext that, as the wife of a convict, she is an unfit mother.

Misfortunes continue to plague the Boy after he is released from prison. He returns to his apartment one day to find his wife being attacked by his former employer, a gang leader known as the Musketeer of the Slums who led him to a life of crime. During the fight that ensues between the Boy and the gangster, the latter is shot by his jealous mistress, the Friendless One, who witnesses the struggle from the window ledge outside the apartment. Subsequently, the Boy is convicted for the gangster's murder on circumstantial evidence and is saved from execution only by the last-minute confession of the mistress.

Jenkins, the capitalist, is depicted as the most powerful individual in his society, exercising an authority comparable to that of a feudal lord or high priest. To emphasize Jenkins' position, Griffith utilizes the long-shot. As the capitalist orders the strike to be crushed, he is shown "like a lord of

The Dear One after her husband has been arrested (the Modern Story).

space, behind his roll-top desk in the center of the vastness of his office, a symbol of Power," and a symbol of the new autocracy of industralism that has come to dominate the modern world.[13] Griffith repeats this shot of Jenkins at different points of the narrative, underscoring the mill-owner's ultimate responsibility for the unfolding tragedy that befalls the hero and heroine. Finally, as the young couple have been brought to the lowest point of their fortunes with the Boy's conviction, "Griffith accentuates it with the cruellest of ironies" as Jenkins is shown being feted at a fashionable gathering where his admirers flatter him by saying, "The people everywhere are singing your praises."[14]

Between the authority figure of Jenkins and his victims stand the analogous characters of Jenkins' sister, Mary, and her associates, and the gang leader, the Musketeer of the Slums. These intermediary characters complement each other, illustrating the hypocrisy of their society through the causality of their relationships; while the Vestal Virgins of Uplift impose a puritanical brand of official morality on the community, the Musketeer of the Slums profits from the proscription of pleasure. Acting upon their belief that morality must be legislated, Mary Jenkins and her fellow proselytizers of moral reform spearhead a drive to clean up the society by enacting laws which prohibit drinking, public dancing and prostitution. With the closure of saloons, dance halls and brothels, the Musketeer of the Slums is able to build an empire from the operation of these forbidden pleasures in the underworld. Instead of accomplishing their goal of moral reform, the zealots of the Jenkins Foundation create an environment in which the gangster flourishes. The Musketeer of the Slums gains so much political influence that, when the Boy leaves the gang to "go straight," the underworld czar, in order to avoid possible prosecution for illegal activities, "buys" the judicial system by sending the youth to prison on a false charge of theft. While the intermediary characters are portrayed as agents of oppression as they interact with the powerless in the film, their authority is hierarchical. It is derived from the actions of Jenkins, the monopolistic capitalist who remains unscathed by social conflict although, in Griffith's view, he is the ultimate perpetrator of intolerance in his community.

The hero and heroine are depicted as hapless victims caught up in situations over which "they have little or no control."[15] They do not directly interact with the people in power like Jenkins, but "they are affected by the decisions and actions of ... those whose power leads them to intolerance."[16] They are ordinary people who, in the beginning of the film, are shown leading a simple and serene existence until powerful forces in society obstruct their freedom, destroying their happiness and making them the "playthings of intolerance."[17] Although their problems are rooted in society, not within themselves, they are unable to present a tangible challenge to the system that threatens to crush them. The Boy, an unconventional heroic figure, does not shape his destiny; instead, he falls into the traps laid for him by forces of social intolerance. The suppression of the strike, the big-city crime fostered by political corruption and a system of laws that is perverted by an inhumane society are all circumstances beyond his control that bring him to the brink of destruction. His wife not only shares in his tribulations but endures her own suffering when she is persecuted by the women of the Jenkins reform group who snatch her child from her.

The Judean Story

From the contemporaneous narrative, Griffith weaves his historical analogies, shifting from one era to another to emphasize the injustice that

The Boy is saved from the hangman's noose (the Modern Story).

has characterized all societies since antiquity. The Judean Story, the second epoch to be introduced, has no dramatic structure independent of the Modern Story, existing solely as a series of brief scenes to comment on the injustice and intolerance of the religious establishment in Christ's time as it is paralleled with the self-righteous morality in twentieth century America. Griffith chose not to include a fictional plot, relying instead on episodes from the Gospels to develop his theme. Among them are the Pharisees denoucing Christ, the wedding feast at Cana, Christ saving an adulteress, and the trial and crucifixion of Christ.

By intercutting between the Judean Story and the Modern Story,

The wedding feast at Cana (the Judean Story).

Griffith stresses that the true spirit of Christianity as illustrated by Christ's life is antithetical to the priestly despotism of the Pharisees and is betrayed by the actions of those who profess to uphold Christian values in contemporary society. In an opening sequence, the Pharisees, demanding that all action stop while they pray in public, loudly proclaim, "Lord, I thank thee that I am better than other men!" Like the moral reformers in the Modern Story who set up the Jenkins Foundation to enforce their brand of morality, the Pharisees advertise their claims to moral and spiritual superiority. In a later sequence, Griffith again parallels the hypocrisy of the Vestal Virgins of Uplift with the self-righteousness of their Judean counterparts; expressing their disapproval of the wedding feast at Cana when Christ turns water into wine for the celebrants, the Pharisees declare, "There is too much pleasure-seeking among the people."

When the Pharisees condemn Christ for wining and dining with the publicans, the film cuts to a scene of the pharasaic reformers closing the saloons. With the subtitle, "Now let us see how this Christly example is followed in our story of today," Griffith switches from a shot of Christ saving the adulteress from a mob to the moral reformers in the Modern Story raiding the brothels, then leading the prostitutes to jail. Again, as the Dear One's baby is taken by the members of the Jenkins Foundation, Griffith draws a "touching and poignant parallel," reverting to the Judean Story, and "without any linking title or images ... superimposes over a picture of Christ surrounded by children the title: 'Suffer little children.' "[18]

To illustrate the injustice of capital punishment in light of Christ's example, Griffith analogizes the conviction and crucifixion of Jesus with the conviction and near execution of the Boy. With the title, "An eye for an eye, a tooth for a tooth, a murder for a murder," reflecting his view of capital punishment, Griffith cuts from the Boy's death sentence at the trial to a shot of the judgment of Christ; then, again, near the end of the film when the Boy is led to the gallows, "Griffith cuts directly to a shot of Calvary Hill and three crosses in the background."[19]

The French Story

The French Story, the third to be introduced in the film, has a more fully developed narrative than the Judean Story, with the didacticism integrated within the framework of the plot. It dramatizes the power struggle at the royal court of Charles IX between Admiral Coligny, who heads the minority Protestant Huguenot faction, and Catherine de Medici, the queen-mother of France and champion of the Catholic cause. The conflict, which culminates in the infamous St. Bartholomew's Day Massacre, develops amid the festive atmosphere of the marriage of Henri of Navarre to Marguerite de Valois and the joyful expectations of the Huguenot lovers, Prosper Latour and Brown Eyes, the fictional protagonists of the story and counterparts of the Boy and the Dear One in the Modern Story.

The scene of a French soldier forcing his attentions on Brown Eyes, who spurns his advances, foreshadows the fate of the lovers inexorably bound to the actions of Catherine de Medici. Catherine persuades her son, Charles IX, to sign an order authorizing the slaughter of the Huguenots, whom she regards as a subversive element. A flashback depicts the Protestant atrocities against the dominant Catholic faith as the queen reminds her son that the existence of the Huguenots should not be tolerated. Reluctantly yielding to her pressure, Charles shouts, "By God's death, since you wish it, kill them all! Kill them all! Let no one escape to upbraid me." In a dramatic transition, Griffith cuts to Brown Eyes and her sister preparing for bed while "outside unknown to them, the mercenary soldiers mark the house with white paint, showing that the inhabitants are Protestants."[20] The soldiers' sweep through the city, as they massacre the unsuspecting Huguenots, climaxes this segment of the film. Brutally forcing their way into the home of Brown Eyes and her family, the soldiers slaughter everyone in sight. Prosper Latour, arriving too late to save his sweetheart, also falls at the hands of the royalist troops.

Using masterful editing techniques, Griffith constantly points up the historical continuity of the suffering inflicted on ordinary people by the intrigues of the powerful. Through a series of transitions, Griffith links the

The massacre of St. Bartholomew's Day (the French Story).

destinies of the young couples in the French and Modern stories. To underscore the parallel, he cuts from Prosper Latour and Brown Eyes, blissfully making plans for their marriage against the backdrop of the royal wedding and the court infighting, to Miss Jenkins laying the groundwork for the proposed foundation, followed by shots of the Dear One at the mill workers' dance, as unaware as the Huguenot couple of an imminent threat to her happiness. Griffith relates the fortunes of the couples, shifting from a lighthearted scene of Prosper Latour and Brown Eyes listening to her father read to the Boy and the Dear One enjoying a "Coney Island day."[21] Extending the comparison, he accentuates the similarity between the machinations of Catherine de Medici and the women reformers of the Jenkins Foundation, cutting from a poignant scene of the Dear One, deprived of her own child, peering through windows to observe the happiness of others, to Catherine attempting to induce her son to agree to the massacre. Finally, he connects Prosper Latour's failed attempt to rescue his fiancée, who dies at the hands of the mercenary soldier, with the Dear One's effort to save her husband from execution, intercutting scenes of the brutal attack in the French Story with the race between the governor's train and the car carrying the Dear One and the confessed murderess, the Friendless One.

An obvious parallel with Jenkins in the Modern Story, Catherine de Medici is the most powerful figure in the French Story and Griffith's ultimate villain. Through constant badgering, she is able to persuade her son to consent to an assault on the Huguenots, whom she sees as a threat to the traditional religious-monarchical hierarchy of medieval France. Similarly, Jenkins responds with violence to a challenge to his authority, ordering the militia to fire upon the striking workers.

The Babylonian Story

The Babylonian Story traces the last days of the ancient Mesopotamian civilization and its fall to the invading forces of Cyrus the Great, the Persian ruler, in 539 B.C. Prince Belshazzar, acting ruler of Babylon at the time of its conquest and a champion of religious liberty and the cult of Ishtar, antagonizes the established priestly class of the rival sect of Bel-Marduk. The High Priest of Bel, leader of the sect, in the words of a subtitle, "sees in the establishment of Ishtar loss of his religious power. He angrily resolves to reestablish his own god—incidentally himself." Rather than risk the loss of his privileges and authority, the priest betrays his city to its Persian enemies, an act which Griffith describes as "the greatest treason in all history by which a civilization of countless ages was destroyed and a universal written language (the cuneiform) was made to become an unknown cipher on the face of the earth."

Within the historical setting is the personal story of the Mountain Girl, a brave, madcap tomboy devoted to Prince Belshazzar. Scorning the attentions of the Rhapsode, a young poet and an agent of the High Priest of Bel, the girl takes part in battle against the besieging Persians. Her antics provide a contrasting comic touch that serves to humanize the remote period of the story.

The fatal flaw in Belshazzar and his court is their failure to adequately comprehend the danger that threatens them. After repulsing the Persians in a spectacular battle, the Babylonians celebrate their victory in a round of feasting, unable or unwilling to foresee the imminence of their collapse. Griffith underscores the tragic irony of their situation as he shows them on the eve of their fall making elaborate plans for "tomorrow." Only the Mountain Girl makes a heroic but futile effort to warn the court of the approach of the Persian army brought about by the treachery of the High Priest of Bel. When Cyrus' forces enter the city, Belshazzar and his consort commit suicide rather than face capture. The Mountain Girl is fatally wounded by a Persian arrow; Griffith's shot of the dying girl with a toy chariot pulled by doves at her feet is the definitive image of a fallen civilization, its peace and accomplishments laid waste by invasion and conquest.

Griffith juxtaposes sequences from the Babylonian Story with the other stories to stress the similarity between the powerbrokers of the different eras. Introductory shots of the Babylonian Story, with the High Priest of Bel contemptuously surveying a procession of the worshippers of Ishtar, identifies the forces of authority when preceded by shots of Jenkins monitoring the mill workers at the dance. The ladies of the Jenkins Foundation, congratulating themselves on the success of their moral reforms, accentuate Griffith's commentary on self-aggrandizement when shown alongside a sequence of the High Priest "courting public homage" as he warns the people that their devotion to Ishtar will lead to the ruin of Babylon. Scenes of Cyrus's army in league with the High Priest preparing for battle, followed by the uplifters in the Modern Story making plans to seize the Dear One's child, again link the power structure. Griffith points his finger at those who will impose their will on others no matter what the cost as he cuts from Catherine de Medici egging on her son to Cyrus marching toward Babylon, and from the priests of Bel-Marduk leaving the banquet hall back to Catherine urging her son to sign the order for the massacre.

He also uses parallel action to compare the experience of the victims in the different stories. The return of the Boy to the Dear One after his release from prison intercut with the feast of Belshazzar conveys a sense of "rejoicing and anticipation of more settled times ahead," but is dampened by the feeling of loss affected by the war in the Babylonian Story and the seizure of the child in the Modern Story.[22] In the climax, a series of transitions heightening the suspense as the tempo quickens intermingles the fates of the victims. A shot of Cyrus and the High Priest of Bel plotting the conquest of Babylon is followed by a sequence of the hangmen making preparations for the Boy's execution. Sequences of the Dear One, the Friendless One and a sympathetic policeman attempting to reach the governor's train in time to stop the execution are intercut with the Mountain Girl rushing in her chariot to warn Belshazzar of his imminent danger.

Griffith also uses the narrative structure to compare ancient Babylon and modern America. He sees a similar attitude towards courtship and marriage, drawing analogies between the Babylonian custom of selling women paraded on an auction-block to be judged by potential husbands and the modern American way in which women parade "like peacocks up and down the street in order to attract men." Even the Dear One dons a tight skirt, hoping that "maybe everyone will like me too."[23] By showing Belshazzar intervening in behalf of the people, the director implies that there was greater concern for the common welfare in Babylon than in modern America with its impersonality, detached legal system and a social order that lacks the leadership to control the actions of Jenkins. Griffith's indictment of official morality in America is particularly cogent in his comparison of the treatment of prostitutes; in the Modern Story, prostitutes

Belshazzar's consort, the Princess Beloved, reacts to the Persian siege of Babylon (the Babylonian Story).

are dragged off to jail, but in Babylon, the tradition of temple prostitution makes "women corresponding to our street outcasts, for life, the wards of Church and State."

Belshazzar is depicted sympathetically as a benevolent ruler who, "gaining the loyalty of the people ... abolished religious establishments and protected economic independence."[24] In Lary May's opinion, this portrayal proves that "Griffith does not condemn power per se."[25] While in the characterizations of Jenkins, Catherine and the Pharisees, the director assigns villainy to those who exercise the greatest control over their society, Belshazzar is free from any such taint of malevolence. Demonstrating that power can corrupt in other ways, Griffith, however, reveals a weakness in Belshazzar's character when, after his victory over the Persians, the prince's sybaritic tastes along with his exaggerated sense of invincibility make him vulnerable to the treachery of his enemies.

Griffith sees the High Priest of Bel as the true villain whose traditional monopoly of power is challenged by Belshazzar, a revolutionary upstart. Like his counterparts — Jenkins, Catherine and the Pharisees — the High Priest perceives the new reform movement as a subversive assault on his authority and seeks the aid of Cyrus and his army to overturn Belshazzar's regime. In Griffith's conception, Cyrus is a secondary villain, exploiting the High Priest to further his imperialistic goals, while the priest is the chief perpetrator of intolerance whose actions are decisive in bringing about the fall of Babylon.

The kaleidoscopic structure of *Intolerance* is a triumph of diversity because of the inclusion of four historical narratives in one film, unity because the intercutting of the epochs projects a common theme, a consistent social-historical vision. In Griffith's interpretation of history, the present is inseparable from the past, a quality Vachel Lindsay alluded to in his 1917 commentary on the film:

> There is many a message that is not printed out on the films or put into the apparently explicit publicity matter. And, in like manner, the days of St. Bartholomew and of the Crucifixion signal back to Babylon sharp or vague or subtle messages. The little factory couple in the modern street scene called the Dear One and the Boy, seem to wave their hands back to Babylon amid the orchestration of ancient memories. The ages make a resonance behind their simple plans and terrible perplexities.... The Modern Story is made vibrant by the power of whirling crowds from the streets of Time. The key hieroglyphic is the cradle of humanity, eternally rocking.[26]

Like a mosaic, each segment has its own intricate details which, in aggregation, project the historic reality of the eras. Griffith consulted the historic record, not only to glean the minutiae, but also to gain a broader perspective of the periods he depicted.

3. Historical Sources

The vast design of *Intolerance* necessitated more historical research than any previous motion picture. To create his epic, Griffith drew on widely diverse sources, from archaeological discoveries to contemporary news stories. His organization and use of materials manifests a commitment to accuracy modified by an imaginative approach that employs artistic license or fills in gaps of historical facts in order to convey a generalized impression of historical truth.

Griffith's Approach to Research

To coordinate the enormous amount of data for *Intolerance*, in 1915 Griffith established the first research department in the American film industry. Headed by R. Ellis Wales, the new studio department provided Griffith with "quick-and-ready access to books, magazines, drawings, sketches, maps, statistics and photographs."[1] However, he was not content to rely solely on the department and "continued to perform the research himself."[2]

Griffith encouraged members of his company to participate in the research and to discuss ideas with him. He felt that if the cast and crew shared in the compiling of data they would become more enthusiastic about the project. From a practical standpoint, it relieved him of the burden of gathering all the necessary documentation. Lillian Gish, who contributed to the research for the French Story, recalls: "I read no other books but those dealing with the various periods of history portrayed in the movie."[3] Assistant cameraman Karl Brown helped by studying texts on ancient history for the Babylonian Story. He also remembers Griffith's tireless pursuit of research:

> The desks ... were piled high with books. It would take a full day for anyone to thumb through them even in the most cursory manner. So the significant pictures were cut out and mounted in a scrapbook for ready reference. Then there was another scrapbook, and another, full to the bulging point.[4]

Joseph Henabery, who played Admiral Coligny in the French Story and served as the assistant director for the film, became Griffith's chief research assistant because, as he noted, Griffith respected his ability to "dig in and find things."[5] Henabery pored over innumerable books on Babylonia and Assyria. In one instance, confronted with the problem of how to reconstruct Babylon, Henabery said he used

> logical deduction. Should you have great timbered halls in Babylon? No. Why Not? Because there is no place where such timbers could be found.[6]

When Griffith wanted to build a Babylonian beerhall, Henabery could recall that he had seen an illustration of an Egyptian beerhall but never a Babylonian one. "I had to research into Egyptian history in order to correlate my facts — to see where something might have spread from one country to the other."[7]

Sources for the Modern Story

In the Modern Story, Griffith mirrors his own era, placing it in a historic context by adhering to a realistic depiction of the contemporary scene. Inspired by current news stories of labor unrest, his narrative contains elements of the notorious Ludlow Massacre and the Federal Industrial Commission's investigation of a strike in Bayonne, New Jersey.[8] The sense of realism is heightened by his careful attention to detail, including settings and costumes. His approach in projecting authenticity stemmed, in part, from his previous experimentations with social themes in several of his Biograph films and reflects an awareness of the social problems of his age.

The Federal Industrial Commission's findings in the deaths of the nineteen strikers in New Jersey provided the immediate source for Griffith's narrative. In the actual case, the owner of a chemical factory precipitated discontent among his workers when he refused to raise wages from $1.60 a day to $2.00. The industrialist, who was "fervid in charity and zealous in ecclesiastical activities," hired "goons" disguised as "deputy sheriffs and constables" to put an end to the strike, bringing about the bloodshed that led to the investigation.[9] In adapting this event to his scenario, Griffith establishes a causal relationship between the employer's practice of donating company profits to benevolent causes while denying decent wages to employees; he shows the mill workers suffering cutbacks in pay so Jenkins can finance "charitable" activities that serve to enhance his image in the community.[10]

For the other details of the strike, Griffith turned to accounts of the Ludlow massacre, which was headline news at the time he conceived the plot idea for *The Mother and the Law* in 1914. The bloodiest single incident of the early twentieth century struggles between capital and labor, the confrontation at Ludlow, Colorado, filled the newspapers for days, shocking the nation. The unrest began in September, 1913, with the coal miners of the Colorado Fuel and Iron Company, a Rockefeller holding, striking for higher wages and an eight-hour workday. The situation reached a climax on April 21, 1914, when the state militia, called out by the mine operators, fired into a tent colony of workers, igniting the tents and burning women and children to death. *The New York Times* of April 22 estimated that 45 people, over two-thirds of them women and children, were killed, 20 were missing, over 20 were wounded and more than 200 women and children, separated from their families, became refugees.[11] Order was restored only with the arrival of federal troops sent by President Wilson.

The circumstances of the Ludlow catastrophe that Griffith chose to exclude from his narrative are as significant as those he incorporated. The miners in the Ludlow case struck to improve their working conditions, while Griffith's mill workers strike to protest worsening conditions, a scenario eliminating any ambiguity about the justness of the strikers' cause. In the Ludlow incident. the strikers were well organized and well armed, but in Griffith's portrayal, although some of the strikers have revolvers, the majority are unarmed, appearing almost powerless in comparison to the uniformed troops equipped with rifles.

In both the actual case and Griffith's film, state government cooperated with private interests by sending the militia to suppress the strike, but in Griffith's depiction, the responsibility for the bloodshed falls squarely on the shoulders of the capitalist who commands the militia and his own factory guards to "clear the property." Even his dramatization of unarmed strikers being shot at point-blank range by the militiamen and factory guards demonstrates Griffith's desire to emphasize personal responsibility for the massacre, a point which may have been more obscure had he shown women and children burned in their tents when the stored ammunition exploded during the battle between strikers and the militia. Whatever the variation in detail, the results of the violence in the actual occurrence and Griffith's story were the same, with workers and their families turned into refugees by the callous actions of the forces of capital.

Although the Ludlow massacre necessitated the use of federal troops to quell the violence and the killings in the New Jersey strike prompted a federal investigation, Griffith's narrative avoids any reference to federal intervention. While Griffith may have excluded these facts to accomodate his dramatic construction, using the strike as a springboard to unravel his plot details, he could also have been guided by his intuitive belief that positive change must include responsible acts by individuals. He does not seem to suggest that government intervention is in itself undesirable, since the crisis surrounding the strike is unresolved and the evildoers are unpunished, leaving open the possibility that reform is needed. On the other hand, his interpretation does make quite clear that the ultimate resolution of social problems lies in the spiritual regeneration of the individual, not in government actions as many of the social films of the thirties imply.

To project the physical reality of daily contemporary life, Griffith was attentive to the details of appropriate costuming and authentic settings. Henabery first became involved in compiling data for *Intolerance* when Griffith, intent on reworking *The Mother and the Law* for the Modern Story, asked his advice on how the servants should be dressed at the grand ball hosted by Jenkins and his sisters. Aware that Griffith based this sequence upon the extravagant receptions given by the New York Four Hundred, an exclusive coterie of business tycoons and socialites, Henabery sought out a former secretary to one of the hostesses of the club, who described in detail the servant's uniform, consisting of "knee breeches" and "tails."[12] Having thus won Griffith's confidence, Henabery continued to advise on the particulars of dress throughout the filming, maintaining a standard of accuracy that pleased Griffith. For example, when the rough cut of the Modern Story revealed a discrepancy in the cleric's garb worn by the prison chaplain, Henabery, before recommending the appropriate changes, first consulted with a Catholic priest who had served as chaplain at San Quentin.[13]

Adhering to his commitment to realism, Griffith strove for exact replication for interior settings and shot exterior scenes on location. He visited the San Francisco city jail and the death-house at San Quentin to obtain first-hand research for the prison scenes. Brown, who accompanied him, recalled that the city jail gave them a look at prison squalor, while the San Quentin visit provided them with the details of execution by hanging.[14] When Griffith supervised the construction of the sets for the prison sequences, he was careful to utilize the particulars of his on-site observations. All interior scenes, including the courthouse and the tenements, were equally accurate reproductions built on the studio lot. He brought authenticity to the exterior scenes by filming them on the streets of Los Angeles. Brown remembers that the sequence in which the police and reformers raid a brothel was shot in downtown Los Angeles in the Plaza area between Main Street and the railroad tracks. The strike sequence was also filmed in the poorer section of Los Angeles across the railroad tracks in the warehouse district.[15]

While Griffith was meticulous in his recreation of contemporary social reality, he was purposefully vague about the specifics of time and place of the narrative, since he intended the Modern Story to be emblematic of early twentieth century America. Chronologically, it seems to cover a two-year time span from 1912 to 1914. Although no dates are given, the automobile license plates in the climax bear the year 1914. He describes the story as taking place in a "Western" state, but otherwise makes no attempt to be exact, referring to the location simply as a "city," an allegorical device which he used in naming his characters.

Sources for the Judean Story

The Judean Story adheres closely to the Four Gospels of the New Testament; Matthew, Mark, Luke and John. From these, Griffith selected a few incidents from the life of Christ that point up the theme of his film, presenting Christ as both the opponent and the victim of intolerance. Although he does not deviate from standard Biblical accounts, his narrative structure projects a humanistic view of Christ's life rather than Jesus as the Incarnation or his crucifixion as the central, liberating event, an interpretation intrinsic to traditional Christian historical thought.

As a result, Griffith's treatment of Christ's life is simultaneously orthodox in its presentation and heterodox in its thematic implications. Although nothing in the Judean Story contradicts or refutes sacred history, the incidents Griffith chooses to include as well as those he omits emphasize his view of Christ's ministry in humanistic rather than fundamentalist terms. As Karl Löwith states in *Meaning in History*, the orthodox Christian reading of history

> rests neither on the recognition of spiritual values nor on that of Jesus as a world-historical individual....
>
> Within (the Christian) scheme of salvation, the birth, death, and resurrection of Christ are not a particular now ... but a single once-for-all which happened once-upon-a-time....
>
> ... According to the New Testament view, the advent of Christ is not a particular, though outstanding, fact within the continuity of secular history but the unique event that shattered once and for all the whole frame of history by breaking into its natural course, which is a course of sin and death.[16]

By placing Christ within a cyclical pattern of history symbolized by the cradle endlessly rocking, Griffith departs from the fundamentalist Christian vision of history which sees Christ's ministry, his voluntary martyrdom and resurrection as issuing from his mission to redeem mankind from original sin. Christ's experiences on earth in the traditional Christian interpretation of history defy comparison with any other historical event, but Griffith's narrative structure derives its significance from analogizing Christ's crucifixion with the fall of Babylon, the massacre of the Huguenots and the sufferings of a modern American working-class couple. While he does not reject the eschatological direction of history (as his vision of a future millenium at the conclusion of the film proves), his conception of temporal history, which apparently denies original sin, precludes a metahistorical presentation of Christ's advent.

In Griffith's view, Christ's ministry is to redeem man, not from his innate depravity, but from the corruption of hypocrisy and intolerance in his society. The Crucifixion is the tragic result of the establishment striking back at the "Man among men, the greatest enemy of intolerance," not the climactic event in the divine plan of salvation. In this context, dramatizing Biblical episodes, including Christ's fasting and temptation by the Devil, the raising of Lazarus, the Last Supper, the agony of Gethsemane and the Resurrection, which point up Christ as a willing martyr and victor over sin and death, would have detracted from Griffith's theme linking Jesus' fate with a recurring manifestation of intolerance. Instead, Griffith presents only one of Christ's miracles — the transforming of water into wine at the wedding feast of Cana — thereby asserting his belief in the celebration of life which runs counter to the forces of repression and bigotry. So pointed was Griffith's portrayal of Christ's crucifixion as the consequence of the puritanical Jewish orthodoxy that Howard Gaye, who played Christ, claims that the Jewish authorities in Los Angeles, sensitive to cinematic depictions of the life of Christ, persuaded Griffith to cut the Judean Story from thirty episodes to six prior to the film's release.[17]

To ensure authenticity for his recreation of Palestine in the time of Christ, Griffith consulted the works of Archibald Henry Sayce, author of *Israel and the Surrounding Nations*, James Hastings, author of *The Encyclopedia of Religion, A Dictionary of the Bible* and *The Dictionary of Christ and the Gospels*, and the Semitic scholar Francis Brown.[18] *The Tissot Bible*, with its realistic and meticulously detailed illustrations of Christ's life by the French artist James Joseph Jacques Tissot, was Griffith's chief source for the settings and costumes, according to Henabery and Brown.[19] It was, however, the tradition of popular religious art which portrayed Biblical scenes "with some degree of archaelogical accuracy" and which was familiar to his audience that inevitably influenced Griffith's depiction of the era.[20] His rationale for relying on an orthodox pictorial presentation, Brown contends, was based upon his assumption that the images people had grown up with were true for them and any attempt to change this reality would only confuse the audience.[21] Rabbi Myers and Father Dodd, an Episcopalian priest, were on-the-set consultants during the filming, with the rabbi providing accurate particulars of Jewish ritual and history and the priest's assistance eliminating any possibility that Griffith would be charged with presenting an interpretation that violated the tenets of Christian orthodoxy.[22]

Sources for the French Story

The French Story is built around the St. Bartholomew's Day Massacre of 1572, an event which, until the Holocaust of World War II, was widely accepted as the most notorious example of official intolerance in recorded history. Despite Griffith's apprehensions, his dramatization of an atrocity which had inspired many works of art (including Giacomo Meyerbeer's popular opera *The Huguenots*) evoked little or no controversy in a Protestant-dominated United States. For his scenario, he referred to standard historical works, including François Guizot's *History of France*, weaving into the documented facts the fictional story of a young, ill-fated Protestant couple. Authentication for visual design derived from "old pictures in books in the public library."[23]

Griffith's characterizations of leading historical figures reflects, for the most part, authentic historical accounts. Catherine de Medici, portrayed by Griffith as cruel and cunning, was a woman known in her own time as "the serpent." The historian Henri Noguères, whose work is based on original sources, affirms the filmic depiction of her as a woman embodying "freedom from scruples, trickery and dissimulation, and cruelty."[24] Guizot describes her love of power, her dominance over her sons, and her proclivity for dodging issues.[25] In assigning a political rather than a religious motive for her antagonism towards the Huguenots, Griffith is consistent with historians who agree that her Machiavellian attempts to create dissension between the Catholic and Protestant factions served to maintain her power. His depiction of her sadistic pleasure in the massacre as she emerges from the palace with a triumphant smile on her face to view the bloody victims is confirmed by Noguères's description of her laughing in a self-congratulatory mood as she watched the slaughter from her palace window.[26]

Neither of Catherine's sons is any match for her dominating personality in Griffith's presentation. His characterization of King Charles IX agrees with Guizot's description of him as "a young king of warm imagination and irrepressible and sympathetic temperament but at the same time of weak judgment."[27] He displayed "puerile weakness in the presence of his mother whom he feared more than he trusted," according to Guizot.[28] Griffith points up this weakness in the scene in which Charles signs the decree authorizing the massacre. After initially resisting, declaring "I will not consent to this intolerant measure to destroy a part of my people," he is driven to distraction by his mother and yields to her argument that "our very lives depend upon their extermination." Although Voltaire and other noted historians have argued that Charles participated in the massacre by shooting at the unsuspecting Huguenots from his palace balcony, Griffith does not include this incident, preferring to present the king in a more sympathetic role.[29]

Griffith portrays Henri, duc d'Anjou, the future Henri III and Charles's younger brother, as a decadent, effeminate fop who plays with toys. While his characterization is corroborated by most historians, including De Thou, who attested to Henri's "showiness and effeminacy," Griffith does not show any of the more positive aspects of the prince's divided personality.[30] For example, he omits all references to Henri's reputation as a brave warrior. All the scenes in which he takes part are at the court, where he appears wearing earrings and extravagant attire with puppies in his doublet-top. This representation is validated by the accounts of the Duke of Sully, a member of the court who recalled years after the

Catherine de Medici incites Charles IX to take action against the Huguenots (the French Story).

fateful event of 1572 that "he (Henri) had a sword at his side, a Spanish hood down upon his shoulders, a little cap, such as collegians wear, upon his head, and a basket full of little dogs hung to a broad ribbon about his neck."[31] Griffith's portrait of Henri as a passive and weak character, a mere satellite of his mother who bolsters her call for a massacre and joins her to gloat over the bodies of the victims, also conforms to descriptions of the historical Henri.

Griffith depicts Admiral Coligny, the leader of the Protestant faction at court, as a sincere and upright confidant of the king, his plain dress contrasting with the luxurious costume of Henri. Referred to in a subtitle as "the great Admiral Coligny," his screen characterization harmonizes with Guizot's tribute to the "loftiness of his views" and "the earnest gravity of his character."[32] In the film, his influence with the king arouses Catherine's jealousy, and his appearance in the introductory scene establishes the rivalry at court that leads to the massacre. Historians seem to agree that the competition between Coligny and Catherine, manifesting the widespread factionalization among Protestants and Catholics in France, created the atmosphere that precipitated the violence. According to Noguères, the queen, who feared she was "about to be superseded by the

Ladies of the court dressed in their finery (the French Story).

admiral," panicked and was willing to adopt any means to preserve her authority in the government.[33]

Griffith faithfully documents the actual incidents of August, 1572, tracing the chronology without distortion. His meticulous recreation of the events that culminated with the massacre coincides with the historical record: the schism at court between Catholics and Huguenots; the wedding procession of Henri of Navarre and Marguerite de Valois; the nighttime session in the palace between Catherine and Charles; the soldiers marking the Protestant houses with crosses; the tocsin of St. Germain l'Auxerrois signaling the massacre; the climactic scenes showing the royal soldiers committing all manner of atrocities, including infanticide, on the unprepared Huguenots.

Despite his accurate documentation of incidents, Griffith omits significant facts that might tend to obscure or complicate his thesis. The film makes no reference to Coligny's attempt to influence Charles IX to engage in a war with Spain in order to aid the Protestant revolt in the Spanish-dominated Netherlands. By not alluding to this major goal of Coligny's, Griffith avoids any ambiguity in his interpretation of the role of the Protestant leader. Had he shown him advocating a policy with possible imperialistic aims, Griffith might have found it difficult to justify picturing Coligny as a sympathetic historical figure in the context of a pacifist film. To bring out this fact might also have detracted from Griffith's delineation of Coligny as victim and Catherine as villain. At no point in the film does he rationalize the queen's actions as deriving from policy disagreements over a potential war with Spain; rather he attributes them exclusively to fear and jealousy over a threat to her power. He also fails to show Catherine's initial attempt to have Coligny assassinated, an omission undoubtedly motivated by his desire to simplify the plot rather than to distort the facts. Another point he excludes from the film is the intent of Catherine's original plan, which was, according to the chroniclers, the elimination of key leaders of the Huguenot faction, not the instigation of a wholesale massacre of the Protestants. Instead, Griffith emphasizes Catherine's culpability for the atrocities, reinforcing his contention that crimes of intolerance affecting ordinary people spring from the arbitrary decisions of powerful leaders.

Although he clearly projects the viewpoint of a Protestant republican democracy, Griffith's criticism of a royalist, hierarchical tyranny is balanced, as he acknowledges intolerance on both sides. In a scene at court, Coligny, like Catherine, wishes his opponents would think as he does. Griffith presents Catherine's rationalization for the massacre in a flashback depicting Huguenot brutality in the Michelade at Nimes in 1567, when Protestants destroyed religious artifacts and killed Catholics. When Lillian Gish expressed shock at Catherine's villainy, he replied:

> Don't judge. Just be thankful it isn't you committing some black deed. Always remember this, Miss Lillian — circumstances make people what they are. Everyone is capable of the lowest and the highest. The same potentialities are in us all — only circumstances make the difference.[34]

According to Bernard Hanson, who studied the scrapbook compiled during the film's production: "Nothing indicates that systematic research was done for the visual aspects of the French sequence. Already by 1914 the traditions of the French theater were followed for movies relating to historical France," a practice Griffith had adopted in earlier films with

Opposite: Catherine views the victims of the massacre (the French Story).

French period settings.[35] Brown recollects that old illustrations of sixteenth-century France were used to authenticate the settings and costumes.[36] In addition, Griffith enhanced the visual reality by careful choice of players and attention to makeup to simulate the leading historical figures, Catherine, Charles IX, Henri, duc d'Anjou and Admiral Coligny, as they appear in old portraits.

Sources for the Babylonian Story

With the Babylonian Story, the most spectacular of the four, Griffith aims at nothing less than a total recreation of a lost civilization on the eve of its downfall. Reflecting the modern interest in the nineteenth and twentieth century archaeological discoveries of ancient civilization, this story presents a fresh interpretation of antiquity. For his narrative, he turned to the Greek historian Herodotus and contemporary scholars of ancient history, including Archibald Henry Sayce and Morris Jastrow, Jr., then used his imagination to complete the gaps in regard to the events and personalities surrounding the fall of Babylon to Persian forces in 539 B.C. His scenario differs sharply in details and interpretation from the Old Testament account in the Book of Daniel. For his depiction of Babylonian civilization—its religion, customs, costumes and architecture—he relied on the archaelogical excavations of his time.

Griffith's fresco of Babylonian life represents the tremendous appeal of the archaeological excavations to the Western imagination. Scholars gained first-hand knowledge and new insights into the history and culture of the ancient Middle East beginning with the discovery of the Rosetta Stone in 1799, which led to the deciphering of Egyptian hieroglyphics by Jean François Champollion in 1822. In the early 1800s, Claudius James Rich, a British diplomat stationed in Baghdad, initiated the modern interest in Mesopotamia with his careful survey of the ruins of Babylon, resulting in the first detailed map of the abandoned city. The excavations in the 1840s of Paul Émile Botta, a French consul in Iraq, and Sir Austen Henry Layard, a British explorer, as they uncovered the long-buried Assyrian empire, generated great excitement in the West. Botta's *Monument de Ninive* (1849), and Layard's *Nineveh and Its Remains* (1849) were widely read, indicative of the public's growing fascination with the origins of civilization. In the early 1850s, Sir Henry Creswicke Rawlinson, a renowned British soldier and scholar, announced his decipherment of cuneiform writing, a monumental breakthrough in the study of Mesopotamia. Successive archaelogical excavations in the nineteenth and early twentieth centuries uncovered the remains of the ancient Sumerians, founders of the Mesopotamian civilization, and the Hittites, builders of a great empire in the Middle East in the second millenium B.C. In 1899, Robert Koldewey, a German archaeologist, began the systematic excavation of Babylon, which continued until 1917, when World War I brought a halt to his expeditions. Koldewey's findings were published in his 1914 book, *The Excavations at Babylon.*[37]

Griffith was able to amplify his conception of the Babylonian ruling class and its culture through his study of works based on the new discoveries of cuneiform writing. They included *Lectures on the Origin and Growth of Religion as Illustrated by the Religion of the Ancient Babylonians* (1887), and *Babylonians and Assyrians* (1900), by A.H. Sayce, and *Aspects of Religious Belief and Practice in Babylonia and Assyria* (1911), and *The Civilization of Babylonia and Assyria* (1915), by Morris Jastrow. Since information concerning the historical individuals involved in the fall of Babylon is fragmentary, Griffith elaborated on the facts, creating partially fictionalized characterizations of leaders who dramatize the clash of personalities in the Persian conquest.

Nabonidus, the king of Babylon, who gained power through a revolution and reigned from 555 to 539 B.C., is a comparatively irrelevant figure in *Intolerance*. He is shown announcing his discovery of the foundation-stone of the early Mesopotamian ruler, Naram-Sin, a historical incident verified by a cuneiform inscription in which the king states "how he trembled with excitement and awe when he read on (the stone) the name of Naram-Sin ... who, he says, ruled 3200 years before."[38] Absorbed in his archaeological find, the filmic Nabonidus displays his lack of concern for the affairs of state when he offhandedly mentions that the Persian forces are approaching the city of Babylon. The validity of this aspect of his personality is supported by Robert William Rogers in *The Religion of Babylonia and Assyria* (1908) who says that Nabonidus "was without military skill or interest" and that he "busied himself chiefly with the restoration of temples."[39]

Adhering to historical fact, the film makes clear that Prince Belshazzar has assumed the rule of Babylon from his father, Nabonidus. Cuneiform documents of the time attest to Belshazzar's administrative abilities as regent of Babylon. Griffith is at variance with history, however, in showing Belshazzar as the initiator of religious reform. Although the prince undoubtedly continued his father's policies, it was King Nabonidus who began a revolutionary religious reform "to undermine the local character of [Babylonian religion] and create a universal religion," a move which brought about a schism between the priests and the central government.[40] Griffith's characterization of Belshazzar as an enlightened leader attracting the love and devotion of his people contrasts with the dissolute wastrel described in the Book of Daniel whose fall is foretold by the handwriting on the wall. While adapting from the Biblical episode a picture of Belshazzar delighting in wine, women and song, Griffith does not present the prince's epicureanism on the eve of his city's fall in the same light as the Old Testament. Consistent with his humanism, he sees Belshazzar's revelry as a lapse in judgment rather than an example of pagan debauchery. No hand appears on the wall to warn Belshazzar of his imminent destruction, a fate resulting, not from the vengeance of God, but the treachery of man. The prince is, in Griffith's conception, a nobler character than his enemies, and in this way resembles the more austere Admiral Coligny in the French Story. Since the historical record of Belshazzar is sketchy, Griffith is free to ascribe heroic qualities to him. Film historian Jean Mitry, in defending the accuracy of the film, says Belshazzar "governed with much practical sense" although he was destroyed by the priestly class for carrying out his father's reform policies.[41]

The High Priest of Bel, the chief villain, is a product of Griffith's ingenuity in designing a character embodying historical forces. Historically, the priestly class, the most powerful group in Babylonian society, was headed by a high priest or "shangu nakhkhu" in the Babylonian language. According to Jastrow, Nabonidus antagonized the priests of Bel-Marduk, causing them to seek revenge by aiding "the advance of Cyrus who was hailed by them as the deliverer of Marduk."[42] Since there is no documentation establishing or refuting the culpability of a high priest in the betrayal of Babylon, Griffith was at liberty to create a character representing the hostility of the theocracy toward Belshazzar's leadership.

Cyrus's characterization represents the most striking departure from traditional accounts of all the historical figures in the Babylonian Story. Overlooking Cyrus's positive reputation in history, Griffith's subtitles refer to him only as Cyrus the Persian, never as Cyrus the Great. His appearance on the screen, with his hulking figure and fierce demeanor, emphasizes Griffith's conception of the Persian leader as a cruel warrior. The titles reinforce the visuals, calling Cyrus's sword "the most potent weapon forged in the flame of intolerance," and describing his preparations for battle with: "And Cyrus repeats the world-old prayer to kill, kill, kill. And to God be the glory, forever and ever, Amen."

The Bible and Jewish tradition, Herodotus and other Greek writers, and Cyrus's cuneiform inscriptions present a picture of the Persian monarch which contradicts Griffith's portrayal. Jewish tradition honors Cyrus for liberating the Jews from Babylonian captivity, allowing them to return to their homeland. The Greek historians, basing their interpretations on Persian accounts, also present Cyrus favorably. Herodutus describes Cyrus's leniency toward his enemy, Croesus, the king of Lydia, whom he conquered in battle. *The Cyropoedia*, a biography of Cyrus by Xenophon, a Greek historian who lived in Persia in the fifth century B.C., glorifies the Persian conqueror as wise and tolerant, an ideal ruler. The inscriptions of Cyrus justify his conquests, praising his tolerance and mercy and his overthrow of the heretical Nabonidus and Belshazzar. Working from these sources, most historians to the present day have extolled Cyrus as one of the most brilliant and merciful leaders in antiquity.

Although Griffith's characterization of Cyrus might appear to be an extreme distortion, drawing a full picture of the monarch's personality is difficult since the traditional conception is based on incomplete data and biased interpretations. In a recent book on Babylonian history, Joan Oates states that "the Greek accounts are based on Persian sources, which all betray an understandable bias against Nabonidus."[43] She describes Cyrus's "blatant propaganda campaign throughout the Babylonian empire, winning support for what were presented as his liberal policies."[44]

Undoubtedly, Griffith's perception was modified by his anti-imperialist attitudes stemming from his Southern background, but he seems to have deliberately excluded any positive aspects of Cyrus's personality in order to cast him in the classic mold of the conqueror. While he shows him as a fierce warrior, he does not ascribe to Cyrus acts of brutality or plunder which would be a total violation of historical fact. The historical gaps in the record gave him the freedom to evolve Cyrus's character to accomodate his dramatic scheme. From the perspective of the Babylonians, Griffith's portrayal of Cyrus may not be as much at variance with history as has been assumed. Cyrus's skillful use of propaganda to rationalize his restless ambition and continual aggression would seem to indicate a personality more complex than the traditional representations of the model ruler. Later empire builders, including Alexander the Great, Julius Caesar, Charlemagne, Genghis Khan and Napoleon Bonaparte, are the subjects of a far more detailed, varied and even contradictory historical literature, alternately depicted as tolerant, statesmanly heroes and bloodthirsty despots. Considering that the more fragmentary record of Cyrus derives from a single perspective which excludes the comments and criticism of his adversaries, Griffith's view of the conqueror cannot be dismissed as historically invalid. Even the favorable accounts attest to his ferocity in battle. The cuneiform inscriptions state that "when Cyrus fought at Opis on the Tigris river against the troops of Akkad (Babylonia), the people of Akkad he destroyed by means of a conflagration; he put the people to death."[45] And, as Griffith's interpretation suggests, Cyrus's tolerance for the established systems in the lands he conquered may have helped to prevent change within those societies.

Griffith synthesized his source material on the incidents of the Persian conquest of Babylon to produce an imaginative scenario which embellished or altered the meager facts in accord with his vision. The dissension between the priests of Bel-Marduk and the Babylonian government in the film had been brought to light by the cuneiform inscriptions excavated at the site of Babylon in the nineteenth century. His spectacular battle scenes were influenced by Herodotus and Xenophon. Both contend that the Babylonians engaged the Persians in battle near Babylon, followed by Cyrus's siege of the city. In describing this confrontation, Herodotus wrote: "The Babylonians had taken the field and were awaiting his (Cyrus's) approach. When he arrived near the city they attacked him, but were defeated and forced to retire inside their defenses." A siege dragged on with no sign of progress; "Cyrus was beginning to despair of success"

and, acting on a plan, he withdrew his forces to another area.[46] Xenophon argues that the Persians were unable to surround the extensive walls. "On this account Cyrus withdrew his soldiers to their tents in the face of missiles from the Babylonians."[47] Drawing on these accounts, Griffith depicts Persian forces besieging the city and meeting fierce resistance from the Babylonians, who engage them in hand-to hand combat outside the walls and defend themselves with bows and arrows from their ramparts. The conflict ends with a resounding victory by Babylon over Persia, a version which more closely reflects Xenophon than Herodotus, who records that the siege ended in a stalemate. The "Nabonidus Chronicle," a cuneiform account of the fall of Babylon, refers to battles fought elsewhere in the empire but makes no mention of a battle and siege outside Babylon, leading some historians to speculate that the Greeks may have confused Cyrus's conquest of Opis on the Tigris with a struggle for Babylon. However, as Raymond Philip Dougherty comments in his study *Nabonidus and Belshazzar*, "the text of the 'Nabonidus Chronicle' is extremely terse, and there is no assurance that it contains a complete statement of all that occurred in connection with Cyrus's conquest of Babylon."[48]

According to Herodotus and Xenophon, Cyrus devised a scheme for capturing Babylon in which the Euphrates River was diverted into a marsh, allowing the Persians to enter the impregnable city by following the riverbed. While the cuneiform tablets record only that the Persians took the city "without fighting," Jastrow and Sayce infer from the hints in the inscriptions that the fall of Babylon was accomplished by a conspiracy between the priests of Bel-Marduk and Cyrus. Ignoring the Greek accounts of the Persians entering the city through the shallow Euphrates riverbed, Griffith partially based his interpretation of Babylon's conquest on the deductions of Jastrow and Sayce. In the film, the High Priest of Bel journeys to the Persian camp to inform Cyrus that the gates will be left open while Belshazzar and his followers are distracted by the feast celebrating their recent victory over the Persians. Herodotus, Xenophon and the Book of Daniel are consistent in their contentions that the Babylonians were taken by surprise while in the midst of a great feast. As Herodotus writes, the Babylonians "knew nothing of what had chanced, but as they were engaged in a festival, continued dancing and revelling until they learnt the capture but too certainly."[49] Xenophon's book confirms that, as in the film, Cyrus waited to storm the city until the overconfident Babylonians were absorbed in their revelry.[50]

The sources disagree on the extent of the resistance offered by the Babylonians, with Xenophon claiming that a drawn-out battle ensued, the cuneiform inscriptions stating that the occupation was entirely peaceful, and Herodotus and the Book of Daniel indicating that there was no prolonged struggle. Influenced by Herodotus and Daniel, Griffith shows scat-

Opposite: Persian forces lay siege to Babylon (the Babylonian Story).

tered and ineffectual resistance by the unprepared Babylonians. Daniel and Xenophon claim that Belshazzar died when Babylon was taken, with the former recording he was slain but providing no details and the latter relating that he was killed by Cyrus's lieutenant, Gobryas. With available information inconclusive, Griffith chose to embellish his narrative, portraying Belshazzar, his consort and their servants committing suicide, a common practice of nobles in antiquity to avoid the disgrace of capture. Deviating from the cuneiform inscriptions, Griffith alters the chronology by telescoping the details in the climax. According to the "Nabonidus Chronicle," Gobryas led the Persian troops into the city, with Cyrus making his triumphal entry seventeen days later, hailed by the priests of Bel-Marduk as their deliverer. Griffith shows Cyrus and Gobryas joining forces to lead the attack. Cyrus makes his entry into Babylon immediately after he seizes the city, at which time he is acclaimed by the High Priest of Bel as "the king of kings and lord of lords."[51]

The only comprehensive criticism of Griffith's treatment of history in the Babylonian Story to appear at the time was the commentary by the Reverend Canon William Sheafe Chase, rector of Christ's Episcopal Church in Brooklyn. Chase argued in a letter to *The New York Times* that the Babylonian Story "misrepresents the historical facts, beyond what dramatic license can justify." In attempting to refute the validity of Griffith's interpretation, Chase contended that Cyrus's conquest benefited Babylon by restoring stability to the government. To support his arguments, he quoted from L.W. King's *History of Babylon* (1915) which states that the "tranquility of the country under Cyrus formed a striking contrast to the unrest and intrigue" of the reign of Nabonidus and Belshazzar. He provided further evidence for his position, quoting from *Passing of the Empires* by Gaston Maspero: "Babylon suffered in no way by her servitude and, far from being a source of unhappiness, she actually rejoiced in it." While he acknowledged "There is some evidence on the cuneiform inscriptions ... that the heathen priests betrayed Belshazzar," Chase emphatically denied that the civilization was destroyed by religious intolerance. Ignoring the fact that the Babylonians' periodic revolts against Persian rule caused Shah Xerxes I to plunder the city in 482 B.C., he claimed that Babylon continued to flourish until the time of Alexander the Great, with its eventual decline coming from "a gradual and purely economic process" when the center of trade shifted to nearby Seleuceia.[52]

Chase's critique must be weighed against his background as a highly reactionary fundamentalist cleric who inveighed against "indecency" in films and supported the enactment of Prohibition. In the 1920s, he sympathized with the revived Ku Klux Klan, calling it a strong "patriotic organization" that defended the U.S. Constitution and opposed immorality in society.[53] His real motive in criticizing the Babylonian Story, as becomes apparent in his concluding remarks, may have arisen from his objection to Griffith's attack on Prohibition in the Modern Story:

In Mr. Griffith's opinion, it is intolerance which has induced eighteen
states to enact prohibitory laws and has driven 500 saloons out of
New York during the last year. He represents that these reforms have
been caused by the same spirit which incited the massacre of the
Protestants in France on St. Bartholomew's Day and which brought
about the crucifixion of Jesus.

Mr. Griffith has a right to exhibit such absurd ideas if he really
holds them, but to proclaim that intolerance destroyed Babylon is
too ridiculous to be accepted without protest.[54]

Although it is impossible to fully assess the accuracy of historical
detail due to the fragmentary record, Griffith's film conveys generalized
emotional and historical truths of the final days of the great early
Mesopotamian civilization. Despite Chase's critical evaluation buttressed
by historical references, many scholars conclude that the Persian conquest
ended this civilization by interrupting its indigenous development.
Dougherty maintains that "the disaster which brought the Neo-Babylonian
empire to a close" was a turning-point which "introduced a new pre-
dominating influence in ancient Oriental developments."[55] Oates points
out that, with the Persian conquest, "new religious and political ideas were
gradually replacing those of ancient Mesopotamia."[56] Herodotus writes of
"the poverty which followed upon the conquest with its attendant hardship
and general ruin."[57]

Following the Greek historian, Griffith presents the fall of Babylon as
a great historical tragedy. While the Persian conquest may not have been
an immediate disaster for Mesopotamian civilization as Griffith implies,
the long-term consequences of Persian domination indisputably eroded
the cultural autonomy of the Tigris-Euphrates river valley. The glory of
mankind's first great civilizations ended with the incorporation of Egypt
and Mesopotamia into a greater Persian empire. The ancient literature of
Mesopotamia was forgotten, since the Persians "had their own literature
and were apparently very little sympathetic to the history and legends of
their late enemy."[58] Babylon itself "survived only as a minor provincial
capital" and "slowly vanished into oblivion."[59] With the conquest of the
Persian empire by Alexander the Great in the fourth century B.C., the
torch of civilization was passed to Greece and Rome in the West and India
and China in the Far East. Not until the rise of Islam a millenium later did
the entire Middle East reassert its cultural independence. With the
establishment of the Abbasid Caliphate of Baghdad in the eighth century
A.D., the Tigris-Euphrates river valley reemerged, for the first time since
the fall of Babylon, as the center of a flourishing, Semitic-speaking
civilization.

Chase's contention that religious intolerance played no significant role
in the destruction of Babylon is not only in conflict with Griffith's interpretation but contradicts the reality of Middle Eastern cultural history.
Civilization in the Middle East is characterized by theocentric absolutism

in contrast to the humanism of European and East Asian civilizations and the pantheism of South Asian civilization. Consequently, the civilizations of the Middle East tend to draw rigid distinctions between God and man, viewing attempts to alter the divinely ordained religious structures as heresies. The reform movement of Nabonidus and Belshazzar "constituted a religious innovation which proved exceedingly unpopular with conservative elements in Babylonia."[60] In Egypt in the fourteenth century B.C., this type of ideological schism was evident in the bitter opposition of the priestly hierarchy to the unsuccessful efforts of the pharaoh Akhenaton to establish a new monotheistic religion. Succeeding Egypt and Mesopotamia as the leading center of Middle Eastern culture, Persia was also dominated by a religious hierarchy—the Zoroastrians—who suppressed the reform movement of Mazdak in the early sixth century A.D. Even in the twentieth-century Middle East, this pattern has continued as the Muslim modernists have failed to modify the rigidity of the entrenched Islamic fundamentalism in countries such as Saudi Arabia, Iran and Pakistan.

The validity of Griffith's view that the fall of Babylon was rooted in religious intolerance has broader historical implications for the Middle East as a whole. The ancient pre–Islamic civilizations of Egypt, Mesopotamia and Persia died out as a result of the fossilization of their religious structures, which would not tolerate change from within. Much of the equally theocratic Islamic Middle East has lagged behind the rest of the world in adapting its religious culture to a modern, more pluralistic society. Griffith's grasp of the historic problems of the Middle East demonstrates what James Agee described as the director's intuitive perception "of the memory and imagination of entire peoples" that he used to project "an absolute and prophetic image of a nation and a people."[61]

Griffith's most ambitious undertaking was his attempt to recreate the remote Mesopotamian civilization resurrected from oblivion with the archaeological excavations of the nineteenth century. William K. Everson notes that "Griffith's handling of the Babylonian sequences is masterly." Coupling his rich imagination and ingenuity with the historical data, he "builds up an astonishingly convincing picture of Babylonian life."[62] His reproduction encompasses the religion, customs, class and governmental structures, military technology and architecture of ancient Babylon. His view of antiquity represents a radical departure from the traditionalist conceptions of the Biblical epics of Cecil B. DeMille and his imitators and the silent Italian spectacles. DeMille's projection of antiquity, emanating from the fundamentalist Judeo-Christian heritage, shows the early civilizations as pagan tyrannies lacking moral and ethical standards. The Italian films reflect the European-centered perspective, which views classical Greece and Rome as the true fulfillment of early civilization. Griffith's conception of civilization, influenced by the new archaeological findings, recognizes that, in spite of its weaknesses, a non–Christian, non–European society can equal or surpass the accomplishments of the West.

Griffith depicts Babylon as a society dominated by its religion. In the film, most elements of the civilization, including the government, the customs and ceremonies, and the arts, as confirmed by archaeological discoveries, are reflections of religious values. Historically, the cities of Mesopotamia originated as population centers grouped around the temples or ziggurats. Each city was consecrated to a particular deity in the belief that man's primary function was to serve the gods.[63]

Babylon's chief deity was Bel-Marduk, a solar god who, after gradually absorbing the characteristics of the other divinities, was elevated by Hammurabi to the head of the Mesopotamian pantheon in the eighteenth century B.C., when Babylon emerged as the dominant power in the Tigris-Euphrates Valley. Dating from that time, Bel-Marduk was extolled as the king of the gods by the Babylonians. Indeed, worshipping other deities in his place was considered heresy.

Although Bel-Marduk was revered by his followers as a protector of mankind, Griffith emphasizes only his supremacy in the traditional pantheon. The first reference to Babylon's official cult occurs when the High Priest appears in his temple tower above the city. Accompanying the shot is the subtitle: "The priest of Bel-Marduk, the supreme god of Babylon, jealously watches the statue of the rival goddess, Ishtar, enter the city, borne on a sacred ark." To the right of the High Priest is a huge statue of Bel-Marduk, surrounded by a cloud of incense. The overall effect of the visual composition accentuates the divinely ordained authority of the priesthood over the city. The administrator of the largest temple complex in the empire dedicated to the Supreme Deity, the High Priest presides over a hierarchy that includes assistant priests and agents who carry out his orders. Griffith's conception of the power invested in the priesthood derives in part from Jastrow's contention that the Babylonian priests "virtually held in their hands the life and death of the people" as intermediaries between God and man.[64]

Griffith is more definitive in his portrayal of the rival cult of Ishtar, the goddess of love and fertility, presenting a union between spiritual and sensual conceptions of love more common to the civilizations of the East than the Christian West. Linking sexuality with mysticism, a part of all Eastern religions, is alien to Christianity, which has the Virgin Mary as its leading feminine object of adoration. The shot of a fire burning in the temple tripod, a metaphor for passion inspired by the veneration of fire in many ancient religions, accompanies a scene of temple prostitution. Griffith's camera reveals naked and seminaked young women consecrated to the goddess in Ishtar's Temple of Love and Laughter as the subtitle paradoxically calls them "Virgins of the Sacred Fire of Life." In the midst of this erotic imagery, Belshazzar says to his consort, the Princess Beloved: "The fragrant mystery of your body is greater than the mystery of life." A daring interpretation in the context of the Christian culture, Griffith's depiction again relied on Jastrow and Sayce for supportive material.

Jastrow describes Ishtar as "the goddess of the human instinct, or passion which accompanies human love" and "the mother of mankind ... who awakens passion."[65] Sayce characterizes her as "the fruitful goddess of the earth" and "the patroness of love."[66] A Mesopotamian hymn praises her as "the queen of women, the greatest of all the gods ... clothed with delight and love ... full of ardor, enchantment and voluptuous love."[67] Jastrow points out that she was "attended by maidens who appear to be her priestesses."[68] Sayce notes that these priestesses engaged in prostitution, which "became a religious duty whose wages were consecrated to the goddess of love."[69]

The cult of Ishtar also underlies the religious ceremonies in the film. Since knowledge of Mesopotamian rituals is incomplete, Griffith collaborated with Ruth St. Denis, a famous choreographer familiar with the heritage of Oriental dance, to create the elaborate religious dance performed in the courtyard during Belshazzar's feast. The dance, according to the subtitle, commemorates the resurrection of Tammuz, Ishtar's departed lover, who returned to the goddess from the underworld. The authenticity for this sequence originates with Sayce, who writes that "the resurrection of Tammuz had once been commemorated as well as his death" in Babylonia.[70]

While he stresses Ishtar's role as a goddess of love, Griffith also acknowledges her warlike qualities. In history, she is known as "the deity who furnishes aid in war and battle" and "is called 'the warlike Ishtar.' "[71] This dualism is revealed in the film during the Persian siege of Babylon when the priests of Ishtar, throwing animal sacrifices into a temple fire, exhort her to "seize now the flaming sword," and again, when the Princess Beloved beseeches the goddess to fight for her lord. Additionally, Belshazzar ascribes his triumph in battle to the aid of Ishtar.

Griffith posits that a conflict between the entrenched theocracy of Bel-Marduk and the ascendant cult of Ishtar brought about the fall of Babylon. For the purpose of illustrating the eternal struggle between repressive orthodoxies and the liberating forces of love and tolerance, he modifies and simplifies the nature of the religious controversies wracking the late Neo-Babylonian empire. In one sequence, the High Priest of Bel admonishes the people that they will bring about the ruin of Babylon if they continue to follow the cult of Ishtar. He sends his agent, the Rhapsode, to the tenement district "to convert backsliders to the true cult of Bel." While watching the great feast from his temple tower, the High Priest vows to Bel that, although they worship Ishtar now, "Cyrus, your servant, will avenge you."

In actuality, the religious strife had broader ramifications, arising when Nabonidus turned away from Bel-Marduk and attempted to establish a new religious structure centered around the worship of the moon-god, Sin, whom the king proclaimed the most important deity. Associated with Sin were his son, Shamash, the sun-god, and his daughter,

Ishtar, a link confirmed by a stele excavated in 1956 showing Nabonidus worshipping the three deities.[72] Nabonidus' devotion to the cult of the moon-god angered the priests of Bel-Marduk, and his efforts to secure a unified religion antagonized the priesthoods throughout the country when he moved the images of the local gods to Babylon, placing them on an equal level with Bel-Marduk. The hostility of the priesthood toward Nabonidus and Belshazzar served to aid Cyrus, who styled himself as the restorer of Mesopotamian religious values, and ultimately doomed the Neo-Babylonian Empire.

In concentrating on the cults of Bel-Marduk and Ishtar, Griffith omits salient aspects of the total religious picture in the Middle East during the sixth century B.C. He stresses the joyous rituals of Ishtar, making only passing reference to the darker, more pessimistic side of Mesopotamian religion. Its fatalistic belief that, after death, man is destined to a shadowy existence in Hades appears at the end of the Babylonian Story when Belshazzar, the Princess Beloved and their servants commit suicide, knowing they will enter "the death-halls of Allat," the goddess of the underworld.

Even more striking is Griffith's omission of the Jewish religion in Babylon. His narrative does not include the Babylonian captivity of the Jews and the prophecies of Daniel even though in Judeo-Christian tradition these events are held to be the most significant in the history of that period. Because the Bible credits the Persians with liberating the Jews from Babylonian oppression Griffith undoubtedly reasoned that any reference to the Jews might inadvertently shift audience sympathy away from Belshazzar to Cyrus.

Griffith makes no mention of the lofty tenets of Zoroastrianism in his portrait of the Persians, indicating they were sun-worshippers in a scene in which a revolving image of the sun dominates their religious rites. Although Zoroastrianism was beginning to spread in Persia at this time, his omission cannot be regarded as a distortion since there is no evidence to support some historians' claims that Cyrus was an adherent of Zoroastrianism. In fact, the religion did not replace the ancient Iranian nature-worship until the reign of Darius I.[73]

Babylonian society in the film is highly stratified, a representation verified by Jastrow, who notes that the Mesopotamians maintained a strict demarcation between the higher and lower classes.[74] To dramatize the societal structure, Griffith uses a series of contrasts: the elegant manner of Belshazzar and the Princess Beloved appears even more elegant juxtaposed against the rowdy behavior of the Mountain Girl, a member of the lower classes who has migrated from a rural setting to the capital city; the banquet in the great hall with its delicacies and "spiced wine, cooled with snow from the mountains" for Belshazzar and the lavishly attired nobles of Babylon including Egibi of the historical, wealthy banking family, seems all the more extravagant when intercut with the simple repast of the Mountain Girl in her humble quarters. The historicity for Griffith's intuitive representation of the conspicious consumption of the Mesopotamian upper class is found in a cuneiform description of a ninth century B.C. feast given by the Assyrian king, Ashurnasirpal II, in which immense quantities of meat dishes, bread, beer and wine, side dishes and dessert were devoured.[75]

The potential threat posed by the gap between the aristocracy and the commoners is held in check in the film partly because they share a common danger from the Persians. More significantly, however, any widespread discontent is mitigated by Belshazzar's sense of responsibility toward his subjects, an aspect of the leader's rule substantiated by Jastrow, who contends that, whatever its shortcomings, the government recognized "obedience to ethical principles as the basis of well-being."[76] Griffith implies this sense of justice springs from the Code of Hammurabi. As he points out in a courtroom scene, "in the oldest known court in the world" justice as contained in the Code was designed to protect the weak from the strong. Excavated in 1901, the Code of Hammurabi, in Griffith's time, was believed to be the first "legal text," and its discovery enhanced Hammurabi's reputation as a ruler devoted to the welfare of his people.[77] Greatly impressed by the protection afforded the people by the governments in Mesopotamia as revealed in the Code, Griffith indicates that the benevolent leadership in Babylon contributed to the relative harmony in the society. Indeed, he was so intent on trying to project the concern for the public's welfare inculcated by Hammurabi's laws that he avoids any reference to the harsh penalties prescribed by the Code.

Griffith presents such a pervasive picture of the society that a scene inserted mainly for comic relief becomes an accurate illustration of the marriage market as described by Herodotus. When the Mountain Girl's brother, who is also her guardian, takes her to court complaining she is incorrigible, the judge rules she is to be placed on the marriage market. Griffith introduces the sequence with the title: "The Marriage Market. Money paid for beautiful women given to homely ones, as dowers, so that all may have husbands and be happy." From this point on, the details in the film correspond with the account of the Babylonian marriage market by Herodotus, who writes:

> An auctioneer then called each one in turn to stand up and offered her for sale, beginning with the best-looking and going on to the second best as soon as the first had been sold for a good price.... The rich men who wanted wives bid against each other for the prettiest girls, while the humbler folk, who had no use for good looks in a wife, were actually paid to take the ugly ones ... The money came from the sale of the beauties, who in this way provided dowries for their ugly and misshapen sisters.[78]

After panning the girls making up for the auction, the camera focuses on the playful antics of the Mountain Girl trying to discourage potential suitors. She is released from her obligations only when Belshazzar appears on the scene, handing her a legal document with the royal seal which gives her "freedom to marry or not to marry — to be consecrated to the goddess of love or not — as thou choosest."

Belshazzar's kindness to the Mountain Girl is emblematic of the bond between the king and his people and his paternalistic concern for their welfare. Not only in the marriage market sequence but throughout the Babylonian Story, Griffith suggests that Belshazzar is a champion of the people who commands popular support. Many historians, however, including Sayce, contend that the religious policies of Nabonidus and Belshazzar stirred discontent among "the great mass of people," resulting in a lack of resolve in the Babylonian resistance to Cyrus's onslaught.[79] Whether Griffith was indulging in his thematic parallelism to show the evils of theocratic despotism or employing logic to conclude that the absence of open revolt signified popular acceptance of the regime, his interpretation cannot be disproved because of the paucity of data. As is true with so much of history, the feelings and opinions of the ordinary people, who are Griffith's heroes and heroines, were unrecorded. Cyrus's inscriptions give the impression that the Babylonian people welcomed Persian intervention, but "since a campaign was instituted to blacken the name and reputation of the last Babylonian king," and reminders of his reign were systematically destroyed, it is impossible to accurately assess the degree of public support for the government of Nabonidus and Belshazzar.[80]

Dougherty adds credence to the soundness of Griffith's assumptions, pointing out the possibility the Persians exaggerated the extent of public discontent with the Babylonian government to justify their conquest of the country. He also argues that, if opposition to the regime were widespread, "the Babylonians would have known how to end the dynasty without looking to Cyrus for aid."[81] Furthermore, he refutes the claim by other historians that Cyrus's troops entered Babylon virtually unopposed and cites fierce resistance in some parts of the country as an indication that the Babylonian government was able to command the loyalty of its people. As additional proof that the people were not totally alienated from their government, Dougherty mentions that Nidintu-Bel and Arahu, both claiming to be Nebuchadnezzar, son of Nabonidus, were able to rally public support for revolts against Darius I.[82]

While historical evidence is inconclusive regarding the level of Babylonian resistance to the invading Persians, the record reveals that both sides possessed efficient fighting machines, using advanced military technology developed by the Assyrians. Fascinated by the early achievements in the mechanization of warfare, Griffith staged a spectacular siege of Babylon complete with "ancient instruments of war," prompting a contemporary critic to note that "the attack of surging Persian hosts indicates that the modern war is not such an advance on ancient

Griffith's depiction of ancient warfare (the Babylonian Story).

conflicts as some war correspondents would have one believe."[83] For source material, he relied primarily on Layard's *Nineveh and Its Remains*, which annotates "the engines and materials necessary for the siege of the cities and the strategies used by the combatants."[84]

In Griffith's reconstruction of the siege, the Persians attack Babylon from great moving towers, engaging the Babylonians in battle on the ramparts. Layard confirms that "movable towers which held warriors and armed men" were made use of to put the besiegers in a better position for archers to harass the defenders and warriors to mount the walls. In the film, Persians operating from the siege towers utilize huge pincers to move a battering-ram in place to smash the city gate. Again Layard corroborates this depiction, stating that "the first step in attacking a hostile city was probably to advance the battering-ram" which could be "without wheels ... constructed on the spot" or "joined to movable towers." With the

Babylonians distracted by the assailants from the siege tower, Griffith shows hordes of Persians scaling the walls with ladders. This adheres to Layard's account, which notes that "mounting to the assault by ladders was constantly practiced and appears to have been the most general mode of attacking a castle." The catapult, too, assisting the advancing Persians, is modeled on Layard's description of "a kind of catapult ... (which) threw large stones and darts against the besieged."[85] Griffith, however, departs from Layard when he shows elephants in combat, a Persian innovation, as they push one of the siege towers into place. Nor does Layard contain collaborative material for the Persian archers with giant crossbows, a detail Griffith incorporates to illustrate the historic supremacy of the ancient Persians in archery.

The Babylonians in the battle sequence endeavor to fend off their attackers, firing arrows, hurling boulders from the ramparts and pouring oil on the battering-ram and the warriors below. They also set fire to the siege towers and topple them with long beams. According to Layard, "the besieged ... sought to destroy [the battering-ram] and threw lighted torches and firebrands upon it," and "manned the battlements with archers and slingers who discharged their missiles against the assailants." The boiling oil and boulders were suggested by Layard's description of "large stones and hot water" which were dropped on the foes.[86] Griffith's most striking deviation is his depiction of a Babylonian flame thrower mounted on wheels, which burns Cyrus's towers and succeeds in driving off the Persian forces. This weapon seems to have come from Griffith's imagination, although it is true that the Greeks developed a flamethrowing device for use in war some centuries later.

While the battle scenes display the destructive capabilities of the ancients made possible by technological advances in war, Griffith's recreation of the art and architecture of Mesopotamia pays tribute to the civilization's creative achievements. Collaborating with stage carpenter Frank Wortman and scenic designer Walter L. Hall, Griffith sought to reproduce Babylon as it might have appeared in the sixth century B.C. — dominated by towers and temples adorned with intricate designs reflecting the mythological beliefs of its people. To achieve their objective of an authentic presentation, Griffith and his associates studied the works of Layard, Sayce and Jastrow along with *Ancient Times: A History of the Early World* (1916) by James H. Breasted and the two-volume *A History of Art in Chaldea and Assyria* (1884) by Georges Perrot and Charles Chipiez. According to Karl Brown, Griffith and his collaborators combed these authorities "for the most meticulously accurate reproduction of these long-vanished structures. Most of these were highly educated guesses as to what ancient Babylon must have looked like ... but, from bits and pieces unearthed by archaeologists it was possible to make pretty fair assumptions."[87] Thus, Griffith reconstructed Babylon "as a pastiche of more-or-less authentic details," assimilating artistic and architectural designs from

Babylonia, Assyria and Persia and using his ingenuity when information was lacking.[88]

Like the ancient fortified city, the filmic Babylon appears impregnable, encircled by inner and outer walls reinforced by towers. To open the massive gates requires slaves working in unison to set in motion the cogs and gears that activate the hinges. Based on Herodotus, a subtitle notes that Babylon's walls were "300 feet in height and broad enough for the passing of chariots." Griffith, however, built walls 90 feet high, a dimension more in accord with contemporary scholars, who estimate that they were a maximum of 65 feet in height. The walls of Griffith's Babylon were wide enough for Belshazzar to ride across the summit in a chariot drawn by two horses. Commenting on Griffith's use of proportion in replicating Babylon, Jean Mitry states that it conforms perfectly to the facts as set forth by a modern historian, Marguerite Rutten.[89]

The gate of the inner wall of Imgur-Bel is a reproduction of the southeastern gate of Sargon II's palace in the Assyrian city of Khorsabad. Near the summit, its towers are decorated with winged sun-disks first used by the Assyrians. Standing at the bottom of the towers guarding the city are sculptures of human-headed winged bulls. Between them are "larger-than-life-size images of Gilgamesh holding a lion under his left arm," symbolic figures frequently found in Mesopotamian art.[90] With rosettes, palmettes and mosaic reliefs adorning the walls, Griffith carefully duplicates the Mesopotamian art uncovered by archaelogy.

Inside the city, the setting for the marriage market is decorated with a glazed-brick frieze of columns topped with volutes and the sacred tree of life, "a noted feature of late-Babylonian palace architecture."[91] The reproduction of the great central courtyard in the palace where Belshazzar holds his feast, reputed to be the most famous set in film history, incorporates authentic details of ancient Middle Eastern art. The staircases on the sides and the center of the courtyard are duplicated from the palace of the Persian monarch, Darius I, in Persepolis.

Throughout the set, Griffith uses the lion motif, common in Babylonian art. Images of lions are mounted on the balustrades of the great central staircase, larger statues of lions are placed at the base of the huge fluted, cylindrical columns, and reliefs of lions flanking a winged figure embellish each of the cornices atop the columns.

Eagle-headed, winged creatures, another recurrent motif in Mesopotamian art, appear as carvings on the massive piers supporting the columns in the foreground and painted at the top of the monumental double arch in the background. The sacred tree of life, also a characteristic Mesopotamian design, a winged genie and rosettes and palmettes complete the ornamentation of the archway. Between the columns on the right is a large statue of Ishtar as the mother-goddess nursing a child.

Opposite: The Great Court at Babylon (the Babylonian Story).

Detailed view of cornice and elephant statue atop one of the columns (the Babylonian Story).

Griffith's major discrepancy, undoubtedly borrowed from the Italian film *Cabiria*, is the inclusion of colossal elephant statues surmounting each of the cornices and at the foot of one of the right-hand columns. Unable initially to find historical verification for this motif, he was delighted when researcher R. Ellis Wales "found someplace a comment about the elephants on the walls of Babylon" and quickly adapted the concept to his set.[92] Despite this imaginative touch, the mammoth Babylonian set creates a convincing impression of the grandeur of ancient Mesopotamia.

Griffith's concern for authenticity extended to the costumes and artifacts, but available information is minimal regarding the specific sources he used in his research. Miss Gish recalls that Griffith "designed and was responsible for many of the costumes,"[93] and Hanson contends that "many of the details of the costumes ... and their embroidery are based on elements found in the scrapbook."[94] Most of the characters are clad in the traditional Mesopotamian "kaunakes," pictured in Middle Eastern art, described by Herodotus as consisting of "a linen tunic reaching to the feet with a woollen one over it and a short white cloak on top."[95] Griffith endeavors to indicate class differentiation in costuming, with nobles wearing elaborately embroidered, fringed and bespangled tunics and headdresses, and commoners dressed in simply designed coarse cloth which, like the Mountain Girl's clothes, looks "as if it were made of whatever stuff would be available."[96]

Like the costumes, the only information available on the sources for the artifacts is in the scrapbook. It contains models for Belshazzar's throne, ornamented by the sacred tree of life and, as Hanson's study reveals, "turned posts, 'pieds-de-biches,' animal heads and carved fringe tassels," all designs from Middle Eastern art. Also in the scrapbook are the illustrations of the original Mesopotamian chariots that Griffith referred to in assiduously detailing replicas for the film.[97]

Differing markedly from the stereotypical picture of a corrupt city designated by the Bible as "Babylon, the Great, the Mother of Harlots and of the Abominations of the Earth," Griffith's presentation of a civilization with high spiritual, ethical and artistic standards was acclaimed for its fidelity to the facts by scholars and film critics alike. Critic Julian Johnson said in *Photoplay Magazine* in 1916, "The Chaldean visions will teach history to college professors." He attributed Griffith's monumental achievement in the Babylonian Story, not solely to its use of spectacle, but to the director's genius "in re-creating the passions, the ambitions, the veritable daily life of a great people so remote that their every monument is dust, their every art-work lost, their very language forgotten."[98] Excerpts from congratulatory letters by historians Sayce and Jastrow appeared in the souvenir programs given out to the audiences during the initial presentation of the film in 1916–17. Commenting on the Babylonian Story, Sayce wrote:

> The Babylonian scenes are magnificent, as well as true to facts. I was much impressed by the attention that had been paid to accuracy in detail. The drama is educational in more than one direction, and the interest it must excite in Babylonian history is especially gratifying to the Assyriologist.

Jastrow, equally impressed with Griffith's production, stated:

You have succeeded in conveying to the audience a remarkably vivid picture of the art, architecture, costumes, public and private life of Babylonia. I was amazed to see how carefully you reproduced our knowledge of the enormous walls of the city, with their battlements and gates, the palace, the battle towers, the battering-rams and other instruments of ancient warfare.[99]

Griffith's interpretation of history blends the cyclical with the progressive. While believing that history repeats itself, he also feels that each turn of the wheel can bring humanity closer to the ideal, a conception embedded in the optimistic resolution of the Modern Story and the millenial epilogue. This fusion is apparent in each of the historical periods he chose to dramatize. Although intolerance besets the innocent in all four, each represents a dramatic change, whether for good or ill, in the history of mankind. The Babylonian Story deals with the collapse of one of the ancient centers of civilization and the erosion of the early Middle East; the Judean Story concerns the appearance of the world religion destined to transform the classical world; the French Story, pitting the Catholic royalty against the Protestant bourgeoisie, depicts the medieval world besieged by the emerging modern society; and the Modern Story portrays the contemporary forces of industrialism and urbanism crushing the age-old village world of personal relationships.

To bring these eras to life entailed exhaustive research to authenticate the facts. Griffith, however, was not a slave to documentation, discarding those facts which did not further his views and emphasizing those that buttressed his arguments. He augmented his interpretation of the past through his study of nineteenth-century art forms, which provided models for ideas and effects that became a part of his vision.

4. Artistic Influences

Utilizing elements from music, painting, theater, poetry and novels, Griffith produced a twentieth-century masterwork, adapting and synthesizing the art forms of the nineteenth century into the new medium of cinema. In addition, he was stimulated by the work of the European filmmakers, absorbing some of their techniques in spectacle and costume productions. As a result, *Intolerance* is a fusion of romanticism and realism. This blending is a distinguishing characteristic of nineteenth-century art, in which intuition, emotion and the exaggeration of incident and action to intensify the theme merges with a commitment to portray life realistically and project believable characters and situations in order to elucidate their social and historical significance.

Music

With Griffith, the use of musical scoring for films attained a new maturity. Deriving from the traditions of the nineteenth-century theater in which music heightened the action and set the mood for popular melodramas and sophisticated stage spectacles such as Sir Henry Irving's productions of Shakespeare, he was meticulous in selecting music to accompany his films. He often worked "for weeks with musicians to find music that would match each character and situation."[1] He believed that music was an integral part of cinema presentation:

> Watch a film run in silence and then watch it again with eyes and ears. The music sets the mood for what your eye sees; it guides your emotions; it is the emotional framework for visual pictures.[2]

Convinced that "The only pure art, if pure art exists, is music," he employed live symphony orchestras ranging in size from ninety pieces in the larger theaters to a minimum of twelve instruments in the smaller houses. He was so certain of the importance of the live orchestra in accentuating the effect of the imagery that in the 1940s he observed: "No sound track will reproduce the true melodic interrelation of instruments in an orchestra."[3]

The premiere of *Intolerance* at the Liberty Theatre was accompanied by a forty-piece orchestra and a chorus from the Metropolitan Opera House. The use of full-scale symphony orchestras for *The Birth of a Nation* and *Intolerance*, marking the maturation of film scoring, was of enormous assistance in catapulting the cinema from the nickelodeon entertainment of the working classes to an art form capable of attracting the most sophisticated circles.

The score for *Intolerance* included classical themes as well as some popular music. Griffith collaborated with Joseph Carl Breil, a composer and arranger who had worked with him on the score for *The Birth of a Nation*. Film historian A.R. Fulton gives a description of the music used in *Intolerance*:

> The music was varied as well as familiar — Beethoven's *Minuet in G* for the peaceful scene in the Huguenot home before the massacre, Handel's *Largo* for the scene in which Jesus is scorned by the Pharisees, "In the Good Old Summer Time" for a day at Coney Island, etc. The film provides opportunity for considerable use of imitative music, such as bugle calls, bells, and gongs, as well as accompaniment to the various dance scenes.[4]

Brown remembers that the "Bacchanale" from Saint-Saëns' *Samson and Delilah* was used to accompany scenes of Belshazzar's feast in the Babylonian Story.[5] Newspaper sources of the time record that Griffith and Breil also used excerpts from Wagner and Rimsky-Korsakov and the popular song, "My Wild Irish Rose," which was the theme for the Dear One.[6]

In addition to making use of music as an accompaniment, Griffith was indebted to the heritage of classical music in helping him to evolve cinematic form. While his other film epics are patterned on the symphonic form, *Intolerance* is often called "the only film fugue."[7] Corresponding to the exposition of the fugue, the theme is introduced in the opening sequences of the Modern Story and repeated in succession in the introductory segments of the other three stories. The Modern Story lays out the basic premise, showing the Vestal Virgins of Uplift initiating their plans for a moral reform campaign followed by shots of the workers peacefully pursuing their daily existence. The theme reappears in the succeeding stories with the Pharisees arrogating righteousness as they interrupt the daily tasks of the people in Judea; Catherine de Medici intriguing at court, followed by shots of the wedding procession and the Huguenot couple; and the Mountain Girl playfully spurning the advances of her would-be suitor, the Rhapsode, intercut with the High Priest of Bel angrily looking down from his lofty tower at the ceremonies of Ishtar.

Continuing to pattern the fugue form in which the exposition is succeeded by the discussion or development, Griffith elaborates the theme as the film proceeds. As the intertwined narrative becomes increasingly complex, he counterpoints the theme of intolerance with subthemes of love, courtship and celebration alternating with violence and loss. Like the windings of the melodic line throughout the fugue, the original theme is always apparent in the various segments of the stories. By the time he reaches the climax of the film, he recapitulates the theme with such rapid intercutting between the stories that, like the stretto of the fugue in which different musical parts overlap, the concluding sequences of each of the stories seem to tumble end over end in a dramatic montage.

Painting

First and foremost a visual artist, Griffith adapted the techniques of the painter, transforming the stationary two-dimensional representation "into the twentieth-century world of moving art."[8] His use of composition to draw the spectator's eye to the central subject of the shot and perspective to create the illusion of distance, combined with his skillful manipulation of light and shadow and color tinting to heighten the mood, demonstrates the capacity of the moving picture to rival painting as a visual art. In addition to utilizing specific paintings in the Babylonian Story, his work is reflective in a general sense of the realistic and romantic schools of painting.

No director has taken more pains to use details of composition to rivet the viewer's attention and create a pleasing visual effect. In the long-shot of the court of Charles IX, the eye focuses on the king seated on his throne with Catherine standing to his right at the apex of a triangle formed by a multitude of lords and ladies in the background. The triangular shape is complemented not only by the page boys kneeling on the left in the foreground, but also by the floor design and the fleurs-de-lis beneath the lavish tapestry. Similarly, in a shot of the Babylonian throne room during the Persian conquest, Griffith enhances the dominance of Belshazzar and the Princess Beloved through a series of rectangular units. In the foreground, the rectangles are apparent in the floor tile and in the grouping of the kneeling servants, a pattern which is repeated in the high window in the background and inverted in the throne itself forming a modified rectangle. In a shot of the strike sequence in the Modern Story, the visual composition stresses the guns of the militia by using the parallel lines of the soldiers stretched on the ground to complement their rifles pointed at the strikers.[9]

Throughout his work, Griffith is adept at using space to add depth to the flat, two-dimensional screen. During the siege of Babylon, the setting is given perspective with the high-angled shots of the towers receding into the background of the open sky as the action of the combatants fills the foreground. The eye of the viewer is directed towards the diagonal lines of the towers directly behind the combatants and through the elongated

Belshazzar and his consort during the Persian conquest (the Babylonian Story).

enclosure created by the series of towers. In a long-shot of Cyrus's troops pouring down the road, Griffith deepens the perspective by showing empty space in the foreground, a technique he often employs in his work.[10]

Griffith augments his compositions with lighting effects and color tints to underscore the emotion of the scene. When the Dear One's father dies, their small one-room apartment is "darkly lit with heavy shadows," conveying a sense of grief.[11] A close shot of the Boy in prison dramatically emphasizes his plight with light playing across his face framed by the bars against the black background of the prison walls. A long-shot of the Massacre of St. Bartholomew's Day is a study in black and white contrasts. The bodies of Huguenots clothed in black and white are strewn across the white cobblestones, reflecting the first rays of the dawn. The armorclad soldiers on their horses are swathed in the morning light as a white sky can be seen peeking through the dark clouds above the buildings that are framed by houses shrouded in darkness. A.R. Fulton points to another example of black and white contrasts in a scene in the Huguenot home in which the white candles and "the headdresses of the Huguenot women contrast strikingly with the dark background."[12] In the original prints, Griffith distinguished the four epochs with specific tints, using amber in the Modern Story, blue in the Judean Story, sepia in the French, and gray-green in the Babylonian. Additionally, moods and atmosphere in each of the four stories were enhanced by the choice of coloring, including flaming red for the shots of conflict in the strike, massacre and war sequences, blue for night scenes and yellow for daylight exteriors.[13]

In a unique adaptation of artistic techniques to the cinema, Griffith employs framing and masking to concentrate on specific details of an image, seldom using "the same shape twice in succession ... so that the eye of the spectator is kept moving."[14] His cameo shots edged in black accentuate the expressions of emotion in his characters such as in the close-up of the delighted Mountain Girl when she meets Belshazzar at the marriage market and the shot of the anguished Dear One at her husband's trial. He uses the vignette, masking the top, bottom, or sides of an image, to add depth and dimension. The long-shot of a train in the Modern Story, masked at the bottom, creates a wide-screen effect comparable to the CinemaScope process introduced in the 1950s. With the iris shot, he duplicates the action of the eye, focusing first on a detail, then gradually enlarging the picture to reveal the full image. For example, he introduces the Babylonian Story with a semi-circular iris shot of a portion of the gate of Imgur-Bel on the lower right of the frame, then opens to encompass the upper left as the full image is disclosed and "the camera retreats through the ages and time rolls backward."[15]

Although it is difficult to determine the extent to which Griffith was influenced by specific schools of art, his photography in the Modern Story contains striking similarities to contemporaneous American realistic painting. His earlier *The Musketeers of Pig Alley*, in the words of Richard J. Meyer, "had the look of the Ashcan School of art," which included the works of painters Robert Henri, George Bellows and John Sloan, who explored the contemporaneous daily life of the city, capturing its essence on canvas.[16] These artists, attracting national attention with their exhibitions in New York in February, 1908 and the Armory Show of 1913, were derisively called the "Ashcan School" of painters by critics who did not appreciate their realistic, unvarnished depictions of the world about them.

In his evocation of the joys and sorrows of lower-class life in the first decades of the twentieth century, Griffith's work parallels John Sloan's, whose paintings and sketches reflect his belief that his mission was to depict the life of his times. Sloan found subject material for his art on the streets of New York. Griffith went to downtown Los Angeles "to search out life at its worst" for scenes in the Modern Story that became, as Brown notes, "one long gray series of pictures in unrelieved monotone."[17] Sloan, who was an art editor and illustrator for the Socialist publication *The Masses* from 1912 to 1916, comments on the same social problems that caught Griffith's attention. In *Before Her Makers and Her Judge*, featured in the August, 1913 issue of *The Masses*, Sloan captures the sternness and hypocrisy of the judge, policeman and onlookers in a sketch of a prostitute in a night-court. "Sloan felt very strongly about the mistreatment" of these women who were regularly entrapped by the police, a procedure condoned by the judicial system.[18] Griffith indicates a similar sentiment in the scene in the Modern Story in which the uplifters and police, after raiding a brothel, herd the prostitutes into a patrol car. *Class War in Colorado*, appearing on the cover of the June, 1914, *Masses*, was Sloan's representation of the infamous Ludlow strike. Depicting a desperate miner firing a revolver as he holds a dead child while a dead woman and her child lie at his feet, it conveys the same powerful emotion as the shot of the Boy in the Modern Story clutching his father who has just been killed by the militia.[19] Reminiscent of Sloan's 1907 *Sixth Avenue and Thirtieth Street*, a painting of New York's Tenderloin District which faithfully records the "drab, shabby, happy, sad and human" surroundings, Griffith's scenes of the mean streets where the Boy first meets the Dear One blends the dreariness and joy of the slums.[20] The simple pleasures of working-class life are subject matter that appeals to both Griffith and Sloan. With a feeling for documentary realism, the painter and director alike are able to catch the exuberant, boisterous atmosphere of the saloons and dance halls where workers found diversion from their monotonous existence.[21]

The love of the sensual and exotic and the taste for violence in the Babylonian Story reflect the romantic school of painting led by Eugène Delacroix, the nineteenth-century master of French romantic art. Delacroix, who inspired many imitators, infused his work with a boldness and intensity of emotionalism that marked a departure from the restraint of the classical tradition. He was intrigued by the Middle East and often chose it as a subject for his art. His paintings *The Massacre at Chios* (1824), showing a Turkish horseman slashing at his helpless victims, and *The Death of Sardanapalus* (1827), with the dying Assyrian king witnessing the suffering of his subjects, are unsparing in their concentration on violence. Similarly, Griffith pictures the carnage in the siege of Babylon with heads being lopped off and fighters impaled. His elaboration of exotic architectural details in the Babylonian settings also bears a resemblance to Delacroix's opulent Moorish interiors and courtyards. Indeed, the French artist's studies of Eastern harem life may have served as a thematic prototype for Griffith's scenes of temple prostitutes in Ishtar's shrine and the undraped women at Belshazzar's feast.[22]

Besides the overall effect of art traditions on *Intolerance*, Griffith's mise-en-scène encompasses specific paintings. In his detailed study of Griffith's assimilation of artistic sources, Bernard Hanson identifies and describes the director's adaptation of nineteenth-century paintings for the Babylonian Story: *The Fall of Babylon* by Georges Rochegrosse, first exhibited in 1891; *Belshazzar's Feast* by John Martin, initially displayed in 1821; and *The Babylonian Marriage Market* by Edwin Long, exhibited in 1875.

Hanson's research, which appeared in *The Art Bulletin*, shows that Rochegrosse's painting of an orgy on the eve of Babylon's fall received a "mixed review" when it was first exhibited. He contends, however, that looking at one of the reviews provides the clue to its adaptability to the screen. Although he noted that the painting demonstrates a high degree of archaelogical knowledge and "ingenuity of reconstruction," the critic cited by Hanson maintained that Rochegrosse's work was so full of details that the central idea was lost, forcing the viewer to scrutinize the "composition piecemeal." When he adapted from the painting, Griffith drew upon its plethoric details, intercutting them between shots of the city being taken by Cyrus's forces and the scenes of the great court of Babylon. While the recreation of "Babylon's last bacchanal" was daring for the time with its scantily clad women, Hanson believes that the filmic adaptation lacks "the grand sweep of the painting ... so that only the 'piecemeal' details remain and the lush opulence of the late nineteenth-century French vision of decadence is lost."[23]

Hailed by David Wilkie, the nineteenth-century critic, for its outstanding treatment of "geometrical properties of space, magnitude and number" and its imaginative reconstruction of architecture, John Martin's *Belshazzar's Feast* provided background particulars for Griffith's spectacular Babylonian set. Thomas Balston, another critic, describes Martin's "multiplication of a few bystanders into an innumerable herd," "the complication of the architecture" and "this wealth of detail and movement." Hanson points out that Wilkie's and Balston's critical evaluations of the painting could also apply to Griffith's Babylon. Griffith, however, was able to free himself from the static confines of Martin's work and, by exploiting movement, give "fuller meaning to the idea behind" the tradition of English historical painting. With the aid of a camera mounted on an elevator, he moves from the vast panorama of the "innumerable herd" of people in the great court of Babylon to close-ups that reveal the characters' emotions.[24]

The influence of Martin's painting can be seen in Griffith's conception of the massive open court of Babylon with its stairways, its columns topped by cornices and its great corbelled arches. Although the painting and the film both create a feeling of "spatial grandeur," the differences between them, according to Hanson, reflect the uniqueness of the respective mediums. The main action in Martin's painting takes place "near the front of the scene and on a terrace reached by a broad flight of stairs above the column-flanked courtyard" while Griffith centers the action "at the top of the stairs and well within the courtyard" in order to utilize the moving camera. His modifications of Martin's design, including the separated cornices and the placement of the stairs between the piers, allow him to make more effective use of space to accomodate camera movement.[25]

With his adaptation of Edwin Long's *The Babylonian Marriage Market*, Griffith, as Hanson states, demonstrates "his genius as an artist

Babylonians feasting as the city falls (the Babylonian Story).

who saw in terms of film ... in the transformation of a static painting into a complex and exciting movie sequence." Hanson notes that Griffith is not only faithful in reproducing the details of the painting, "the slave block, the auctioneer's stance, the metal gate, the gestures, the costumes, and even the expression on the faces of the waiting women," he expands its range of mood by adding a human touch to the scene through the actions of the Mountain Girl on the auction block. Griffith's setting is more crowded than the painting but the director compensates for this, recapturing Long's sweep through skillful use of the moving camera and precise editing. Consisting of sixty shots in all, the sequence is punctuated by three panoramic shots at the beginning, middle and end, evenly spaced between the fifty-seven other shots which are of shorter duration. This rapid cutting enables Griffith to present history "lyrically and humorously transformed, through the looking-glass of nineteenth-century painting, into the reality of the magic world of the movies."[26]

Theater

Griffith's work reveals his indebtedness to the genres of the nineteenth-century theater, including melodrama, spectacle, dramas of intimate and social realism, and opera. In his book *Stage to Screen*, A. Nicholas Vardac contends that Griffith's cinematic achievements culminated more than a century of experiments in staging which emphasized the pictorial, as opposed to the verbal, aspects of theater. Griffith's work also evolved from a dramaturgy that blended realism and romanticism, combining accurate, lifelike details with action and emotion.[27]

No theatrical genre had more effect on Griffith's techniques than the melodrama, providing an example for his scenes of action including suspense-building situations and last-minute rescues. One of the most popular forms of entertainment in the nineteenth century, the melodrama, with its stereotyped characterizations, thrills and narrow escapes, attracted lower and middle class audiences in both urban and provincial America. It often drew on the novel for plots and devices, and perennial favorites in its repertoire included simplified adaptations of *Uncle Tom's Cabin, The Count of Monte Cristo*, and the works of Charles Dickens. Vardac maintains that the melodrama anticipated film narrative in its use of "a progression of pictorial episodes defining a single line of action, or ... crosscutting between two or more parallel lines of action."[28]

Although Griffith frequently attributed his development of parallel action to his study of Dickens, his work clearly indicates that the melodrama played a major role in evolving his cinematic skill. Often the melodrama stage was divided into sections to represent simultaneous lines of action, a technique that anticipated Griffith's use of crosscutting in his last-minute rescues. Vardac cites W.J. Thompson's 1883 melodrama, *A Race for Life*, with the action divided between the heroine downstairs, an old woman upstairs, and a menacing villain outside the house.[29] Similarly, in *The Lonely Villa* (1909), one of the first films in which Griffith employed crosscutting, the parallel action alternates between robbers outside a house threatening a family inside while, a few miles away, the father of the family desperately attempts to find a way to rescue them.

Vardac notes that Dion Boucicault's melodrama *Arrah-na-Pogue* (1864) is a salient example of a theatrical method which was "highly suggestive of the camera." He points to "the crosscutting between three simultaneous lines of action" as a precedent for the film language. The lines of action are cut between a Secretary of State's office, the interior of a prison and a mountain setting outside the prison. In the narrative, a secondary character, after receiving a pardon for the hero from the Secretary of State, attempts to reach the prison before the protagonist is executed. The scene switches to the hero's fiancee waiting outside the prison and then to the hero inside his cell preparing to escape. Two last-minute rescues then occur simultaneously, with the hero rushing to save

Griffith replicated the Babylonian marriage market from a painting by Edwin Long and a description by Herodotus (the Babylonian Story).

his sweetheart from an attack by the villain while the secondary character arrives at the prison with the pardon in time to prevent the hero's recapture and execution.[30]

Such suspense and last-minute rescues were also a part of Griffith's dramaturgy. A classic melodramatic situation occurs in the Modern Story when the Boy, forcing his way through the door, comes to the rescue of the Dear One, who is being attacked by the Musketeer of the Slums. In the climax of the Modern Story, Griffith employs three parallel lines of action as he switches from the Boy in his prison cell awaiting execution to the train carrying the governor, then to the car conveying the Dear One speeding to the rescue. The lines of action merge as the heroine boards the governor's train, leaving the camera free to focus on the final rescue when the governor and the Dear One arrive at the prison.

While he developed his basic editing structure against the background of the melodrama, Griffith's flair for creating epic films with imposing settings and masses of people grew out of the tradition of the stage spectacle, which flourished in the late nineteenth and early twentieth centuries. Transcending the limitations of conventional methods in staging melodrama, the spectacles were large-scale productions that achieved lavish effects through lighting, the use of crowds, and elaborate sets and costumes. Catering to a more metropolitan audience than the melo-dramas, their emphasis on realism and accuracy of detail made them perfect vehicles for presenting historical events such as the destruction of Pompeii and the burning of Moscow. Huge painted panoramas fronted by real houses and trees and special lighting effects from fireworks added authenticity to these productions.[31] Producers striving for greater realism developed complex mechanical devices to stage unusual effects. At the turn of the century, dramatizations of *Quo Vadis* and *Ben-Hur* featured rapid scenic changes and chariot races with live horses on treadmills.[32] These spectacular effects whetted the public's appetite for a pictorial theater, setting up a ready market for mammoth film productions.

Griffith, who insisted upon accuracy of details in his historical productions (as he often reminded his audiences in his subtitles and program notes), derived his concern in part from the example of producers of stage spectacles. Outstanding among these producers was Sir Henry Irving, who achieved photographic realism through careful research. Renowned for his Shakespearean productions, Irving included street scenes which were "faithful representations of familiar localities in Venice" in his 1879 presentation of *The Merchant of Venice*. His 1882 production of *Romeo and Juliet* similarly contained "a photographic reproduction of the time, the place, and the very events of the play." Like Griffith's research for the Babylonian Story, Irving's preparation for his 1888 production of *Macbeth* was extensive and encompassed "the British Museum and all known authorities upon archaeology ... for correct patterns of the costumes, weapons, and furniture of the eleventh century."[33]

The relationship between the silent cinema and the historical stage spectacle was most clearly defined in the work of the American producer-playwright Steele MacKaye. His experiments in the creation of an epic theater were the most ambitious of any of the theatrical producers, exploiting the potentialities of the stage spectacle to its fullest extent and forming a natural link between the stage and the film.

MacKaye's emphasis on elaborate pictorial art, in the words of a contemporary critic, "spoke to the heart as no words of poet, dramatist or historian could speak," minimizing dialogue in favor of action. Vardac points to MacKaye's 1887 play, *Anarchy: or, Paul Kauver*, set in the French Revolution, as an example of the cinematic qualities of his work. Citing a scene in which the heroine's execution by guillotine is enacted with unsparing realism, the reviewers of the time noted that "the production's most skillful invention is a silent picture." The play was also distinguished for its crowd scenes, described by Vardac as "a dynamic, personalized mob which, as a unit, became the most significant single dramatis personae."[34] Griffith's skill in creating momentum and adding forcefulness to his work through crowd scenes is characteristic of *Intolerance*. The angry, rebellious strikers in the Modern Story, the jeering onlookers of Christ's Via Crucis in the Judean Story, the cheering celebrants in the French

Story, the surging mass of Persian troops attacking the walls of Babylon and the festive multitude celebrating their victory in the great courtyard in the Babylonian Story, all react as a single unit to underscore the drama.

Continuing with his innovations in the early 1890s, MacKaye conceived various devices that correlated his staging methods even more closely with cinematic techniques. These contrivances included huge signs to accompany the action (corresponding to silent film subtitles), an "Illumiscope" and "Colourator" for tinting and lighting effects and telescopic and movable stages for changing from panoramas to closer views and from huge sets to intimate scenes. This form of theater, which he called the Spectatorium, enabled him to "present the facts of history with graphic force." His 1893 production, *The World-Finder*, which utilized all of his devices in developing a cinematic style, was a spectacular recreation of Columbus's voyage to America. Ships carrying fifty-foot masts, actors essentially pantomiming the story accompanied by music and told in titles in "flaming letters ... a foot long, a sentence at a time" and a curtain of light which produced dissolve effects and hastened changes of scenery, brought the stage spectacle to a height that could be surpassed only by the resources available to filmmakers.[35]

In the 1910s, Griffith, along with the Italian directors, expanded the potentialities of an epic dramatic form envisioned by MacKaye in his Spectatorium but left unfinished by his early death in 1894. Recognizing the relationship between the stage spectacle and the film, Griffith stated that, in comparison to the stage, "the motion picture ... is boundless in its scope, and endless in its possibilities. The whole world is its stage, and time without end its limitations."[36] He correctly prophesied in 1915 that the cinema was in the process of supplanting the stage as the vehicle for spectacle and the related genre of melodrama:

> The regular theatre ... will, of course, always exist, but not, I believe, as now. The (moving) pictures will utterly eliminate from the regular theatre all the spectacular features of production. Plays will never again appeal to the public for their scenery, or their numbers of actors and supernumeraries. Pictures have replaced all that.
> The only plays that the public will care to see in the regular theatre will be the intimate, quiet plays that can be staged in one or two settings within four walls, and in which the setting is unimportant, while the drama will be largely subjective. Objective drama, the so-called melodrama, will be entirely absorbed in the pictures ...[37]

From the genre of intimate domestic drama, Griffith added to his repertoire of cinematic techniques the capacity to evoke from his players a naturalistic, restrained style of acting and attentiveness to careful reproduction of authentic settings. The intimate drama, distinguished for its photographic realism and use of homey details and sentimental themes, enjoyed its greatest success in the late nineteenth and early twentieth centuries with the work of its principal figure, the producer-playwright David Belasco. While Belasco was also noted for his melodramas and spectacles, his most original contributions to the stage came from his quieter productions stressing characterization and realistic representations of daily life. Griffith, who was a great admirer of Belasco, was often called "the David Belasco of the motion pictures"[38] and, like the producer, "could take obscure people and instill confidence into them," according to Griffith's colleague, the director Marshall Neilan.[39] Indeed, Mary Pickford, one of Griffith's most famous actresses, came to him after working under Belasco.

Vardac cites *The Wife* (1887), which Belasco wrote in collaboration with Henry DeMille (the father of Cecil B. DeMille), as an example of the producer's influence on the intimate style adopted by motion pictures. The play was described by a contemporary critic as "the best example of ... the naturalistic methods of the modern school." Scenes such as the hero courting the heroine as they sat on the bough of an apple tree and, in a room lit only by the fireplace, the wife confessing to her husband she loved another man were so replete with homely details that the play was unique for its uncomplicated but highly personal style.[40]

Griffith adopted this approach throughout his work, delighting in domestic touches to create a sense of intimacy. In the French Story, for example, Griffith presents a picture of domestic tranquility in the Huguenot home in the subtle interaction between Prosper Latour, Brown Eyes, her younger sister and the mother and father: the father reads aloud while the mother rocks a cradle, smiling at her baby; the younger sister munches an apple as Prosper Latour and Brown Eyes exchange tender glances. The silent tête-à-tête of Prosper Latour and Brown Eyes is interrupted when her younger sister throws the core of her apple in their direction. The charming courtship scene in the Modern Story allows the viewer to peer in, as it were, on the romance between the Dear One and the Boy. When the Boy attempts to enter the Dear One's room to say goodnight, she shuts the door in his face, only opening it again to let him kiss her after his promise of marriage.

Zaza, Belasco's 1899 production, demonstrated his ability to give minor characters a life of their own. With his assemblage of sundry characters comprising "a doddering old rake ... a boyish loafer ... a besotted matron ... [and] a shy young debutante," Belasco made each member of the cast equally important in projecting "an aura of real life."[41] His expertise in casting was matched by Griffith, who, in the words of Neilan, "could pick types, as Belasco did, with an unerring eye."[42] Throughout his work, including *Intolerance*, Griffith's minor characters such as the matronly moral reformers, the old men hanging around the bars, or the prisoners on Death Row stand out, like Belasco's, as distinct individuals.

Vardac contends that by exploiting "the intimate and minor details of surface reality," Belasco intensified the effect of his unique, naturalistic style of acting. He notes that David Warfield, who became Belasco's most celebrated actor, "excelled in this itemized pantomime of surface realities." For instance, in *The Auctioneer* (1901), Warfield, surrounded by numerous objects typical of a second-hand store, engaged in lengthy bits of business with these properties, attaining the theatrical effects that Belasco sought.[43]

In both the interior and exterior scenes, Belasco achieved a pictorial reality surpassed only by the film. A reviewer characterized the street scene in *The Auctioneer* as "a simulation of street life as it really exists in busy Gotham" which could be "a motion picture production of the original." *A Grand Army Man*, Belasco's 1907 production, also starring Warfield, was dubbed by a critic "the most realistic play that has been presented in New York City." The "worn benches, bare 'gas fixtures,' strips of dilapidated railing, pulpit-like bench, and a dozen other material details," added to the authenticity of the interior of a rural courthouse.[44]

Belasco's precedent inspired Griffith to break with the limitations of the early films. In place of the melodramatic gesticulations of the actors in the first one-reelers, he introduced a restrained style of acting that became the model for subsequent films. Gradually eliminating painted canvas flats for his background settings, he constructed detailed, authentic interiors that included real properties instead of objects painted on a canvas, and filmed exteriors on location. While Griffith absorbed Belasco's art of stagecraft, the camera enabled him to explore the human emotions through the close-up with an intensity denied the theater and made possible the documentation of reality beyond the restrictions of the proscenium arch as he filmed actual streets and natural landscapes.

Vardac sees Griffith's dramaturgy as emanating primarily from the pictorial theater, but Russell Merritt maintains that it also reflects the influence of the more literary social dramas, particularly in choice of subject matter and symbolic use of inanimate objects. The social drama, revolutionizing the stage in the late nineteenth and early twentieth centuries, dealt with a vast range of conflicts and injustices in modern society. Henrik Ibsen, Hermann Sudermann, Gerhardt Hauptmann, Sir Arthur Wing Pinero, George Bernard Shaw and John Galsworthy were all major social dramatists of the period. As an actor, Griffith had appeared in Ibsen's *Hedda Gabler* and *Rosmersholm* and Sudermann's *Magda* and *The Fires of St. John*, an experience which undoubtedly led to his assimilation of the techniques and thematic dimensions of the social drama.[45]

Galsworthy's plays, *Strife* (1909), depicting a struggle between the forces of capital and labor, and *Justice* (1910), an indictment of the penal system, are built upon themes that parallel the social problems explored by Griffith in the Modern Story. While differing from Griffith in presenting the strike from a neutralist point of view, *Strife*, first produced in the United States in 1910, focuses on the hardships endured by the workers and their families because of the intransigence on both sides of the dispute.

Griffith, on the other hand, attributes the misery of the workers solely to the venality of the capitalist. Galsworthy's highly successful *Justice*, staged in the United States in 1916 with John Barrymore in the lead, concerns a young man of good character who, in order to protect the woman he loves, commits his first offense, the relatively minor crime of forgery, and receives unusually harsh treatment from the law. Like Galsworthy, Griffith exposes the inequity built into the penal system, which seems all the more iniquitous when it victimizes an innocent young man.

According to Merritt, Griffith derived from social dramas "a dramaturgy of signs built around costumes, clothes, hand props and decor." Unlike Belasco, the social dramatist frequently employs inanimate objects as symbols to reinforce the thematic implications of the play. Merritt cites the example of the cut wild flowers in *Rosmersholm*, which are symbolically linked to "Rebecca West's schemes to lure Rosmer away from his dead wife." These "evocative trifles," as Merritt terms them, permeate Griffith's work as well, taking on special significance in the context of the film's theme and adding depth to the characterizations.[46] With the inclusion of a scene in which the Dear One examines "the hopeful geranium," the director signifies his belief in the renewal of life: the girl first mourns the nearly-dead plant, then finds hope in a new shoot growing from the old stem.[47] He builds an ironic motif around the handgun the Boy returns to the Musketeer of the Slums when he renounces a life of crime. It is this same gun that the Friendless One uses to kill the Musketeer, an action leading to the conviction and near-execution of the Boy.

While the social drama provided a model for his "iconography of psychological abstractions," grand opera gave Griffith the inspiration to infuse his work with an emotional quality.[48] The opera's relentless assault on the emotions through the synergetic crescendoing of the music to the unfolding of the plot is analogous to Griffith's heightening of the audience's feelings through rhythmic editing. Whether it is Giacomo Puccini's *La Tosca* with Tosca killing Scarpia to preserve her honor, then jumping to her death from a parapet when her lover is shot, Georges Bizet's *Carmen* with the jealous Don José stabbing the faithless Carmen to death, or Giuseppe Verdi's *Il Trovatore* with the Count ordering the execution of a man who is actually his brother, the audience's emotions are raised to the same level of intensity that Griffith evokes with his films. In the trial scene in the Modern Story, he moves the spectator to empathize with the Dear One awaiting the court's decision, cutting from a close-up of her anxious face to a close-up of her hands twisting and turning in the folds of her dress, then continuing the emotional intensity after the verdict, showing her abject despair. The denouement of the Babylonian Story, in which Belshazzar and his consort commit suicide and the Mountain Girl dies amid the debacle of Babylon's conquest, possesses the same kind of crescendo to catastrophe found in many operas, including the destruction of Valhalla in Wagner's *Die Götterdämmerung*.

A devotee of the opera, Griffith chose subject matter for the French and Babylonian Stories suggesting elements of plots from specific operatic works. Giacomo Meyerbeer's spectacular opera, *The Huguenots*, like Griffith's French Story, has fictional lovers who are caught up in the events of 1572. Both narratives conclude with the deaths of the hero and heroine in the massacre of St. Bartholomew's Day. The Babylonian Story is reminiscent of Verdi's early opera, *Nabucco*, which takes place in the Babylon of Nebuchadnezzar and has among its characters an intriguing High Priest of Bel. Verdi's *Aida* also contains similarities to the Babylonian Story. Both are set in ancient Middle Eastern civilizations and have a High Priest as their pivotal villain. In *Aida*, the High Priest of Isis brings about the death of the hero and heroine, while in the Babylonian Story, the High Priest of Bel is responsible for the fall of Babylon. The priests in *Aida* invoke the gods to protect Egypt in its war with the invading Ethiopians just as the priests in Griffith's film beseech Ishtar's aid to defend Babylon from the Persians. In both the opera and the film, the victors celebrate their triumphs with elaborate festivities and gala performances by dancing girls.

For all his stage background, Griffith was no more indebted to the theater than to any of the other arts. He utilized the rich heritage of the stage, not to imitate it, but to incorporate elements from it to aid him in the creation of a new dramatic-narrative form with its own laws and syntax.

Films

Compared to his absorption of elements from the older art forms, Griffith's borrowing from other filmmakers was superficial, primarily limited to such items as costumes and decors. While his basic editing style and approach to historical film evolved independent of foreign influences, Griffith was impressed with the careful staging he saw in the French "Film d'Art" costume dramas and the Italian epic cinema, prompting him to adopt some of their components for his French and Babylonian Stories.

The Film d'Art, developed in France, influenced filmmakers throughout the world in the 1910s. Dealing with literary and historical subjects, the films of this genre were essentially photographed stage plays with little camera ingenuity. The concentration on elaborate settings and costumes along with the histrionics of the stars brought prestige to the cinema in cultured circles. The dominance of the Film d'Art began with the international success of the one-reel film, *The Assassination of the Duc de Guise* (1908) which Griffith later called "my best memory of the cinema" and "a complete revelation." Depicting an incident from the reign of Henri III (the prince of the French Story), this film, although theatrical, was distinguished for its fine acting and historically accurate sets.[49] Another

The Dear One (Mae Marsh) at her husband's trial (the Modern Story).

celebrated French production in the Film d'Art tradition was the four-reel
Queen Elizabeth (1912) starring Sarah Bernhardt. The American release of
this film simultaneously launched the career of its distributor, Adolph
Zukor of Famous Players, and created a market for longer films in the
United States. As theatrical as *The Assassination of the Duc de Guise,
Queen Elizabeth*, dramatizing the love affair of Elizabeth and Essex, also
provided an opportunity for displaying lavish sixteenth-century costumes
and sets. Although Griffith's dynamic use of the cinematic language in the
French Story went far beyond the stagy techniques of costume productions
like *The Assassination of the Duc de Guise* and *Queen Elizabeth*, his
choice of a sixteenth-century historical subject with the appropriate
costumes and settings owes much to the popularity of the French imports
and his own study of them.

Far more cinematic than the Films d'Art were the Italian spectacles
which established the genre of the epic film. These epics, surpassing the
capabilities of the stage spectacle, recreated historical events including

huge battle scenes and natural disasters and featured thousands of extras and monumental ancient architecture. Although *The Fall of Troy* (1910), a two-reeler directed by Giovanni Pastrone and one of the earliest of these films, had attracted American attention as early as 1911, it was not until the 1913 American screenings of the full-length feature *Quo Vadis*, directed by Enrico Guazzoni in 1912, that the public and critics began to recognize the motion picture's capacity to achieve a scale unknown to the theater. Following *Quo Vadis*, other large-scale Italian productions won acclaim from American audiences and critics, including *The Last Days of Pompeii* (1913) directed by Mario Caserini and *Antony and Cleopatra* (1913) and *Julius Caesar* (1914), both directed by Guazzoni. With their awesome reproductions of ancient Rome, these films revealed that the motion picture could bring history to life. They identified the glories of the Roman Empire with the modern renascent nation of Italy, fulfilling a political goal by giving artistic expression to the resurgence of Italian nationalism.

Giovanni Pastrone's *Cabiria* (1914), the masterpiece of the genre, is an epic recreation of the Punic Wars between Rome and Carthage and an ancient analogy to twentieth-century Italian expansion in North Africa. Upon its release in the United States in 1914, *Cabiria* was hailed by reviewers as an outstanding work of art. It was shown in "legitimate" theaters and had a special screening at the White House. Brown recalls that "The reviews of *Cabiria* had such an effect on Griffith that he and key members of his staff took the next train to San Francisco to see it."[50] He incorporated certain elements from *Cabiria*, including soldiers scaling the city walls while defenders hurl missiles at them, and pet leopards adorning the royal court. He also modeled his giant warrior, the Mighty Man of Valor, who is devoted to Belshazzar, after Maciste, the hairy-chested giant who is the Roman hero's friend and protector in *Cabiria*. The two colossal elephant statues flanking the stairway of a palace courtyard in the Italian film inspired the huge elephants on the cornices that dominate the Babylonian set.[51] In addition, Griffith's elaborate experiments with tracking shots in *Intolerance* may have been stimulated by his study of the extensive use of dolly shots in *Cabiria*.

Despite these relatively minor embellishments adapted from foreign filmmakers, Griffith was so far ahead of the Europeans that his overall style was unaffected by the imported productions. Even in *Cabiria*, the most advanced of the early European historical films, "the editing tended merely to link shots which were complete in themselves."[52] For all their visual impressiveness, the great Italian epics are primarily generalized visions of patriotism and lack the personal vision of history achieved through dynamic editing so characteristic of Griffith's masterpieces. The most significant effect of the early European films on Griffith was in galvanizing him to compete by producing his own full-length spectacles.

Poetry

Poetry was a major influence on Griffith's artistic development; he drew on the master poets for his themes, his images, his characterizations and even his philosophy. At Biograph, he filmed Robert Browning's "Pippa Passes" in 1909 and "A Blot on the 'Scutcheon" in 1911. He also adapted Alfred, Lord Tennyson's "The Golden Supper" in 1910 and directed two film versions of "Enoch Arden" including *After Many Years* (1908) and the two-reel film of 1911, released under the poem's original title. His fictionalized biography of Edgar Allan Poe, made in 1909, and his full-length feature, *The Avenging Conscience* (1914), based on the works of Poe, reflect his admiration for the American poet. He also demonstrated his love for poetry by frequently quoting verses in his subtitles. For example, in *Intolerance*, a shot of the prisoners in the death-house is accompanied by a quote from Oscar Wilde's *The Ballad of Reading Gaol*: "And wondered if each one of us/ Would end the self-same way,/ For none can tell to what red Hell/ His sightless soul may stray."

The preeminent poetic inspiration for *Intolerance* derived from Alfred, Lord Tennyson and Walt Whitman. While Poe and Browning were suitable sources for the content of earlier Griffith films, their concentration on inner conflicts of man was less relevant to the director's projection of a social-historical vision than Tennyson and Whitman, whose works reflect a visual reality more adaptable to his purposes in *Intolerance*. Representing polar opposites, Tennyson, the great British poet-laureate, and Whitman, the great American poet-rebel, are synthesized in Griffith's aesthetic approach, infusing his work with both Victorianism and sensuality. The Victorian values of chastity and domesticity in Tennyson are tempered by the celebrations of the flesh in Whitman. In both poets, however, Griffith found a common thread of love and idealism that harmonized with his own philosophy.

Familiar with Tennyson from his childhood when his father's "orotund voice poured forth the music of Keats and Tennyson and Shakespeare," Griffith imbues his heroines with a kind of Tennysonian Victorianism.[53] Tennyson's maidens are beautiful, chaste, delicate, incapable of malicious or sinful acts, yet sometimes prone to mischief. The Dear One hopping and skipping about and flirting with the Boy, and the Mountain Girl playfully spurning the Rhapsode's advances and impudently chewing onions to discourage suitors in the marriage market, are reminiscent of Tennyson's verbal portrait of Lilian:

> Airy, fairy Lilian,
> Flitting, fairy Lilian
> When I ask her if she love me,
> Claps her tiny hands above me,
> Laughing all she can;

Top: The Mountain Girl (Constance Talmadge) as she meets Belshazzar. Bottom: Brown Eyes (Margery Wilson) and Prosper Latour (Eugene Pallette) on the eve of their wedding (the French Story).

> She'll not tell me if she love me,
>   Cruel little Lilian.
> . . . .
> So innocent-arch, so cunning-simple,
> From beneath her gathered wimple
>   Glancing with black-beaded eyes,
> Till the lightning laughters dimple
>   The baby-roses in her cheeks;
>   Then away she flies.[54]

Brown Eyes in the French Story is the quintessential Tennysonian heroine, a frail, angelic creature whose fidelity to her fiance causes her to resist the savage lust of the mercenary soldier who is ultimately responsible for her death. Tennyson's description of the perfect wife of "chasten'd purity" in the poem "Isabel" might well apply to the faithful, virtuous Brown Eyes:

> Eyes not down-dropt nor over-bright
>   but fed
> With the clear-pointed flame of chastity,
> Clear, without heat, undying, tended by
>   Pure vestal thoughts in the trans-
>   lucent fane
> Of her still spirit; locks not wide-dispread,
>   Madonna-wise on either side her
>   head;
>   Sweet lips whereon perpetually did
>   reign
> The summer calm of golden charity,
> . . . .
>   Revered Isabel, the crown and head,
> The stately flower of female fortitude ...[55]

Tennyson's conception of femininity in "Isabel" reflects his belief that woman possesses qualities which extend beyond conformity to a simple moral code. He characterizes Isabel as having "courage," "prudence," "extreme gentleness," and "a bright and thorough-edged intellect" with the intuitive ability "to part error from crime." In Tennyson's view, woman can redeem man through her role as a "maternal wife,"[56] capable of giving "subtle-paced counsel in distress" and sustenance with her love.[57] For Griffith, too, the power of woman's love can be redemptive, leading man to a higher level of being. In an illustration of this Tennysonian concept in the Modern Story, the Dear One, entreating the Boy to pray with her for strength, convinces him to renounce his criminal pursuits for an honest and upright life.

Not only does Tennyson's admiration for the virtues of woman in the roles of wife and mother add dimensions to his feminine portraits; his poetry shows a reverence for the family unit as the basis for transmitting the values of Christian piety. Instilled in Griffith's consciousness was a deep, abiding respect for family life, which, like Tennyson's, sprang from his mother's teaching of the Protestant ethic. The serenity in the Huguenot home conveys Griffith's feeling for the stabilizing effect of the family unit amid the encroaching internecine conflict that will soon shatter this peaceful domesticity. In both Tennyson and Griffith, "the delights of familial calm occur against a backdrop of frustration, defeat, and impending death."[58]

A poignant illustration of this motif occurs in Tennyson's "Enoch Arden," filmed by Griffith in his own adaptations of the poem, in which the hero, Enoch Arden, returns home from his long sojourn overseas to find his wife remarried. Yearning for the domestic bliss that is no longer his, he peers through the window of the home of his lost love and her new husband, Philip:

> For Philip's dwelling fronted on the
> street,
> . . . .
> With one small gate that open'd on the
> waste,
> Flourish'd a little garden square and
> wall'd:
> . . . .
> And on the right hand of the hearth he
> saw
> Philip, the slighted suitor of old times,
> Stout, rosy, with his babe across his
> knees;
> . . . .
> And on the left hand of the hearth he
> saw
> The mother glancing often toward her
> babe
> Hers, yet not his, upon the father's knee,
> And all the warmth, the peace, the
> happiness,
> And his own children tall and beautiful,
> And him, that other, reigning in his place,
> Lord of his rights and of his children's
> love ...[59]

The mother and father surrounded by their children are "exemplars of a harmony that is sanctioned by, and proof of, a benificent God."[60] Adapting this scene from his own film versions of "Enoch Arden," Griffith shows the Dear One, after her baby has been taken from her, "enjoying the happiness of others" as she gazes longingly through a stranger's window at the tranquil scene of a couple with their child. While undetected by the couple, her smiles and gestures attract the attention of the child who returns her smile. The physical setting of this night scene of a house fronted by a garden so closely replicates Tennyson's description in "Enoch Arden" that Griffith's source for his imagery is unmistakable. In both Tennyson and Griffith, the meanings extend beyond the image to symbolize the melancholy of loss juxtaposed with domestic happiness.

In "Akbar's Dream," one of his last poems, Tennyson manifests a spirit of tolerance that parallels the essence of Griffith's theme in *Intolerance*. The poem concerns the great Indian Mogul emperor who attempted to bring all religions together in a universal faith. Like Griffith, Tennyson expands his theme of spiritual love to a broader perspective glorifying the virtues of tolerance: "when creed and race/ Shall bear false witness, each of each, no more,/ But find their limits by that larger light,/ And overstep them, moving easily/ Thro' after-ages in the love of Truth,/ The truth of Love." Tennyson's description of Akbar in his notes brings to mind Griffith's religious reformer, Belshazzar:

> His tolerance of religions and his abhorrence of religious persecution put our Tudors to shame. He invented a new eclectic religion by which he hoped to unite all creeds, castes and peoples; and his legislation was remarkable for vigour, justice and humanity.[61]

Besides his theme of spiritualized love, another motif that appears in Tennyson's work is his "passion for the past," which enables him to express the sensuousness he repressed within the context of his own time and culture. His tendency to tinge his presentation of the "far, far away" with an exotic lushness of detail extends not only to his portrayal of the heroines but also to their surroundings.[62] While Griffith felt less restricted by Victorian proprieties than Tennyson, he, too, found that the exoticism of the past offered a freedom to revel in sensuous detail. In the Babylonian Story, he projects a voluptuousness denied him in the more repressive or less resplendent periods of the other stories.

Typical of Tennyson's aesthetic indulgence when he conjures up images of the past is his depiction of the heroine, a Persian girl, in "Recollections of the Arabian Nights": "Serene with argent-lidded eyes/ Amorous, and lashes like to rays/ Of darkness, and a brow of pearl/ Tressed with redolent ebony."[63] Griffith's voluptuous portrait of the Princess Beloved, Belshazzar's favorite, displays the same abandonment from the restraints of Victorianism as Tennyson's Persian girl in Caliph Haroun Alraschid's harem.

Tennyson's loving representation of "A goodly place, a goodly time,/ ... in the golden prime/ Of good Haroun Alraschid" compares with Griffith's romantic vision of a lost, glorious civilization. Thus, the pictorial imagery of the mythical Oriental grandeur of Griffith's Babylon is equivalent in its sensual provocativeness to the verbal luxuriousness of the Caliph's palace in Tennyson's poem with its "carven cedarn doors," "spangled floors," "Broad-based flights of marble stairs ... with golden balustrade," and a room containing "six columns, three on either side,/ Pure silver, underpropt a rich throne of the massive ore."[64]

An even more vital influence than Tennyson in molding Griffith's social-historical vision in *Intolerance* was Walt Whitman. Exposed to Whitman as an impressionable youth in Louisville, Griffith's assimilation of the radical morality and individualism permeating the work of the poet undoubtedly played a pivotal role in helping him overcome the limitations of his Victorian-Southern background. Griffith, who "could quote pages of his poetry," often declared in later years that "he would rather have written one page of (Whitman's) *Leaves of Grass* than to have made all the movies for which he received world acclaim."[65] He even attributed his development of tempo and parallel action in his films to his study of Whitman. Although hesitant to openly express his affinity for the work of the robust, sensual poet who had shocked rural America "with his earthy ideas on sex and religion," the director confided to acquaintances that Whitman was even more essential to his evolution as a film artist than Dickens.[66]

A certain coincidental similarity between Griffith the man and Whitman the man may shed light on the director's lifelong fascination with the poet. Raised in the traditions of Jeffersonian and Jacksonian democracy, they both demonstrated an individualistic self-reliance fused with broad social concerns in their personal and political philosophy. With little formal education, both were thrown into the world at an early age, gaining knowledge that would later prove fruitful in their artistic development. Whitman, apprenticing to a printer as a child and later drifting from one editorial position to another, and Griffith, working in a bookstore as a youth and subsequently becoming a traveling actor, exhibited an independence of spirit that typified, not only their lifestyles, but also their conceptions of art. By the time they reached their early thirties, neither had fulfilled his aesthetic aspirations. Not until Whitman, the failed novelist, and Griffith, the failed playwright, abandoned conventional modes of expression to become artistic revolutionaries, did they find their true metier. While their individualism enabled them to expand the horizons of their art forms, their uncompromising adherence to their own inner visions eventually ran counter to the tastes of the mass audience they wished to inspire and led to widely varied critical evaluations.

With their common dedication to the individual, both Whitman and Griffith espoused a form of social democracy that eschewed leftist dogma as well as rightist orthodoxy. Whitman, rejecting the doctrinaire socialism of his day, editorialized in the 1850s that education "is the only true remedy for mobs, emeutes, wild communistic theories, and red-republican ravings."[67] Griffith, in an introductory subtitle in *Orphans of the Storm* (1922), warned the American public to beware of replacing "our democratic government" with "anarchy and Bolshevism." While each was caught up in the great reform movement of his day, each displayed an aversion to what he interpreted as the intellectual tyranny of the left. The intensity with which they opposed the mentality and practices of the traditional oligarchy, however, caused them to fall into a place on the political spectrum that could best be described as "radical social democrats." Paradoxically, their individualistic approach to political philosophy led to greater appreciation for their artistic achievements in the collectivist society of the Soviet Union than in their own country.

Inimical to their sense of social concern and independent spirit were the attempts by government to legislate morality. Griffith's condemnation of those who argue that "we must have laws to make people good" parallels Whitman's attitude towards moral reformers. Denouncing a proposed bill that would punish all practitioners of licentiousness in New York, Whitman stated in an editorial in the 1840s that "You cannot legislate men into morality."[68] This sentiment also appears in his poem "Transpositions," in which he writes that the reformers should "descend from the stands where they are forever bawling" to be replaced by lunatics.[69] He was incensed by another incident in the New York of the 1840s in which fifty prostitutes were arrested and turned again to his editorial pen to protest the "ruffianly, scoundrelly, villainous, outrageous and high handed proceeding, unsanctioned by law, justice, humanity, virtue or religion."[70] His sympathy for prostitutes reappears in his long poem, "Song of Myself" from *Leaves of Grass*:

> The prostitute draggles her shawl, her bonnet bobs on
>   her tipsy and pimpled neck,
> The crowd laugh at her blackguard oaths, the men jeer
>   and wink to each other,
> (Miserable! I do not laugh at your oaths nor jeer you[71]

Reflecting this same sentiment in the Modern Story, Griffith presents prostitutes as victims of pharasaism, departing from the Tennysonian-Victorian view which draws a sharp distinction between virtuous women and temptresses. Again, in the Babylonian Story, his portrait of temple prostitution seems closer to Whitman's belief in the union of body and soul than to Tennyson's with its inherent dualism. While Griffith is Tennysonian in associating the exotic with the sensual, feeling less constrained in a presentation of a far-away era than in his own time, he goes beyond the mere aesthetic indulgence of an inhibited Victorian, imbuing his scenes of the "Virgins of the Sacred Fire of Life" in the Temple of Ishtar with a Whitmanesque quality that becomes a kind of erotic mysticism uniting the spirit and the flesh.

Whitman's attitude toward the penal system represents another area in which his radical morality coincides with Griffith's views. Joining with death penalty abolitionists in the 1840s, he denounced capital punishment in his editorials. Similarly, Griffith expressed his opposition to the death penalty in statements of the time as well as in his films, including *Intolerance*. In their creative work, both exhibit a great compassion for convicts, whom they view, like prostitutes, as among the oppressed in society. Decrying the plight of prisoners in the following poem, Whitman questions the right of society in light of its own misdeeds to pass judgment on these poor unfortunates:

> You felons on trial in courts,
> You convicts in prison-cells, you sentenced assassins
>   chain'd and handcuff'd with iron,
> Who am I too that I am not on trial or in prison?
> Me ruthless and devilish as any, that my wrists are
>   not chain'd with iron, or my ankles with iron?[72]

Griffith interposes his own commentary on the harshness of the penal system in the prison scenes in the Modern Story and again in the epilogue in which he forecasts a day "when cannon and prison bars wrought in the fire of intolerance" shall be no more. In this sequence, the prison walls disappear, "allowing the prisoners to surge to freedom" where, in the words of the final subtitle, "Instead of prison walls bloom flowery fields."[73]

Merged with Whitman's radical morality is his belief in religious humanism, a concept that is at the core of Griffith's *Intolerance*. Whitman, influenced by the teachings of Elias Hicks, the Quaker leader, developed a new religion for himself. Like Griffith, Whitman repudiated original sin and questioned the established church dogmas and official morality as antithetical to the true teachings of Christ.[74] Griffith, however, posits Christ's humanism within the context of a cyclical concept of history, whereas Whitman emphasizes Christ's humanism by freeing him from a historical perspective. The vitality of Griffith's humanism in *Intolerance* emanates from relating Christ's historical experiences and teachings to the present reality. Whitman's contemporary relevance in *Leaves of Grass*, on the other hand, arises from identifying the Christ symbol with himself as the common man who can be his own savior, thereby emancipating Christianity from its Biblical orthodoxy.[75]

The poet's humanism enabled him to embrace all religions, including those regarded as pagan by Christian orthodoxy. He demonstrates his repudiation of traditional Christian claims to exclusive truth in "With Antecedents":

> I respect Assyria, China, Teutonia, and the Hebrews,
> I adopt each theory, myth, god, and demi-god,
> I see that the old accounts, bibles, geneologies,
>   are true, without exception[76]

Again, in "Song of Myself," he pays tribute to all faiths: "My faith is the greatest of faiths and the least of faiths,/ Enclosing worship ancient and modern and all between ancient and modern."[77]

Griffith's assimilation of Whitman's ideas undoubtedly played a role, conscious or unconscious, in liberating him from the confines of the fundamentalist tradition common to the South. In the Babylonian Story, Griffith's depiction of the cult of Ishtar as a religion of love analogous in its essence to Christianity is akin to Whitman's acknowledgment in "With Antecedents" of the verities in all religions, including polytheism. From an orthodox point of view, representing "godless" paganism as possessing spiritual values equivalent to Christianity borders on heresy.

The corollary of this respect for non–Christian religions was the artists' appreciation for ancient civilizations. Just as Griffith found ancient Babylon fascinating, Whitman was captivated by ancient Egypt and included "numerous echoes, allusions and references to Egyptology" in *Leaves of Grass*. His study of the history of the ancient culture at the Egyptian Museum in New York City provided the historic detail appearing in his poetry, and more importantly, gave him "a sense of the continuity of life and human culture," an undercurrent of *Leaves of Grass*.[78]

A similar feeling for the continuity and unity of human experience through the centuries is basic to the narrative structure of *Intolerance* making Griffith's conception of history more Whitmanesque than Tennysonian. Tennyson views the past as a legendary backdrop for romantic escapism or moralistic allegorizing, while Whitman's invocations of remote civilizations are predicated on the theory that the present is inseparable from the past. Although Griffith is Tennysonian in coloring his depiction of Babylon with exotic detail, his total historical conception remains closer to Whitman.

An integral part of Griffith's historical vision is Whitman's view of "flowing time" which anticipates the director's approach in *Intolerance*. Whitman's conception grew out of his belief in an "eternal present" in which "past and present and future are not disjoined but joined." According to Gay Wilson Allen, Whitman's biographer, the artist is a "time-binder" who transcends the limitations of time and space, preserving the wisdom of the past in order to interpret the present and the future, a technique which is embedded in the narrative and ideological development of *Intolerance*.[79] One of the best examples of Whitman's alternation between the past and the present occurs in "Passage to India." In this poem, his homage to the achievements of the past as preparations for the accomplishments of the present becomes a device for revelation:

> Singing my days,
> Singing the great achievements of the present,
> . . . .
> Yet first to sound, and ever sound, the cry with thee O soul,
> The Past! the Past! the Past!
> . . . .

The past — the infinite greatness of the past!
For what is the present after all but a growth out of the past?
(As a projectile form'd, impell'd, passing a certain line,
    still keeps on,
So the present, utterly form'd, impell'd by the past.)[80]

Throughout the poem, Whitman conjures up images of Columbus, Vasco da Gama, Alexander the Great and the ancient Orient alongside the great engineering achievements of his own time, the building of the Suez Canal and the transcontinental railroad. Similarly, Griffith frees himself from the boundaries of time and space, shifting from one era to another in *Intolerance* to discover the underlying pattern of human existence that holds the key to truth.

Griffith also resembles the poet in "Passage to India" in his projection of the future. Both the film and the poem conclude with a future millenium of love and brotherhood. While structurally parallel, each beginning in the present, reverting to the past and ending with a vision of the future, they differ in their internal thematic implications. Griffith's underlying and unifying motif is a tension between harmony and disharmony which is resolved by an ultimate return to man's original state of happiness. Whitman, on the other hand, conceives an uninterrupted progression from past to present to future symbolized by modern transportation and communication linking the continents, a metaphor for the love that will eventually bind the human race.[81]

Another characteristic common to the style of the poet and the director is a blending of the lyric with the epic. Throughout *Leaves of Grass*, Whitman evokes images of vast stretches of time and space encompassing innumerable centuries of history and culture and immense distances in the universe interwoven with the homely details of everyday living. Whitman pictures in "Salut au Monde," for example, "a great round wonder rolling through space," its "mountain peaks," its "Libyan, Arabian and Asiatic deserts," its "huge, dreadful Arctic and Antarctic icebergs." But he also sees "flocks of goats feeding," "the fig-tree, tamarind, date," "fields of teff-wheat," "the incomparable rider of horses with his lasso on his arm" and "the seal-seeker in his boat poising his lance."[82]

In a visual language that emulates Whitman's blending of epic and lyric, Griffith likewise alternates between vast panoramas and close-ups of characters or intimate details. In the Babylonian Story, the long-shots of the colossal set are interspersed with lyrical portraits. At the great feast, for instance, the scene in which the Princess Beloved places a white rose in a toy chariot pulled by white doves to send her gift to the prince on the other side of the table is, as Brown notes, "the big moment of this big set with its big everything."[83] Another example of this technique is the simple, homely scene of the Mountain Girl milking a goat intercut with the shots of epic grandeur and the luxury of the Babylonian court. Like Whitman,

Griffith, while contemplating the vastness of reality, ponders the significance of the small in the belief that "a leaf of grass is no less than the journey-work of the stars."[84]

From these speculations on the cosmic and the confluence of time, the poet and the director come to understand that the individual is the center of existence, a microcosm of the universe. In *Democratic Vistas*, Whitman asserts that in all things, "sooner or later, we come down to one single, solitary soul"[85] and, reaffirming this idea in "By Blue Ontario's Shore," states: "The whole theory of the universe is directed unerringly to one single individual—namely to You."[86] For Whitman, this realization provides the unity for his lyric epic, *Leaves of Grass*. He, as poet-prophet, becomes a common man whose spirituality issues from his identification with people of other times and other places. It forms the basis for his belief that the fulfillment of democratic ideals will come about only through "a real, vital, spiritual democracy" in which the love of individuals for each other fosters the brotherhood of man.[87]

Griffith, too, finds the meaning of existence rooted in "the supreme value of the individual."[88] Although *Intolerance* has no authorial "I" comparable to Whitman's poet-prophet, its truth is revealed in the common experiences of ordinary individuals through the ages. Like Whitman, Griffith believes that the transformation of society occurs through individual acts of kindness that are manifestations of brotherly love.

Whitman's conception of femininity growing out of his belief in individualism may have colored Griffith's portrayal of his heroines. Whitman idealizes the strong, athletic woman who is capable of taking care of herself, a striking contrast to Tennyson's delicate, ethereal women. In "A Woman Waits for Me," Whitman dismisses "impassive women," preferring those who are "warm-blooded and sufficient for me": "They know how to swim, row, ride, wrestle, shoot, run, strike, retreat, advance, resist, defend themselves,/ They are ultimate in their own right—they are calm, clear, well-possess'd of themselves."[89]

These Whitmanesque characteristics appear in Griffith's heroines, profoundly modifying a strictly Tennysonian-Victorian attitude towards women. The Mountain Girl is primarily Whitmanesque despite her touches of Tennysonian sprightliness: she fights valiantly against the Persian invaders, deftly using her bow and arrow, and drives a chariot with lightning-like speed to warn Babylon of its impending doom. Although she does not exhibit this same athletic prowess, the Dear One also possesses Whitmanesque qualities that extend the dimensions of her characterization beyond its Tennysonian elements. Undaunted after the death of her father and the imprisonment of her husband, she manages to survive, manifesting the strength and endurance that Whitman so appreciated in women.

The pivotal poem in *Leaves of Grass* is "Out of the Cradle Endlessly Rocking" which, for the first time, sets forth the central themes, repre-

"Out of the cradle endlessly rocking."

senting a transition from materialism and individualism to a spirituality that embraces the totality of existence.[90] In this poem, Whitman uses a mother rocking a cradle as a metaphor for the sea; the sea becomes a symbol for life and death. The persona of the poem is a boy who matures with his understanding of "the absorption of the individual into the soul of nature or the universe" when he observes two nesting mocking-birds on the beach.[91] He shares their joy together and their grief when they are forever separated. Contemplating the significance of death as he wanders by the sea, the boy gains insight that enables him to become a poet-prophet.

This poem so profoundly affected Griffith that he adopted its image of a rocking cradle for his own metaphor in *Intolerance*. The image of a young woman rocking a cradle with the indistinguishable three Fates in the background represents the eternal cycle of life and death. Freed from any identification with a specific historical period, this image opens and closes *Intolerance*. Throughout the film, it is used as a transitional device virtually every time Griffith cuts from one era to another, reinforcing the unity of the work. Adapting from Whitman's lines

> Out of the cradle endlessly rocking,
> ....
> I, chanter of pains and joys, uniter of here and hereafter,
> ....
> A reminiscence sing.

he either quotes or paraphrases these lines at several points in the film.[92] When the cradle image first appears, it is preceded by the title, "Out of the cradle endlessly rocking" and is followed with the paraphrased title: "To-day as yesterday, endlessly rocking, ever bringing the same human pas-sions, the same joys and sorrows." Later in the film, the words "Endlessly rocks the cradle/ Uniter of here and hereafter./ Chanter of sorrows and joys" is superimposed over the image. Griffith repeats the lines to underscore the idea of continuity associated with the image. Additionally, the line "Chanter of sorrows and joys" may indicate his wish to enlighten his audience through his authorial presence. Much as Whitman, the poet-prophet, seeks to reveal the truth through his reminiscence of personal ex-perience, Griffith shares with his audience the historical experiences of other human beings.

Novels

Griffith's approach to narrative construction, indeed, his overall social and historical vision, owes much to English and American novels of the nineteenth century, particularly the works of Sir Walter Scott, James Fenimore Cooper, Charles Dickens and Frank Norris. As Jack C. Ellis notes in *A History of Film*:

> The fusing of fiction with history ... was standard with Sir Walter Scott and other historical novelists; Griffith drew more or less con-sciously on nineteenth-century literary precedents for the shaping of his stories.[93]

Acknowledging his indebtedness to Dickens, Griffith once said he com-posed novels in pictures.[94] He maintained that "the Motion Picture is a novelizing or story-telling form, not strictly a stage form."[95]

Griffith's assimilation of Scott's methods of depicting historical themes and characters seems to have been largely intuitive, arising from his Southern heritage. The first great novelist of the nineteenth century and the most important since Cervantes, Scott set a literary precedent that radiated across the Western world from America to Russia. In America, he enjoyed particular popularity in the South, where marked similarities to his native Scotland led to identification with the spirit of his work. Com-pared to the urbanized, industrialized and wealthy northern United States, the South seemed rural, feudalistic, and impoverished, as did Scotland in contrast to the neighboring England. Both had suffered disastrous defeats at the hands of the more advanced adjacent regions. In the South in the aftermath of the Civil War, the vivid narratives of the defeats of heroic Scottish rebellions had a particular appeal to the heart of a Dixie cherishing the memory of a lost cause.

By the time Griffith was growing up in the South, Scott had become central to the literary and cultural heritage of the region. Steeped in

Southern traditions, Griffith was introduced to the novelist at an early age
when his father read Scott's works aloud to the family. Indeed, the genesis
of his treatment of historical narrative can be traced to Scott's example.
Like Scott, he intermingles his fictional protagonists with actual historical
personages. Also, like Scott, he creates characters representing social
forces who articulate his historical perspective of any particular moment
in history. David Brown's description of Scott could apply to Griffith as
well:

> Scott's great originality ... lies not only in his intuition that an in-
> dividual's life is fundamentally affected by the age in which he lives,
> but also in a complementary intuition that the most significant
> manifestation of the forces at work in society at any one time will
> be in the lives of ordinary individuals ... Scott attempts to illuminate
> the underlying movements common to society as a whole at the par-
> ticular moment.[96]

Similarly, Stanley J. Solomon states in *The Classic Cinema* that *Intolerance*, like Griffith's other historical films, concentrates on

> the problems and emotions of ordinary individuals who reflect the
> values and attitudes of their culture ... as we watch the Persian
> assault on the walls of Babylon or the massacre of the innocents on
> St. Bartholomew's Day, for example, we are always aware of a par-
> ticular individual's struggle against the dehumanizing forces of his
> age.[97]

Henry Morton, Scott's hero in *Old Mortality*, exemplifying the forces
of Presbyterianism in rebellion against the royalist authority, parallels
Griffith's Prosper Latour, who embodies the Huguenots' struggle against
the allied forces of church and state. While historical figures like Catherine
de Medici in the French Story and Claverhouse in *Old Mortality* symbolize
vast forces of repression attempting to thwart and subdue the perceived
enemies of the power structure, the narrative emphasis in both Scott and
Griffith always returns to the ordinary individuals in their brave struggle
against their oppressors. Henry Morton, siding with the Covenanters
during their revolt against the crown, twice saves the life of one of his com-
patriots; Prosper Latour vainly attempts to rescue his sweetheart in the
midst of the St. Bartholomew's Day Massacre. The Dear One, manifesting
the heroic qualities of the common people as she pleads for her husband's
life amid the class conflicts of the Modern Story, recalls Jeannie Deans,
the humble peasant girl in Scott's *The Heart of Midlothian* who, caught
up in the dissension brought about by the Porteus riots, endeavors to save
her sister, demonstrating "the rich humanity and simple heroism of a really
great human being."[98]

Griffith also seems to have drawn from James Fenimore Cooper, the other great historical novelist of the early nineteenth century. The only direct evidence of Cooper's impact on the director is Griffith's one-reel adaptation of *The Leatherstocking Tales* for Biograph, but, given Cooper's stature as the first great American novelist, it is reasonable to assume that his literary precedent may have been as important as Scott's in shaping Griffith's narrative concepts. In his early films of pioneer and Indian life, his themes and settings suggest he may have used Cooper as a frame of reference. In addition, Cooper's use of action to highlight the recreation of historical events and his tendency to infuse his work with a moral purpose are characteristics that can be found in Griffith's work.

In his stories of frontier life and Indian Wars, Cooper is a master at creating suspense through vivid descriptions of flights, pursuits and rescues to propel the action, providing a prototype adaptable to filmic methods. A typical example of his technique occurs in the climax of *The Last of the Mohicans*. During a wilderness battle in the French and Indian Wars, tension mounts as one dramatic incident follows another. The Indian hero, Uncas, and his friends, Natty Bumppo and a British officer, pursue the villainous Iroquois, Magua, and his fellow tribesman, fleeing through the rugged mountainous terrain with their captive, Cora Munro. Cora, refusing to go farther, is killed by Magua's companion just as Uncas drops from a high ledge to knife Cora's murderer. Magua first stabs Uncas, then attempts to leap to safety only to miss his mark and hang precariously over a precipice. The action concludes with Natty Bumppo shooting the Iroquois, who falls into the abyss below.

In Griffith, too, events coalesce to add momentum and suspense. Griffith's most advanced use of this narrative device, surpassing Cooper in scope, appears in the climax of *Intolerance* when, as Lewis Jacobs observes,

> action follows action ... as the rhythm sweeps along. Christ is seen toiling up Mount Calvary; the Babylonian Mountain Girl is racing to warn her king of the onrushing enemy; the Huguenot is fighting his way through the streets to rescue his sweetheart from the mercenaries; the wife is speeding in an automobile to the prison with a pardon for her husband who is about to be hung.[99]

Another similarity between Cooper and Griffith is their intense religious moralizing. Although Griffith presents a religious perspective imbued with Whitmanesque humanism that is broader and more eclectic than Cooper's doctrinaire approach, in many of his films he infuses his social and historical view with moral overtones. Iris Barry calls *Intolerance* "an epic sermon" with Griffith citing scriptures to make his point, presenting his moral conclusions in didactic subtitle, drawing a clear distinction between good and evil in his characters and manifesting his seriousness of purpose in an epilogue prophesying the Millenium.[100] Similarly, Cooper blends breathtaking entertainment and epic historical recreation with his own moral and religious convictions as in the conclusion of *The Deerslayer*:

> We live in a world of transgressions and selfishness, and no pictures that represent us otherwise can be true; though happily for human nature, gleamings of that pure spirit in whose likeness man has been fashioned, are to be seen, relieving its deformities, and mitigating, if not excusing, its crimes.[101]

Cooper, like Griffith, sees the possibility for mankind's redemption amid all its evils. Unlike Griffith, however, Cooper believes that land ownership, the law, the social hierarchy, the traditional high church are sacred and that "the devaluation of the sacred inevitably leads to the degeneration of civilization."[102] Although Cooper's philosophy contrasts with Griffith's prerevolutionary view in *Intolerance*, in which traditional hierarchies pervert or obscure the sacred, moral qualities inherent in the individual; both artists conceived their work and their interpretation of history as a means of reaffirming a moral conception of man originating in the religious experience.

The most singular influence on Griffith among novelists was Charles Dickens. Griffith's favorite novelist, Dickens played an important role not only in the development of his cinematic techniques, but also in shaping his overall social and historical vision. In their use of characterizations, their attitude toward established institutions, their sympathy for the downtrodden in society, their emphasis on pathos to highlight their narratives, and their ability to depict the sweep of historical events through the passion of crowds, Dickens and Griffith show a concern for social justice and a commitment to rectify the wrongs. As Lary May points out, Griffith, like Dickens, sought "to show the way the world ran and inspire the viewer to change it."[103]

Griffith often attributed his development of parallel editing to his study of the great English novelist. While the director's most elemental use of crosscutting in his earliest films may have derived from the melodrama, his more sophisticated narrative construction drew on Dickens's precedent as he stated in 1922:

> It was the reading of his [Dickens's] works that convinced me of the effectiveness of this policy of "switching off." It is to be found throughout his books. He introduces a multitude of characters and incidents, and breaks off abruptly to go from one to another, but at the end he cleverly gathers all the apparently loose-threads together again and rounds off the whole. It occurred to me that the method would be far more suitable to films than the straightforward system borrowed from plays which was then in vogue, and I put it into effect.[104]

An episode in *Oliver Twist* in which Oliver, on an errand for his benefactor, Mr. Brownlow, is recaptured by a gang of thieves illustrates the technique Griffith described. A series of transitions accompanies the action. As the episode begins, Oliver is leaving the Brownlow house where Mr. Brownlow and his friend await the boy's return. The action then cuts to a scene in a tavern disclosing the thieves, Fagin, Bill Sikes and Nancy. After Nancy and Sikes leave, the setting switches to the streets where Oliver is blithely carrying out his mission for Mr. Brownlow when he is suddenly accosted by Nancy and Sikes. A brief cutback to Mr. Brownlow and his friend still waiting for Oliver is followed by the street scene in which the boy is led away by Nancy and Sikes to Fagin's den. Inspired by the Dickensian form, Griffith perfected his method of crosscutting, enabling him to evolve the cinematic editing which became the basis for narrative film.

The link between Dickens and Griffith in delineating characters is analyzed by Sergei M. Eisenstein, the Russian film director, in his famous essay, "Dickens, Griffith and the Film Today." He notes that "striking figures of sympathetic old men, noble figures of sorrow and fragile maidens, rural gossips and sundry odd characters in the Dickens tradition" abound in Griffith's work "and grow from episodic figures into those fascinating and finished images of living people in which his screen is so enriched."[105] Dickens endows even his incidental characters with memorable traits, such as the opinionated old lady in *David Copperfield* who thinks all sailors are nothing but "meanderers" and the disreputable old shopkeeper from the same novel who haggles with David over the price of clothes. These characters, like the myriad others who people the Dickens world, are used by the author for comic relief. Like Dickens, Griffith punctuates his drama with unforgettable incidental characters. In *Intolerance*, the bit-players humanize the theme and make satirical comments on the pretentiousness and hypocrisy around them. For example, in the Judean Story, an old man momentarily stops munching an apple, his face reflecting the absurdity of the situation when the Pharisees demand that all activity cease while they pray in public.[106] Again, in the Modern Story, a grizzled old man's sly wink ridicules the self-righteous Vestal Virgins of Uplift as they lead the police raid on a brothel.

Another similarity in character development between Griffith and Dickens is their preference for youthful protagonists to emphasize the social themes. The innocence of the aspiring young heroes and heroines is accentuated when contrasted with the harshness of their societies. In *Nicholas Nickleby*, Dickens exposes the oppressive nature of provincial schools by juxtaposing the young hero, an assistant teacher, with his overlord, the sadistic schoolmaster, Squeers. Again, in *Bleak House*, Dickens highlights the chicanery of unscrupulous lawyers by showing the downfall of young Richard Carstone, who is destroyed by his entanglement in a lengthy chancery suit. The injustice of debtors' prison is underscored in *Little Dorrit* as Dickens portrays the heroine growing up in the prison where her father is incarcerated. Griffith likewise strengthens his statement against injustice in the Modern Story by counterpointing the naivete of the Dear One and the Boy reveling in the simple pleasures of life with the self-righteousness of the reformers, the avariciousness of the capitalist, and the impersonal cruelty of the law. The horror of the St. Bartholomew's Day massacre in the French Story is vividly conveyed to the audience through the fate of the young couple who are slaughtered on the eve of their marriage. In the Babylonian Story, the viewer is sensitized to the futility and destructiveness of war through the depiction of the Mountain Girl sacrificing her life in battle for a lost cause.

Both the novelist and the director developed a gallery of villains to project the corrupting and destructive forces in society. Jenkins, his sister and her associates in the Jenkins Foundation display the same kind of pharasaism that Dickens portrays in the arrogant, heartless industrialist, Josiah Bounderby, in *Hard Times*, who loudly proclaims the official morality while boasting that he is a self-made man. Griffith's characterization of the Musketeer of the Slums combines the shrewd, conniving leadership of Fagin, chief of the underworld in *Oliver Twist*, with the menacing appearance and manner of Fagin's chief lieutenant, Bill Sikes. Fagin is able to achieve his ignominious position by recruiting poor boys and girls to carry out his thievery. Like Fagin, the Musketeer of the Slums thrives upon social outcasts to build his empire, enlisting those who have been dispossessed because of the strike. Thus, the criminality of Dickens's and Griffith's underworld figures becomes an indictment of poverty and corruption, the conditions in society which allow the criminals to flourish.

Dickens's and Griffith's inclination to show "morally degraded characters who have sudden flashes of goodness" is apparent in the analogous portraits of Nancy in *Oliver Twist* and the Friendless One in the Modern Story.[107] Both are criminals' mistresses who manifest an inherent goodness enabling them to rise above their sordid milieu. To save Oliver Twist, whom she has befriended, Nancy turns against her gang, an act of self-sacrifice that leads to her death at the hands of Bill Sikes. Her Griffithian counterpart, the Friendless One, redeems herself by saving the innocent Boy from execution on the gallows when her conscience forces her to confess to the murder of her paramour.

Both Dickens and Griffith express an immediate and passionate concern for the social ethos, a motif lacking in Scott's detached historical view and Cooper's religious didacticism. They are able to communicate sympathy for the downtrodden and stimulate outrage at social injustice by creating scenes of pathos to stir the emotions of the audience. Mingling comment on social inequities with a sense of loss is typical of both Dickens and Griffith. In *Great Expectations*, Dickens impresses upon his reader the unnecessary human devastation that results from society extracting its pound of flesh when he creates empathy for Abel Magwitch, an old convict who, after befriending the young hero, Pip, dies a broken man in prison. Dickens poignantly dramatizes the results of society's neglect of the poor in the scene in *Bleak House* in which Jo, the little sweeping-boy, dies from a disease brought on by his life of poverty. Comparable scenes in *Intolerance* arouse the spectator to Griffith's perception of the corrosive effects of poverty: the death of the Dear One's father, reduced to indigence by the suppression of the strike, becomes a strong indictment of the monopolies; the Boy's gravitation to the underworld when he cannot find work after his father's death at the hands of the militia dramatically illustrates Griffith's belief that poverty leads to crime.

An underlying distrust of established institutions is a dominant theme in both Dickens and Griffith. They view the Establishment as a potential instrument for oppression. In his satirical depictions of popular religious and moral movements in *Bleak House* and other novels, in his expose of the alleged "charitable" workhouse system in *Oliver Twist*, in his attack on governmental bureaucracy in *Little Dorrit*, and in his many other indictments of societal injustice and hypocrisy in his works, Dickens established a precedent for the socially conscious artist. Griffith, who had taken up this challenge from his earliest days at Biograph, uses the Modern Story to condemn the motives and practices of capitalist-sponsored charitable foundations, the brutal treatment that labor received at the hands of monopolists, the connection between political corruption and the underworld, and the inequities built into the legal system. He reinforces his expose of twentieth-century abuses through his historical analogies.

Frank Norris, the powerful social novelist who seems to have had the strongest impact on Griffith of any of the turn-of-the-century American writers, augmented the Dickensian legacy. Regarded as a literary revolutionist, Norris was a transitional figure between American Literature of the nineteenth and twentieth centuries, introducing uncompromising realism to portray the life of his time and becoming one of the first voices of Progressivism.

The seeds of the vast organization of the historical and social vision of *Intolerance* can be traced directly to Griffith's 1909 Biograph one-reel film, *A Corner in Wheat*, based on "A Deal in Wheat," a short story by Norris, and several sequences from Norris' great novel *The Octopus*, published in 1901. When he adapted a chapter from *The Octopus* for *A Corner in Wheat*, Griffith greatly advanced film language by using Norris's method of alternating scenes to dramatize an idea. Indeed, before *A Corner in Wheat*, Griffith's experiments in parallel editing or crosscutting had been used primarily for creating suspense and unfolding his narrative.

The Norris model enabled Griffith to express a social vision through parallel editing which went beyond the melodramatic structures of his earlier films. *A Corner in Wheat* manifests "a firm and obvious rhythm ... based on the ideological content of each shot."[108] In *The Octopus*, a novel about the oppression of farmers by the railroad monopoly, Norris repeatedly cuts between feasting at the mansion of a railroad executive and a starving woman and child wandering in the city streets, victims of the railroad's war on the farmers. From this source, Griffith evolved his form of editing to express a philosophical and ideological conception of society in *A Corner in Wheat*, in which he cuts between the banquet of a wealthy wheat capitalist and the breadlines of the poor who suffer from the executive's manipulation of the stock market. In succeeding films, Griffith continued to experiment with this technique. It reached its apogee with his "drama of comparisons" in which he not only cut between the oppressors and the oppressed within the individual stories but used thematic cross-cutting between the four stories to reinforce the unity of his historical vision.

The overwhelming force of industrialism crushing the helpless victims in its path is a dominant theme in both Norris's *The Octopus* and Griffith's Modern Story. Adopting the epic form, Norris presents a struggle between the wheat farmers and the railroad over the land in California's San Joaquin Valley. In the end, the monopoly prevails, leaving the farmers broken men as their ranches are "seized in the tentacles of the octopus." With comparable epic vision, Griffith shows in the Modern Story that the force of capitalism, strewing its course with ruined lives, is able to quell the budding labor movement.

Despite similarities in their perception of social conflict, their basic philosophic values lead them to different conclusions. A sympathetic but detached observer of his time, Norris is an optimistic determinist. He believes that "the individual suffers but the race goes on" as he shows that the wheat harvest is destined to feed thousands of the famished in India. Viewing the railroad as necessary and inexorable to facilitate delivery, Norris concludes that out of evil comes good (the wheat) "untouched, unassailable, undefiled, that mighty world-force, that nourisher of nations."[109] Griffith, his roots in an agrarian society defeated by industrialism, maintains that the race will survive only through the triumph of the individual. Thus, the optimistic conclusion of *Intolerance* derives, not from any coincidental beneficence of industrialism, but from the survival of the young couple in the Modern Story over the forces of capitalistic oppression. Reflecting the Jeffersonian and Whitmanesque tradition, Griffith believes that the system is good only if it respects the individual.

As artists, Norris and Griffith stand at the conjunction of realism and romanticism. Both combine depictions of the minutiae of daily life and social and historical analysis with action, emotion and intuition. Norris's style, which has been described as "primitivism," stresses "a faith in instinct and emotion" with "action rather than the mind the center of existence."[110] It became "a central force in the modern American novel," and was inherently suited to the visual medium of film.[111] It was through Griffith, intuitively incorporating the more compressed style of the modern novel, that "primitivism" became the characteristic mode of expression in the cinema.

Norris and Griffith held a common belief that, as artists, their mission was to instruct the people in the truth about life as they saw it. Donald Pizer writes that Norris

> believed that the best fiction does not merely describe or amuse. Rather, it serves the practical moral purpose of revealing both the primary truths of human experience and the full extent of human injustice and deprivation, so that man might learn and mend his ways.[112]

In Norris's own words, he saw his role as a novelist as

> one who reaches the greatest audience. Right or wrong the People turn to him the moment he speaks, and what he says they believe ... The People have a right to the Truth as they have a right to life, liberty and the pursuit of happiness. It is not right that they be exploited and deceived with false views of life ... (The novelist) has a heavy duty to perform, and tremendous responsibilities to shoulder, and he should address himself to his task, not with the flippancy of the catch-penny juggler at the county fair, but with earnestness, with soberness, with a sense of his limitations, and with all the abiding sincerity that by the favor and mercy of the gods may be his.[113]

Griffith demonstrated a similar earnestness of purpose in commenting on the role of filmmaker in his pamphlet *The Rise and Fall of Free Speech in America*, written as a protest against censorship, which he feared would limit the screen to "slap-stick comedies, the ridiculous, sentimental 'mush' stories, the imitation of the cheap magazines." The director stated:

> The world-wide acceptance of moving pictures means the introduction of the most popular and far-reaching form of education the world has ever known.... Censorship demands of the picture makers a sugar-coated and false version of life's truth.... We have no wish to offend with indecencies or obscenities, but we do demand, as a right, the liberty to show the dark side of wrong, that we may illuminate the bright side of virtue.[114]

As many commentators have implied, Griffith is a transitional figure, drawing upon nineteenth-century art forms to create a twentieth-century art. His work, then, reflects a continuity with past achievements, yet his choice of artistic models is congruent with his times. In particular, such authors as Dickens and Whitman, with their celebrations of the common man and condemnation of injustice, harmonize with the democratic idealism of Jeffersonianism and the spirit of the Progressive Era. Indeed, Griffith's assimilation of nineteenth-century art forms to project a social-historical vision underscores the link between the democratic idealism of the 1800s and the Progressive movement of the early 1900s.

5. Influence of the Progressive Movement

The dominant contemporary influence on Griffith's historical vision was the Progressive movement. A diverse collection of groups and individuals demanding liberal reform in politics and society, the movement flourished from the turn of the century until the U.S. involvement in World War I. The movement incorporated a restatement of democratic Jeffersonian traditions and had as its foremost national exponents William Jennings Bryan, heir to the agrarian Populist movement of the 1890s; Robert M. La Follette, the radical reform governor and senator of Wisconsin; Theodore Roosevelt, advocate of a strong, centralized national reform administration; and Woodrow Wilson, the idealistic synthesizer of Bryan Populism and Roosevelt New Nationalism. In the forefront of the battle to improve the lot of the laboring man were Eugene Debs, radical leader of the Socialist Party, and Samuel Gompers, the more conservative head of the American Federation of Labor.

"Muckraking" journalists and novelists, sociologists and theologians provided the underpinnings and added momentum. So pervasive was the movement that new capitalists such as William Randolph Hearst and Henry Ford sought to improve their standing with the public by supporting Progressive causes, and long-established capitalists like John D. Rockefeller and Andrew Carnegie attempted to win public approval by setting up philanthropic foundations.

The Progressive movement contained more contradictory viewpoints in its ranks and is subject to greater diversity of interpretation by historians than any subsequent reform period. Progressives held widely differing views on such issues as war and peace, racial relations, moral reforms, and centralized federal authority versus states' rights. To the extent that there was a Progressive consensus in the years between the U.S. conquest of the Philippines and World War I, it was a recognition among Progressives that America's major priority was domestic social reform. All favored government intervention to control big business but were divided on how it should be done. Rooseveltian New Nationalists sought regulatory measures, Democrats called for a restoration of an open economy favoring small business, and Socialists argued for public ownership of business.

Historians in later decades have disagreed over the efficacy of Progressive reforms. Radicals maintain that Progressive legislation was cosmetic change that actually strengthened big business under a veneer of reform, while liberals assert that Progressivism helped to fulfill the promise of American democracy by curtailing the power of the corporations.

Despite the differing opinions on the gains of Progressivism and the divergence within the movement itself, there can be no doubt that the spirit of Progressive reform permeated American society. Caught up in this spirit, Griffith expressed the movement as he interpreted it in *Intolerance*, which, infused with the dynamics of the era, became an amalgam of Progressive trends. Through his masterpiece, he was able to expound the "aesthetics and social goals of a great movement."[1] For this achievement, he was alternately called a "communist" or an advocate of the "lost cause" of "laissez-faire" in his own time and suffered his first financial setback. Never again did he undertake to "produce a film that advocated the transformation of the industrial system through a mass movement."[2]

Bryanism

The Populist Party, an agrarian-based Southern and Western group hostile to the Eastern moneyed interests, was a harbinger of the Progressive movement and served as a catalyst for reform. Arising in the wake of the depression of the 1890s, it was largely absorbed into the mainstream of American politics when William Jennings Bryan, the Populist-minded Democrat, was first nominated by the Democratic Party as their presidential candidate in 1896, running on a platform that called for the free coinage of silver.

Bryan continued to represent his party over the next three decades. He was particularly popular in the Midwest and South, where "farmers and small townspeople ... basked in his prairie-like simplicity and whole-souled sentimentality, and three times bestowed upon him ... the Democratic presidential nomination."[3] Griffith, who came from an impoverished farm family and, like most Southerners at that time, supported the Democratic Party, undoubtedly assimilated the tenets of the Populist-Bryan movements. His "lively correspondence" with Bryan, who was a "great admirer" of Griffith, offers evidence that he acknowledged Bryan as a spokesman for a political perspective that harmonized with his own.[4]

An undercurrent in much of Griffith's work is the restatement of Jeffersonian ideals embodied in Bryanism, which defended the "old and simple life of America," and, Walter Lippmann argued, was antithetical to the new industrialized society. Bryan hated the corporate structure, blaming it for the economic conditions which had "destroyed village loyalties, frustrated private ambitions, and created the impersonal relationships of the modern world."[5]

Griffith, like Bryan, "gloried in the past when self-sufficiency was the rule," tending to idealize the simpler, more personal relationships of a preindustrial society.[6] He often imbues his work with an element of nostalgia for a lost innocence that he implies is undermined by industrialization and urbanization. A manifestation of Bryanesque idealism, the bucolic imagery of the heroine romping with chicks and geese in the opening scenes of the Modern Story conveys Griffith's affection for a way of life soon to be shattered by the forces of capitalist oppression and urbanization. Again, extending the Bryanesque mood of the "old and simple life" threatened by industralism, a shot of the Dear One nonchalantly sipping a soda at the mill workers' dance is intercut with the foreboding image of Jenkins alighting from his long limousine to check on the revelers.

Another similarity between the director and the politician is their conception of man's relation to society. Griffith's juxtapositioning of the powerless and powerful reinforces a view that corresponds to Bryan Democracy. According to his biographer, Louis W. Koenig, Bryan believed that

> Man is intrinsically good; but man is corrupted when he is embraced by man-made institutions, above all, the business corporations. These institutions, powerful, immoral and brutally manipulative, spread deprivations and misery.... In Bryan's perceptions, the common man was suffering, meritorious, and heroic ...
>
> Greedy men, moving behind the scenes and lacking any vested legitimacy, manipulated society and public policy to their own immense profit and brought misery to the general citizenry.[7]

Koenig's exposition of Bryan's convictions could also explain Griffith's depiction of the power structure in *Intolerance*. As he shows heroic common people throughout history destroyed by those who seek to enforce their power over society, he accepts Bryan's view of the causes of social and economic inequities. Griffith's common people are good, enduring, brave, warm and self-sacrificing; they meet with disaster, not because of personal flaws, but because of the machinations of the powerful. The "autocratic industrial overlord," as the mill-owner is dubbed in the Modern Story, Catherine de Medici and the High Priest of Bel are Griffith's visualizations of Bryan's view of "greedy men, behind the scenes, manipulating society and public policy."

Theodore Roosevelt and Executive Leadership

Theodore Roosevelt, who became president in 1901 and remained the central figure in American political life until his defeat in the 1912 election, "was so impressed with the relevance of Bryan's proposals that he made many of them the warp and woof of his administration's major policies."[8] A charismatic, dynamic leader whose style and personality affected not only the political scene, but also had an impact on the pioneering film industry, Roosevelt personified the spirit of Progressive reform, which sought to alleviate abuses stemming from the unrestrained power of large corporations. Through legislation, personal mediation and compelling oratory, he established a modern national reform administration that served as a precedent for other progressive presidencies.

In his famous New Nationalism speech of 1910, Roosevelt defined the office of the presidency as "the steward of public welfare." He believed that "every man holds his property subject to the general right of the community to regulate its use to whatever degree the public welfare may require it."[9] During his administration, he instigated over forty lawsuits against giant corporations such as the Northern Securities Company and the Rockefeller oil trust in an attempt to bring the monopolies under government regulation. Legislation passed with his support included the Hepburn Railway Rate Act, the first Pure Food and Drug acts, and laws to conserve the natural resources. Climaxing his career as a Progressive leader, he articulated the ideals of the movement in the campaign of 1912:

> We are for liberty. But we are for the liberty of the oppressed, and not for the liberty of the oppressor to bind the burdens on the shoulders of the heavy laden. It is idle to ask us not to exercise the powers of government when only by that power of the government can we curb the greed that sits in the high places, when only by the exercise of the government can we exalt the lowly and give heart to the humble and downtrodden.[10]

The concept of a strong executive leadership, which characterized the Roosevelt administration and later became the hallmark of the Wilson presidency, inspired the reformist activism of Progressive governors, including Robert M. La Follette and Hiram Johnson. The most influential senator and governor in the Progressive Era, La Follette as governor of Wisconsin instituted direct primaries, equalized taxation and controlled railroad rates, setting a pattern for the liberalization of state government. Johnson, the leading political figure in California when Griffith reached his zenith in Hollywood, followed La Follette's example in his term as governor from 1911 to 1917. Johnson, who was Roosevelt's running mate in 1912, distinguished himself during his administration in his fight against corporations and was responsible for breaking the power of the Southern Pacific Railroad in California. Woodrow Wilson, who had been a reform governor of New Jersey, continued the role of the president as the champion of public welfare, enacting an impressive reform program to implement his view that laws were needed to "prevent the strong from crushing the weak."[11]

Griffith's characterization of Prince Belshazzar in the Babylonian Story is analogous to the reform governors and Presidents Roosevelt and Wilson. Like the Progressive leaders, Belshazzar's championship of the people brings him into conflict with the special interests of his society, the entrenched theocracy of the priests of Bel-Marduk. The Prince promotes religious freedom to diminish the monopolistic control of the cult of Bel in the same spirit in which the Progressives strove to foster economic freedom by breaking the power of the trusts. And, like the Progressive leaders, he institutes reform through a bloodless revolution within the context of the traditional values of his culture. Just as the Progressives sought to fulfill the aspirations for greater freedom set forth in the Declaration of Independence and the Constitution, Belshazzar attempts to reanimate the goals of his civilization contained in the Code of Hammurabi to "protect the weak from the strong."

Not only did Roosevelt's concept of a strong executive concerned for the public welfare help shape Griffith's interpretation of Belshazzar; his style and forceful rhetoric conveyed a sense of drama to social issues which acted as a stimulus to early filmmakers, including Griffith. In assessing Roosevelt's effect on the American silent cinema, film historian Kevin Brownlow describes him as "a man whose spirit and example imprinted themselves indelibly upon the minds of the prewar generation."[12] His penchant for defining the ills of society as a struggle between good and evil characters parallels Griffith's own treatment of social and historical conflicts. While Wilson spoke in abstract terms about "the wrongs of a system" rather than "the wrongs which individuals intentionally do,"[13] the flamboyant T.R. denounced "the representatives of predatory wealth," labelling them "the criminal rich," "those rich men whose lives are evil and corrupt," and "malefactors of great wealth."[14] Griffith, who wanted to portray societal injustice in palpable terms that audiences could comprehend, chose the Rooseveltian mode, focusing on evil resulting from the wilful acts and decisions of individuals occupying positions of power; evil and good are clearly delineated in his characters.

Wilsonism

Despite his affinities with Roosevelt, Griffith's ties to Woodrow Wilson were more significant in determining the philosophical viewpoint of his feature films including *Intolerance*. Like Griffith, Wilson and many members of his cabinet were Southerners, a regional link which helped the director develop a personal relationship with the administration. While Wilson was in the White House, Griffith met with the president on several occasions and also was friendly with two other fellow Southerners: Secretary of the Navy Josephus Daniels, and Secretary of the Treasury

William G. McAdoo, Wilson's son-in-law, who was associated with Griffith in the formation of United Artists.[15] Wilson's papers reveal that at least on one occasion Griffith corresponded with the president, seeking his assistance in the production of future epic films which would further the cause of Wilsonian Progressivism. Griffith's letter, dated March 2, 1915, reads in part:

> If we carry out the proposed series of motion pictures dealing with matters historical and political, of which I spoke to you, I should be happy to have someone representing your views to pass upon our ideas before beginning the initial work.[16]

Griffith timed the release of *Intolerance* to help "Wilson and the Democrats defeat the Republicans" in the 1916 election.[17] He greatly admired the president, hailing him as "a man we all revere or ought to."[18] His admiration sprang, not only from a mutual Southern heritage, but also from a philosophical compatibility championing the individual in his struggle against the burgeoning power of the monopolies. While Bryan's belief in individualism was tempered by his subordination of the individual to the values of the community, and Roosevelt's appreciation of individual effort was modified by his admiration for a large, efficient government, Wilson's view that the integrity of the individual should be a central consideration in social organization underlay his far-reaching reforms. In Wilson's view, the chief evil of the corporate structure was its impersonality, as he declared in his 1912 campaign:

> Today the everyday relationships of men are largely with great impersonal concerns, with organizations, not with other individual men....
> We are all caught in a great economic system which is heartless. The modern corporation is not engaged in business as an individual. When we deal with it, we deal with an impersonal element, an immaterial piece of society.... [19]

Griffith's vision, like Wilson's policies, sought to humanize the social order. Both Griffith and Wilson believed that the "humanization of business and industry ... could come only through a renewed recognition of human individuality."[20] The emphasis on the value of individuals in *Intolerance*, in which their acts of goodness are counterpointed against unjust, dehumanized systems, extends Wilson's view of human relations to Griffith's art. In the Modern Story, Griffith conceptualizes corporate impersonality in his portrayal of Jenkins, a remote figure who has no personal contact with his workers. Jenkins, who sees his workers as so many objects to be manipulated for his own profit, remains aloof and unaware of the effect on the individual of his suppression of the strike. While Griffith is Rooseveltian in personifying evil in the character of Jenkins, he is Wilsonian in showing that the injustice emanating from the capitalist's policies results from detachment rather than personal vindictiveness against any one individual. The Boy is first victimized by the impersonality of the tycoon when he is forced out of work and his father is killed, then by the judgment of a detached legal system which puts his life in jeopardy for a crime he did not commit. He is saved only through acts of individual kindness. The devotion of the heroine for her husband, the friendly policeman convinced of the Boy's innocence, and the confession of the real culprit because of pangs of guilt, are the only real bulwarks against a dehumanized system with its resulting intolerance.

Griffith's sympathy for Wilson's New Freedom, which united workers, farmers and small businessmen against the power of the trusts, was also apparent in his attempt to maintain his independence as a small entrepreneurial artist. Simultaneous with Wilson's first year in office, Griffith left Biograph, establishing his own studio to gain more freedom and autonomy. When the film industry came under the control of giant corporations, Griffith's career came to an end partially because of his unwillingness to submerge his individuality to the demands of the large studios. According to his cameraman, Billy Bitzer, Griffith felt he could not "be his own man" in an efficient corporate system, an intransigence which made it impossible for him to accomodate himself to the new Hollywood.[21] Wilson, too, rejected control of the individual by an efficient, impersonal corporation, declaring in his 1912 campaign:

> You know what happens when you are the servant of a corporation. You have in no instance access to the men who are really determining the policy of the corporation. If the corporation is doing the things that it ought not to do, you really have no voice in the matter and must obey the orders ... Your individuality is swallowed up in the individuality and purpose of a great organization.[22]

Although Wilson was unable to fulfill his campaign promise to dissolve the trusts and restore the open competition that existed in pre–Civil War America, his administration climaxed the Progressive Era with impressive legislation to curb corporate abuse and reform the governmental structure. His persuasive leadership resulted in the passage of the Underwood Tariff Act, which lowered or lifted tariffs on many imports; the establishment of the Federal Reserve System to reform the banking structure; the enactment of the Clayton Anti-Trust Act to monitor big business practices; the creation of the Federal Trade Commission to protect consumers; and the passage of the Federal Farm Loan Act to aid farmers in securing government loans.

In the midst of these accomplishments, the great war engulfing Europe threatened to undermine Wilson's efforts to create a more humane America with respect for individual freedom. Griffith, reflecting the widespread apprehension of many Progressives that American involvement in World War I "would weaken the reform impulse at home and do irreparable damage to the crusade for social and economic justice," depicts war as the destroyer of an advanced civilization in the Babylonian Story.[23] He shared the hopes of the Progressives who supported Wilson's reelection in 1916 believing that he could keep America out of the European fray and continue the policy of neutrality he had fostered in his first term. Enthusiastically expressing his support for the president's reelection, Griffith said: "Wilson kept us out of war. I would rather have him reelected than have *Intolerance* a success."[24]

Muckraking Journalism

The legislative programs proposed and enacted by Progressive statesmen were partly in response to the widespread demands for reforms generated by a new school of journalism which Roosevelt termed "muckraking." This reciprocity between politics and journalism enabled the print media to play a more significant role in molding American public opinion during the Progressive Era than at any time before or since. From the big-city national newspaper chain of William Randolph Hearst to the small-town journal of reform activist William Allen White, journalists "produced voluminous and effective exposures of corruption, crime, waste, brutality and autocracy in the dark corners of American life" in the hope that the public's social conscience would be aroused to correct these evils.[25] With a newly emerging urbanized population looking to the mass circulation publications to replace "village gossip and local politicking," these exposes stimulated competition between newspapers and magazines, which resorted to ever-increasing sensational revelations to garner the market for readers.[26]

Griffith saw the potential in motion pictures to parallel the press in dramatizing the corruption and abuses exposed by the muckrakers. He stated in his pamphlet attacking censorship that "the moving pictures are, in fact, a pictorial press, performing in a modern and entertaining and instructive manner all the functions of the printed press."[27] As Lillian Gish confirmed, he saw his own role "as similar to a newspaper editor, in a position to affect not only his country but also the world ... and he took an editor's responsibility for his point of view."[28] On a worldwide scale, he viewed the motion pictures as having a greater potential for impact than language, whether printed journalism or the oratory of statesmen, because images in films "have gone beyond Babel, beyond words. We have found a universal language, a power that can make men brothers and end war forever."[29]

Armed by his faith in the capacity of the motion picture to transform society, Griffith was inspired by the work of the muckraking journalists "to dramatize every major concern of the day."[30] The dynamics of the muckraking revelations, including Ida Tarbell's expose of the Rockefeller oil trust in *The History of the Standard Oil Company* (1904), Lincoln Steffens's documentation of civic corruption in *The Shame of the Cities* (1904), and Upton Sinclair's hard-hitting attack on the meat-packing industry in his 1906 novel *The Jungle*, set the tone for Griffith's arraignment of the injustices and corruption in contemporary American life, from his Biograph shorts to the Modern Story of *Intolerance*.

Drawn from leading stories in the newspapers of the time, the Modern Story is a virtual anthology of the kinds of abuses exposed by the muckrakers. Griffith's picture of the brutal suppression of labor by the archetypal industrialist and the sham charity foundation he establishes to enhance his image suggests the influence of Tarbell's trendsetting detailed study of Standard Oil appearing in *McClure's* which brought public attention to the "ruthless methods by which some great enterprises and great fortunes had been built" and the exploitation of "business competitors and industrial workers alike" by "captains of industry."[31] Also serialized in *McClure's*, Steffens's probing examination of crime and high-level corruption in some of America's larger cities, including New York, Philadelphia and St. Louis, may well have served as a prototype for Griffith's depiction of the link between the gangster element and corrupt officials.[32] The Musketeer of the Slums, who gains control of the community through his monopoly of the liquor traffic, uses his political influence with "higher-ups" to frame the Boy when he quits the gang. The journalistic crusades focusing on ameliorating the slum life of the poor may have stimulated Griffith's unvarnished picture of the meager, threadbare existence of his hero and heroine living in a tenement. Social worker Robert Hunter's book, *Poverty* (1904), the most shocking report of the extent of poverty in this time, contended that ten million people were "barely able to survive."[33] The criticism of the prison system and the death penalty in the Modern Story punctuates the calls for penological reform by muckrakers such as Charles Edward Russell.

Ross's Sociology of "Criminaloid" Types

The "criminaloid" theory propounded by Edward A. Ross, leading sociologist of the Progressive Era, whose work attracted the attention of Bryan and Roosevelt, comes to life in Griffith's portrayal of villains who maintain an air of respectability while committing crimes against society through their misuse of power. In his well-known study of 1907, *Sin and Society*, Ross argues that there is a new type of transgressor against society who, unlike more recognizable criminals such as adulterers, murderers and thieves, is invariably a pillar in the community, a transgressor the sociologist terms "criminaloid":

Fortified by his connections with "legitimate business" ... he may
even bestride his community like a Colossus ... Do we not hail him
as a "man who does things," make him director of our banks and
railroads, trustee of our hospitals and libraries?....

Too squeamish and too prudent to practice treachery, brutality
himself, he takes care to work through middlemen....

The upright may fall slack in devout observances, but he cannot
afford to neglect his church connection. He needs it in his business....

Likewise the criminaloid counterfeits the good citizen.... Full well
he knows that the giving of a fountain or a park ... will more than
outweigh the dodging of taxes, the grabbing of streets, and the corrupting of city councils.[34]

Jenkins exemplifies Ross's description of the criminaloid type—a
pious man, he bears all the trappings of the outstanding citizen of his community, heading a flourishing industry as he achieves the capitalistic
American goal of success. Increasing his prestige in the society by cloaking
himself in the mantle of the public benefactor, he establishes a charitable
foundation which then attempts to enforce public morality. When his
workers strike to protest a reduction in wages, he calls on the state militia
and his factory guards who, as middlemen acting under his orders, fire
upon the strikers.

Although there were many capitalist "robber barons" in late nineteenth and early twentieth century America, the most obvious exemplifica-
tion of Ross's criminaloid was John D. Rockefeller. Bryan saw Rockefeller
as the "chief villain" of the social order whose misdeeds were not counterbalanced, in his opinion, by the capitalist's "good works." In a particularly
strong indictment, Bryan once asserted that "no criminal now incarcerated
... for larceny has shown more indifference to human rights and property
rights than this same Rockefeller." He was not impressed with
Rockefeller's contributions to colleges and churches, considering them
bribes to silence opposition to his unscrupulous methods in building his
empire.[35] It was no wonder that Bryan was attracted to Ross's ideas,
agreeing with the professor's concept of "social sin" originating with the
absence of any genuine social conscience among wealthy transgressors like
Rockefeller.[36]

Film historians Arthur Lennig and William K. Everson claim that the
character and actions of Jenkins were suggested by Rockefeller who, along
with his son, slashed workers' pay, inciting strikes they brutally suppressed. Even Jenkins's twofold purpose for creating a charitable
organization parallels the Rockefellers' campaign to stamp out vice in New
York City and establish philanthropic foundations in order to hide behind
the good citizen image characteristic of Ross's criminaloid type.[37]

Griffith's depiction of the criminaloid is also apparent in the villains
of the other stories. While Ross takes the view that the criminaloid is a
relatively new social phenomenon, the director demonstrates that this type

of individual is a historical constant. The Pharisees, Catherine de Medici and the High Priest of Bel perpetrate their crimes through middlemen or agents, while they are to be found "in the assemblies of the faithful, zealously exhorting and bearing witness."[38] From their exalted positions in Judaism, the Pharisees bring about the crucifixion of Christ; Catherine de Medici, as a title states, "hides her political intolerance of the Huguenots beneath the cloak of the great Catholic religion"; and the High Priest of Bel exploits his hierarchical position in his cult in his conflict with Belshazzar. By showing hypocrisy in high places, Griffith substantiates Ross's contention that "because so many good men are pious, the criminaloid covets a high seat in the synagogue as a valuable private asset."[39]

Social Gospel Christianity

The liberal theologians of the Progressive Era added to the fervor of the muckrakers and statesmen. They advanced the doctrines of the social gospel of Christianity based upon the unity of religion and social consciousness. Imbuing the Progessive movement with a messianic impulse to awaken the public to the wrongs in the nation, the social gospel theologians, including Washington Gladden, William Dwight Porter Bliss and Walter Rauschenbusch, excoriated the materialism of contemporary American society that sanctioned the crimes of the "robber barons" against labor and ignored the growing gulf between the affluent few and the deprived millions forced to live in the degradation of the city slums. Gladden, pastor of the First Congregational Church in Columbus, Ohio, denounced the "tainted money" and conspicuous consumption of the wealthy from pulpits and college campuses across the country as he sought to inject Christian ethos into the social order. An Episcopalian cleric, Bliss, who was "among the more radical advocates of the social gospel," attempted to ally Christianity with socialist principles, founding a church in Boston for the laboring classes, an organization advancing the cause of labor under the auspices of the church, and the Society of Christian Socialism.[40] Rauschenbusch, a professor at the Rochester Theological Seminary and a Baptist minister who gained first-hand knowledge of poverty from his pastorate in the slums of New York City, articulated most fully the ideals and goals of the social gospel in his writings. Called "the towering intellectual figure" of social gospel Christianity,[41] Rauschenbusch believed that the ministry should be used to foster social consciousness:

> He (the minister) can infuse the spirit of moral enthusiasm into the economic struggle of the dispossessed.... he can strengthen the consciousness that the working-people have a real grievance.... and

awaken among the wealthy a sense of social compunction and moral uneasiness....

The spiritual force of Christianity should be turned against the materialism and mammonism of our industrial and social order.[42]

In accordance with the crusading spirit of social gospel theology, *Intolerance* weds Christian ethics to social awareness. Contrasting the lavish furnishings of the Jenkins mansion with the dingy surroundings of the tenements, Griffith, like the social gospel theologians, attacks the deplorable disparity between the privileged and impoverished classes. His juxtaposition of the actions of the moral reformers with the scenes from Christ's life unmasks them as hypocrites devoid of genuine concern for the plight of the poor. In a potent illustration of the incompatibility of capital punishment with Christian mercy, Griffith links the agonizing trial and sentencing inflicted on the Boy by the modern legal system with the martyrdom of Christ. When asked by an interviewer, Henry Stephen Gordon, whether he regarded the Modern Story as an attack on courts and judges, Griffith replied:

> I certainly do not because it is not.... judges do not make the laws; you, I, everyone are responsible for the laws ... What has seemed peculiar to me about the law is that after so prolonged an experiment with the principles of Christianity, we still find as was found through all the ages that justice demands if a man kills another he in turn should be murdered.[43]

In the epilogue of *Intolerance*, Griffith implies that the forward movement of humanity through Progressivism can attain the apocalyptic vision of the Christian ideal, a millenium of love and peace when prisons are replaced by flowery fields. This conclusion is not surprising in a work of art assimilating the aspirations of the Progressive Era, since much of the optimism of even the secular thinkers was inevitably the result of the mutual interchange of ideals between secularists and social gospel theologians. Indeed, Griffith's whole conception of an art that would bring about the brotherhood of man corresponds with Rauschenbusch's view of the pulpit as a force for peace and justice: "The influence of the Christian ministry, if exercised in the spirit of Christian democracy, might be one of the most powerful solvents and the decisive influence for peace."[44]

While Griffith's insight derived from his personal experiences and background and his cultural heritage, his relationship to the reform movement of his time confirmed the direction his vision took. Much of his early popularity, in fact, stemmed from his sensitivity to the mood of the times. But like his choice of facts to illustrate his theme, he incorporated those elements of Progressivism that were most congruous with his basic philosophy. For this reason, he was especially attracted to Wilsonism, which seemed to offer the greatest hope for the realization of individual freedom fused with a concern for the well-being of the people as a whole. At the same time, he rejected those aspects of Progressivism, such as moral reform, that threatened the integrity of the individual. Perhaps because of the wide diversity among Progressives, it was inevitable that *Intolerance*, under the impact of World War I, should become a casualty of the deeply divided movement. Yet the reception of the film by audiences and critics in 1916 attests to Griffith's success in conveying a vision in consonance with Progressive idealism.

6. Impact of *Intolerance*

When *Intolerance* was first presented in the United States in 1916-17, the reaction of audiences and critics was indicative of the fragility of the Progressive consensus, which was rapidly disintegrating as America moved toward war. The most significant work of art of the Progressive Era, *Intolerance* symbolized the climax of the movement, synthesizing its basic philosophical tenets and commenting on immediate issues of the era. Yet it is usually described as a major box-office failure in the United States, although the reasons for its failure or the degree to which it failed remain in dispute. Some historians claim that *Intolerance* was an immediate failure upon its initial showing at the Liberty Theatre in New York on September 5, 1916, an impression that Griffith himself gave credence to in statements in later years. In actuality, however, *Intolerance* played to packed houses throughout the United States, far exceeding the popularity of average program pictures of the time, and was a commercial triumph in foreign countries. Unlike its predecessor, *The Birth of a Nation*, a box-office success for years, the American popularity of *Intolerance* waned after a few months. The reasons for its failure are as complex as the film itself: the expense of production; the unusual narrative structure; the impact of World War I; a conservative backlash against Progressivism; and the factionalization within the movement itself.

Audience Reaction

As Kevin Brownlow comments: " ... at first, audiences in America supported the picture."[1] Reports of theatrical showings throughout the United States in *The New York Dramatic Mirror* confirm Brownlow's assessment of early audience reaction. From September, 1916, to April, 1917, when America entered the war, *The Dramatic Mirror* reports that *Intolerance* was playing to capacity houses from Portland, Oregon, to New Orleans. In an advertisement appearing in the February 24, 1917, issue of *The Dramatic Mirror*, Wark Producing Corporation (the company formed by Griffith to distribute the film) announced that twelve road-show companies were touring America and that the film had completed a five-month run at the Liberty Theatre. It also ran for four months in Chicago,

Opposite: Advertisement in the "New York Dramatic Mirror," February 24, 1917.
This page: Advertisement in New York newspapers at the time of the film's initial
screenings in September 1916.

producing earnings in excess of *The Birth of a Nation* for a similar period of time. It had equally sensational engagements for several months in San Francisco, Philadelphia, Pittsburgh and St. Louis. Despite blizzards and less favorable critical reviews, it was "the hit of the season" in Milwaukee with the receipts for its two weeks' screening surpassing *The Birth of a Nation*. It had return engagements in Indianapolis and Oakland, an impressive indication of its popularity. In smaller cities such as El Paso, Texas, San Jose and Modesto, California, Decatur and Elgin, Illinois, Elmira and Syracuse, New York, limited engagements also played to packed houses. After the United States entered the war in April, *Intolerance* was still drawing crowds in May when it opened in Baltimore and Washington, D.C., and the smaller city of Appleton, Wisconsin.[2]

A full-page editorial in *The San Francisco Bulletin* of October 19, 1916, entitled "The Eternal Obstacle — Intolerance" on the significance of the film describes its effect on audiences of the time:

> Crowds gaze at *Intolerance* day by day; at times they break into laughter and hand-clapping as though the figures on the screen had life and could hear the praise.... They have seen a great truth — perhaps the greatest of truths — greatly expressed. They recognize it as a truth....
>
> Griffith's film moves thousands of persons each day to tears, to applause, to noble and fine emotions....[3]

The first indication of a falling-off in popularity of *Intolerance* was reported in the May 12, 1917, issue of *The Dramatic Mirror*. While the report from Scranton, Pennsylvania, still described its screening as having "thrilled capacity houses" in late April, a report in the same issue records a simultaneous limited engagement in Fort Dodge, Iowa, as drawing "only fair patronage." The June 9 issue also gave indications of diminishing audience enthusiasm, with a Denver correspondent writing that, in spite of its magnificence, *Intolerance* did not match *The Birth of a Nation* in popularity, closing after a run of only eight days in Denver.[4] Lillian Gish recalls that, after a surge of popularity for several months, attendance had declined during the last weeks of the film's run at the Liberty, a pattern that was repeated in other cities where *Intolerance* had lengthy runs. "It was obvious to us all that the film was failing," she states.[5]

It was by far the most expensive motion picture made anywhere in the world prior to the 1920s and needed a run for several years in order to recoup its cost. On the occasion of its San Francisco opening on October 9, 1916, Griffith, in the first flush of apparent success, predicted to critic Thomas Nunan of *The San Francisco Examiner* that "however successful *Intolerance* may be, even though it surpass *The Clansman (The Birth of a Nation)* in extended runs throughout the country, it will never pay back the money expended on it."[6] Griffith persisted in road-show presentations with full orchestral accompaniment in "legitimate" theaters, which "ate up the profits." Karl Brown says, "It did not fail as compared with the grosses of other pictures. It failed only because it cost much more than even an enormously successful picture would have brought in."[7] Within a year of its opening, Griffith was financially ruined; even with subsequent successful productions, it was years before he finished paying off the debts incurred by *Intolerance*.

Some film historians claim that the film failed because it was difficult for cinematically unsophisticated American audiences of 1916–17 to grasp the meaning behind its complex structure. Their contention is supported by critics of the period who found the film confusing or bewildering. Julian Johnson, an otherwise sympathetic critic, observed in *Photoplay Magazine*: "[It] results in positive mental exhaustion. The universally-heard comment from the highbrow or nobrow who has tried to get it all in an evening: 'I am so tired.' "[8] This argument, however, fails to explain the reports of favorable audience reaction that extended beyond its initial screenings. It also does not account for the resounding popular success of *Intolerance* several years later in foreign countries, including Russia and Japan, where audiences were less familiar with Griffith's earlier works and were less cinematically sophisticated at this time than audiences in the United States. Further evidence that the structure was not solely responsible for its ultimate failure in America is the lack of audience enthusiasm for the re-cut versions of the Modern Story, *The Mother and the Law*, and the Babylonian Story, *The Fall of Babylon*, which Griffith released as separate features in 1919.

Despite its overall commercial failure as the United States entered the war, *Intolerance* continued to be a popular attraction in some American communities as late as the spring of 1918. In September, 1917, Griffith's company announced plans to distribute the film to the smaller "representational" theaters or "neighborhood houses" devoted exclusively to motion pictures.[9] Edward Wagenknecht recalls that *Intolerance* was shown in the second-run "neighborhood houses" in Chicago during the fall of 1917.[10] *The Dramatic Mirror* reported return engagements in Pittsburgh, Omaha and Milwaukee during the winter and spring of 1918 and recorded successful revivals in Boston and Cincinnati in the same period. In March of 1918, *Intolerance* attracted record-breaking crowds in its return engagement in Louisville, Griffith's hometown, and played to capacity houses, standingroom only, during a limited run in the small city of Crawfordsville, Indiana.[11]

Critical Reception

Concomitant with the legend of its immediate box-office failure is the myth that *Intolerance* was an overwhelming critical failure upon its release. In reality, however, while some reviews were more favorable and more appreciative than others, the preponderance of critical opinion heralded Griffith's cinematic genius. Indeed, some reviewers were particularly perceptive in their appraisal of Griffith's achievement, disproving later claims by some film historians that critics of the period were insensitive to film art.

Reviewers in the trade press were lavish in their praise. *Film Daily* called *Intolerance* "stupendous, tremendous, revolutionary, intense, thrilling ... the most stirring human experience that has ever been presented to the world."[12] Frederick James Smith wrote in *The New York Dramatic Mirror*:

> *Intolerance* ... stands at the outpost of the cinema's advance. It has an idea. It has a purpose. From a structural standpoint, the handling and interweaving of four plots are revolutionary.[13]

Newspaper reviewers were equally enthusiastic, O.L. Hall of *The Chicago Journal* declaring that "it discounts all else the theater has shown."[14] *The New York Evening Post*, which had registered its opposition to *The Birth of a Nation* by refusing to advertise it, described the new Griffith epic as "the highest achievement which the camera has recorded ... a spectacle that no one should miss seeing, because it marks a new epoch in the progress of this form of entertainment."[15] Dorothy Dix in *The New York Journal* marveled at "its magnitude and grandeur, its poetry, its whirlwind action" and wondered how it could have emanated "from the brain of one man."[16] Walter Anthony of *The San Francisco Chronicle* likened it to the wonders of nature or a Beethoven symphony, noting its musical structure:

> There is a grandeur which in nature takes the breath away—a glimpse at Niagara, a sight of the Yellowstone canyon or the canyon of the Colorado....
>
> There is something of that quality in *Intolerance*. You gasp at its very immensity and meekly bow to the daring and vision of the man who conceived it....
>
> Such pictures as *Intolerance* come like a Beethoven set of symphonies—once in a century....
>
> It is handled in four streams of pictorial counterpoint. And like good polyphony, each melody or theme is the equal of any of the others. And, to continue the musical simile, each is complete in itself, though woven into the web of the whole.[17]

Because *The Birth of a Nation* had been a national event and an unprecedented commercial success, widely praised and condemned, recognized as an object of controversy and a landmark of film art, *Intolerance*, as Griffith's next monumental effort, was eagerly awaited by critics and public alike. The verdict of a wide number of critics in 1916 was that *Intolerance* surpassed the earlier film. *The New York Herald* maintained that *"The Birth of a Nation* is to *Intolerance* what the old one-reel motion picture is to the present day feature"[18] while *The San Francisco Call-Post* said that, in comparison with *Intolerance*, its Civil War predecessor was "colorless and mediocre."[19] Harry Carr of *The Los Angeles Times* agreed, stating that *"Intolerance* ... makes *The Clansman* look like a fishing smack when a dreadnaught sweeps into a harbor."[20]

Nevertheless, like *The Birth of a Nation*, *Intolerance* generated controversy although considerably less vehement than the furor surrounding the earlier film. One of the harshest appraisals of the new film appeared in *The New Republic*, reflecting, perhaps, its earlier hostility towards *The Birth of a Nation*. The review by George Soule, whose editorial specialty was economics rather than literary or dramatic criticism, dismissed *Intolerance* as having "no human emotion except visual amazement," comparing its attempts to "gorge the senses" to a Barnum and Bailey production.[21] More appreciative of Griffith's cinematic skill than Soule but equally disdainful of the theme of *Intolerance*, Heywood Broun commented in *The New York Tribune*:

> David W. Griffith is an immature philosopher, a wrongheaded sociologist, a hazy theologian, a flamboyant historian, but a great movie man. As a picture, *Intolerance* is quite the most marvelous thing which has been put on the screen, but as a theory of life it is trite without being true.[22]

In the same vein, Alexander Woollcott in *The New York Times* regarded *Intolerance* as "Unprecedented and indescribable splendor of pageantry ... combined with grotesque incoherence of design and utter fatuity of thought." He contended that its philosophy of history was flawed by taking "any historical fact" as an example of intolerance and placing it "in an extraordinary jumble under one magic name." The *Birth of a Nation* controversy, which was still plaguing Griffith, may also have influenced Woollcott's criticism, since he argued that "Mr. Griffith was scarcely entitled to berate *intolerance*, even in this confused manner, after the offensively bigoted Simon Legreeism of his own *Birth of a Nation*."[23]

Commentaries on *Intolerance* by poet Vachel Lindsay, author of *The Art of the Moving Picture*, Walter Anthony and Frederick James Smith demonstrated greater sensitivity for the aesthetics of the film than those by Broun and Woollcott, who were primarily stage critics. Smith refuted the critics who characterized *Intolerance* as incoherent or confused, arguing in *The Dramatic Mirror* that "it builds its structure securely ... in a new fashion."[24] Critic Ashton Stevens of *The Chicago Examiner* also countered reviewers who failed to recognize the art of the film and judged it incomprehensible:

It is terrifyingly difficult only to the man who attempts to describe it in a column of words.

It confuses nobody but the critics, who are accustomed to the muzzle-loaded, single-barrel type of drama and photo-drama....

Instead of imitating my theatre, my drama, he (Griffith) invented one of his own.[25]

A review in the Socialist newspaper, *The Masses*, by Floyd Dell, the distinguished writer and critic, and the editorial comment appearing in the strongly Progressive *San Francisco Bulletin*, repudiated the denigration of the film's theme by Soule, Broun and Woollcott. Dell wrote:

No one who didn't have a genuine and deep emotion of anger at the way we misuse the gift of life, could have produced the film-play at the Liberty Theatre.... It seems to me the expression ... of a mind which loves life and beauty and joy, and is moved to rage and pity by the deliberate malice with which, in all ages, life and beauty and love is destroyed....

There is much of loveliness in the play, both of spectacle and of human nature.... But the thing which makes *Intolerance* more than a gorgeous and exciting spectacle is the portrayal of the most violent and extreme and terrible emotions. It requires one who loves beauty and tenderness to exhibit the horror of death and the fear of death, without offense: Mr. Griffith does it with the splendor of a great sincerity.[26]

In praising the film and Griffith's contribution to the cause of peace and tolerance, *The San Francisco Bulletin* observed the relevance and immediacy of its message:

What is intolerance? Griffith shows us that as it was in Babylon, so it is today—that outward forms of life have changed, but the spirit remains the same. Babylon, with its pride, was overthrown by a mightier hatred; Christ, who looms alone as the one Man of Perfect Tolerance, was crucified by those who could not "live and let live"; His followers, finding different answers to the question of worship, turn to slaughter; the worn man of the prisons, the weary girl of the streets, repeat the tale today. We do not slay Dissenters; but we hang prisoners. We do not crucify Christ; but we imprison Karl Liebknecht and jeer at Henry Ford. While as to conquering Babylon—Babylon is striving to conquer Babylon today in Europe, and both are falling....

Griffith's film comes powerfully to strengthen the hands of the believers in love. Overwhelmingly he preaches the lesson that no action inspired by hate can be other than wrong....

If only one-half of one percent of [its audiences] remember the film and its message after they have returned to their daily tasks, its effects upon America's civilization will be endless. There is no grander work that can be done than the liberation of the all-powerful forces of love. Once liberated, they will never cease.[27]

Effect of World War I

Pointing to the parallel between the conflict in the Babylonian Story and the turmoil that convulsed Europe at the time, *The San Francisco Bulletin*, like Floyd Dell, maintained that the pacifist motif interwoven throughout the fabric of the film was a manifestation of Griffith's sympathy for the peace movement. Griffith asserted in later years that, caught up in the debate between the militant and pacific factions of Progressivism, the film suffered at the box office because of its anti-war views, a claim echoed by Miss Gish and Brown in their books on Griffith. On the other hand, the pacifist elements that ultimately contributed to its commercial failure may have been responsible for its initial success at a time when the sentiment for peace was still very strong throughout the country and the screen had become a forum for debate over the war.

From the outbreak of World War I in the summer of 1914 until the end of 1916, a majority of American Progressives favored neutrality and were sympathetic with the peace movement, an attitude that was particularly prevalent in Griffith's native South, where people still remembered the horrors of the Civil War and Reconstruction. Nevertheless, a growing minority of Americans, led by Roosevelt, supported military preparedness and advocated outright military intervention in the European war. They were not strong enough, however, in 1914–16 to counter the combined forces of the majority of Progressives and Socialists, the traditionally isolationist Westerners and Southerners, the anti–British Irish-Americans and German-Americans who opposed involvement in the war. The anti-war forces, headed by Bryan and La Follette, were cautiously supported by President Wilson and endorsed by the influential capitalists Hearst and Ford. This made the militarists' fight for majority opinion an uphill struggle until Germany's resumption of unrestricted submarine warfare in February, 1917, brought about a turnaround in public sentiment culminating in the declaration of war by the United States in April, 1917.[28]

The American screen, emerging from its nickelodeon swaddling-clothes, became a battleground between the militarists and the pacifists as the debate over the war raged in 1915–16. While the richness of *Intolerance* precludes strict classification, it represents a climax in the series of films inspired by the controversy between the pacifists and the interventionists. The universal model for this series was Griffith's own *The Birth of a Nation*. Although the storm over its racial attitudes obscured its pacifist intent, ironically generating vehement criticism from noted pacifists Jane Addams and Oswald Garrison Villard, the graphic portrayal of the horrors of war and military occupation, in the words of Rev. Dr. Charles H. Parkhurst, "conveys an indelible lesson to all who have been bewitched by those who have decked out the naked hideousness of war with tinsel drapery."[29]

The example of *The Birth of a Nation*, with its spectacular battle scenes and controversial viewpoint, stimulated other filmmakers, hoping to equal its success, to tackle the provocative issues surrounding the conflict that was tearing Europe apart. The first round in the debate, fired by the pro-war forces, was *The Battle Cry of Peace*, a production by J. Stuart Blackton of the Vitagraph Company. The film advocated U.S. military preparedness and forecast an invasion of America by an unnamed European power, an obvious reference to Germany. A huge box-office success, it was first shown in September of 1915. The film was supported by Roosevelt and aided the immediate cause of the militarists at a time when they sought President Wilson's authorization for preparedness measures. In retrospect, the underlying motive for Blackton's production was its more comprehensive goal of encouraging the United States to abandon its policy of neutrality.[30]

Another attempt to emulate *The Birth of a Nation* was Thomas Ince's production, *Civilization*, which premiered in April of 1916. A response to the militarists, the film was an elaborate pacifist allegory with a European setting. Wilson was so impressed with its theme about a man imbued with the spirit of Christ who tries to stop war that he gave the film his endorsement. Racking up huge grosses at the box office, *Civilization* is credited with having helped reelect Wilson, who campaigned under the slogan, "He kept us out of war."[31]

While they did not rival *The Birth of a Nation* in size or box-office receipts, other films reflecting the ongoing debate on war and preparedness received their share of popularity and public attention. *War Brides*, directed by Herbert Brenon in 1916, was highly respected for its pacifist view, depicting the devastation of modern war in Europe. In contrast, *The Fall of a Nation* (1916), which showed an invasion of the United States by a German army and ridiculed peace advocates like Bryan and Ford, was produced by the staunchly pro-war Southern author Thomas Dixon, despite the disapproval of his friend President Wilson.[32] Contrary to Griffith's personal commitment to the peace movement, his studios released *The Flying Torpedo* in 1916, a film combining a preparedness statement with a "yellow peril" theme in which American cities are bombarded by the guided missiles of an unnamed Asian power. *Patria*, another film built around a "yellow peril" motif, was produced by Hearst. An elaborate serial appearing in late 1916 and early 1917, it was made to distract attention from the European conflict as it depicted an invasion of the United States by the combined forces of Mexico and Japan.[33]

Appearing in the midst of the whirlwind of point and counterpoint surrounding the war issue, *Intolerance* paradoxically resembles the militant films of the era even though its pacifist message links it philosophically with *Civilization* and *War Brides*. Like *The Battle Cry of Peace, The Fall of a Nation, The Flying Torpedo* and *Patria*, which attempted to arouse Americans to the menace of alien powers bent on conquering the United

States, *Intolerance* shows the devastation of a prosperous, progressive civilization by a foreign invader aided by internal enemies. Indeed, when the film was shown in England in 1917, Babylon's fight against Persia "was seen by English audiences as supporting their fight against Prussian intolerance."[34] Undoubtedly, the immense proportions of the clash in the film between two great empires as an endless procession of Persian soldiers attempting to scale the mammoth walls and storm the gates are met with the determined resistance of the Babylonians, armed with flame-throwers, represents an ancient parallel to the titanic struggle sweeping across Europe.

Griffith was unsparing in detailing the carnage of warfare. His shots of hand-to-hand combat, in which soldiers are decapitated or impaled with lances, are so vivid that, at a revival screening twenty years later, dowagers "especially wilted under the bloody moments." According to Paul O'Dell, Griffith uses "the horrors of war, not for their sensationalism, but to turn us violently against what he depicts."[35] Griffith, confirming O'Dell's assessment, asserted at the time: "If moving pictures properly done of the horrors of war had been innoculated in all the nations of Europe, there would be no bodies of men lying on European battlefields."[36]

The destruction of a civilization by war in the Babylonian Story mirrored the disintegration of Europe as it descended into the madness of World War I, causing apprehension and dismay among men of Progressive faith, who wondered if modern civilization could survive the conflagration. John Haynes Holmes, a social gospel theologian, said of the European conflict, "three hundred years of progress is cast into the melting pot," and questioned whether "social progress" would be replaced by mere "social survival."[37] David Starr Jordan, distinguished president of Stanford University and a leading pacifist Progressive, wrote at the outbreak of war in 1914, "thorns and thistles grow in the harassed mind as in the devastated field."[38] As the war continued, he wondered whether Europe could "build up a solid foundation of peace amid the havoc of greed and hate."[39] Fighting until the eleventh hour to keep America out of the war, he expressed his appreciation for the pacifist theme of the new release, *Intolerance*, in a letter to Griffith:

> A really amazing piece of work ... The general lesson of the play, that of the evils of intolerance and of carelessness as to the feelings and rights of others, is an excellent one, a piece of work inherently great and sure to be successful with the public.[40]

Jordan's prediction of the film's success proved accurate only in the first months after its release. As the war-clouds gathered, there were some indications of slipping popularity as early as January, 1917, with attendance plummeting toward the end of its run at the Liberty Theatre. The major decline coincided with the U.S. entry into the war in the spring, when *Intolerance* failed in several communities. By the summer of 1917, there were few, if any, major theatrical showings. The film that embodied pacifist Progressivism became a commercial disaster, its indictment of war out of tune with the times.

During the war, Griffith went to England and France to shoot documentary footage in 1917 for films he made supporting the Allied cause. Of these, the most famous was *Hearts of the World*, a 1918 release about a French village overrun by German soldiers. Although originally intended as propaganda for the war effort, Griffith's first-hand observation of the front, confirming his feelings about war, prompted him to modify his anti–German, pro-war motif to include pacifist messages. Sequences like the shelling of a village described in an accompanying title, "War's gift to the common people," were strong indictments of war in spite of more propagandistic scenes of atrocities committed by German officers.[41]

Griffith regretted his public support of the war and in 1919 told Max Eastman, then a leading radical anti-war dissenter and editor of *The Liberator*, successor to *The Masses*:

> You are a braver man than I am. I would say the same things you do if I had the courage. I served in the war and made a famous war film, but I don't really believe in wars. I think they're always wrong on both sides.[42]

Factionalization and Disintegration of Progressivism

The schism in the Progressive movement in 1915 and 1916, brought on by the dispute between the militant minority headed by Roosevelt and the neutralist majority which looked to Wilson for leadership, represented a weakening of the Progressive consensus that had dominated American politics in the prewar years. As war fever and intolerance spread throughout the land, engendered by the U.S. entry into the war, Progressivism was perverted, leading to the increased factionalization and disintegration of the movement.

The mood of the country in the war and postwar years was antithetical to the didacticism on the evils of social inequities and repression illustrated by Griffith in *Intolerance*. Leading Progressive statesmen degenerated into advocates of intolerance, often in the sincere conviction that repressive measures were necessary to defend their ideals. Roosevelt's wartime rhetoric became increasingly bellicose toward the enemy and demagogic toward dissenters. Bryan devoted more time to his crusade for Prohibition and his championship of fundamentalist religious values. Wilson, the liberals' main source of inspiration, allowed the imprisonment of antiwar dissidents, including Socialist leader Eugene Debs.

In this atmosphere, films like *My Four Years in Germany*, distributed by Warner Brothers, and Metro's production *To Hell with the Kaiser*, enjoying transient box-office success in 1918, mirrored the bigotry and hatred that permeated the American consciousness at the time. Because of its opposition to the war, *The Masses* was suppressed by the government, leading to its demise. Robert Goldstein, a former associate of Griffith, was imprisoned for making *The Spirit of '76* (1917), a film which focused on the villainy of the British in the American Revolution. It was increasingly clear that Griffith's cogent portrayal of the dire consequences of bigotry, exemplified in the French Story when Catherine de Medici orders the massacre of the "subversive" Huguenots, did not fit into the climate of a society conducting witch-hunts against all forms of dissent.[43]

Even more than his dramatization of historic evils, Griffith's treatment of two of the most controversial Progressive issues, capital punishment and Prohibition, ran counter to the tide of public opinion during the war and postwar years. Under the impetus of the war, reformers' attempts to abolish the death penalty suffered a severe setback, while the movement to institute national Prohibition triumphed with the passage of the Eighteenth Amendment in 1919.

By 1917, which "promised to be the wonder year of abolition," the movement to abolish capital punishment had gained strength throughout the country. To many Progressives seeking to build a more humane society based on individual freedom, executions were regarded as outmoded barbarism. Defense lawyer Clarence Darrow and the reform mayor of Toledo, Brand Whitlock, who wrote a novel attacking the death penalty, were among the most outspoken leaders of the abolitionist cause.[44] Many governors of the era, including Hiram Johnson of California, sought to put an end to the reign of the gallows and the electric chair in their states. Also many of the newspapers, including *The San Francisco Bulletin* and the Hearst press, campaigned against capital punishment. Motion pictures joined in the crusade as well. In addition to *Intolerance*, the decade produced several abolitionist films, such as *Capital Punishment*, released by the General Film Company in 1915, *The People Vs. John Doe*, produced by Universal in 1916, and *Who Shall Take My Life?*, made by Selig in 1917.[45]

As the movement gained momentum in the 1910s, several states, including Minnesota, Washington, Oregon, North Dakota, South Dakota, Tennessee and Arizona, abolished the death penalty. The Missouri legislature voted to outlaw the death penalty in April, 1917, several weeks after *Intolerance* began its lengthy run in St. Louis with the premiere attended by the governor and other dignitaries. However, in the wake of the vigilante atmosphere induced by the war, the abolitionist cause floundered, then retrogressed as several states, including Missouri, voted to reinstate capital punishment.[46]

Griffith's personal attitude toward capital punishment was compatible with the abolitionist sentiment. He maintained that "If all the people of today were really educated and knew the history of the world since the beginning of time, there would be no wars, there would be no capital punishment."[47] In order to impress the public with the horrors of executions, he shows harrowing scenes of the Boy's trial, the haunted faces of the condemned men on Death Row and the Boy's narrow escape from hanging for a crime he did not commit. To heighten the suspense, Griffith uses close-ups of the executioners' trembling hands holding the knives poised to cut the cords that release the gallows-trap. The director, attempting to put his players in the proper mood and striving for greater authenticity, even took his cast to visit the gallows prior to shooting these sequences.[48] In the trial scene, Griffith points to society for the blame it must shoulder in sending an innocent man to his death because he is too poor to afford an experienced lawyer.

At the time of the film's release, the Stielow case was headline news throughout the country. By sheer coincidence, in an instance of life imitating art, the case resembled the situation in the Modern Story, as Griffith noted:

> Stielow was convicted of a murder and sentenced to die; four times he was prepared for the chair, four times he and his family suffered every agony save the final swish of the current. What saved him was exactly what saved The Boy in my picture; the murderer confessed; the final reprieve arrived just as the man was ready to be placed in the chair, his trousers' leg slit for the electrode.
>
> Three times the reprieve came at the very last minute. If I had shown scenes like that on the screen it would have made the public laugh as impossible....[49]

The glaring injustices of the legal system exemplified by the Stielow case and the progress of the reform movement made the times amenable to Griffith's criticism of capital punishment. But as the war became a watershed in redirecting America towards a more tightly controlled society in 1917–20, Griffith "offended prevailing views on law and order by calling a prison a 'sometimes House of Intolerance' and questioning the legal system that condemns an innocent youth to death," an attack that contributed to the plunging box-office receipts of *Intolerance*.[50]

In contrast to the movement to abolish capital punishment, Prohibition, a Progressive reform cause congruent with the conformist, censorial climate of wartime society, experienced its most decisive victory at this time. Although it was foredoomed to fail, many Progressives saw Prohibition as a means of eradicating the evils of alcoholism and the corrupting influence of liquor interests on politics. It had long been one of the most divisive issues in Progressivism, supported by the rural South and Middle West and strongly opposed by the urban, industrialized Northeast. Among the ardent Prohibitionists were Midwestern Progressives William Jennings

Bryan and William Allen White, and among the staunch opponents, Clarence Darrow and Samuel Gompers, representing the consensus of labor and immigrant opinion. Adding their support to the temperance crusade were evangelical Christians and many big businessmen. The lure of the saloons was viewed by evangelicals as undermining morality and by capitalists as interfering with the job performance of their workers. By showing Christ in the Judean Story, in the words of a subtitle, "consorting with wine-bibbers" and turning water into wine at the wedding-feast of Cana with the title explaining that "wine was considered a fit offering in the Jewish religion," Griffith refutes the evangelical position that any consumption of liquor negates Christian values. He also condemns capitalists who attempt to exert feudalistic control over their workers by regulating their off-duty activities when he shows the Jenkins Foundation closing down saloons, dancehalls and brothels.

As a Southerner and a film producer, Griffith was a maverick in his attitude towards Prohibition. The influence of evangelical Christianity, combined with the racist intent to use Prohibition to control the Negro, made the South a bastion of the movement with state after state adopting Prohibition laws. Motion picture producers tended to favor Prohibition, believing that eliminating the saloon would remove competition to the film theater.[51] While Griffith recognized that motion pictures could "keep men away from saloons and drink" and directed a number of films for Biograph exposing the evils of drink, his belief in individual freedom, reinforced by his experiences as a traveling actor and laborer, made him a firm adversary of Prohibition.[52] He once said that "should Christ reappear in Prohibition America, he would be jailed as a bootlegger."[53] In 1922, with Prohibition established as the law of the land, Griffith declared:

> Prohibition has only intensified the quantity and horror of drunkenness in America. And so we see today more than ever before in matters national and domestic the eternal curse of intolerance; and we labor — we must labor — towards its conquest by the forces of love and understanding.[54]

In a revealing look in *Intolerance* at the futility of the temperance crusade, Griffith presages the inevitable corruption that follows Prohibition, with "each man his own distiller" and the gangster element controlling the liquor traffic. He had expressed his opposition to Prohibition as early as 1913 in the Biograph film, *The Reformers: or, the Lost Art of Minding One's Business*, when he showed self-righteous moral reformers shutting down the saloons. *The Struggle*, his final film, contains a sharp critique of the Prohibition Era.

In his review of *Intolerance* in *The Los Angeles Times*, Harry Carr commented: "Whether it was done with deliberate intent on Griffith's part or not, it is about the most brilliant and vivid propaganda the anti–Pro-

INTOLERANCE

—THE BLUE PERIL—

HERE IN CALIFORNIA we are quite familiar with the "yellow peril." We have heard it discussed from many angles and have listened to those who believe we are face to face with danger, as well as to those who believe there is no yellow peril.

There is an element of uncertainty about the "yellow peril," but there can be none about the BLUE PERIL with which this State is confronted. The BLUE PERIL owes its existence to the spirit of the INTOLERANT blue laws of the Puritans. Its promoters are the members of the Anti-Saloon League—Puritans of the extreme school two and a half centuries out of date.

The founders of the Puritan Commonwealth acted upon the theory that man was made for law, not that law was made for man. They undertook to make human nature conform to impossible standards. They forged shackles upon the liberty of the individual, suppressing many natural and healthy instincts of the race, imposing a narrow and burdensome theocracy instead of fostering those religious and political liberties which are component essentials of every true democracy.

The Puritans failed, just as the prohibitionists will fail, in inflicting laws which are not rooted in the hearts and wills of the people. We are living today in an era of foolish laws. One of the greatest evils confronting us is the spread of the monstrous theory that law can take the place of the moral education of the individual.

Entire religious denominations have apparently given themselves ever to political propaganda. The whole scheme of prohibition is un-Christian, and yet it draws its sustenance from certain of the evangelical Christian churches. Thousands of such churches in this country are political recruiting stations and supply depots for the Anti-Saloon League, in spite of the fact that all history proves that never yet has the cause of Religion or the cause of the State been benefited where the one has tried to usurp the province of the other.

To say that the Prohibition movement is moral and social instead of political in its essence is to beg the question. Whatever it may be in theory, it has become a political issue in practice, due to the activities of the Anti-Sanity League. Its leaders boast that they have invaded every political precinct in the country. They have thrust the Church into politics. The political campaign has taken the place of moral suasion. Practical Christianity, with certain denominations, expresses itself in votes for regulatory laws. Nothing is left to free will. You must be made "good" by law, and behind the law stands an army of professional and amateur reformers.

In what essential are these methods different from those employed by the misguided religionists who framed the Blue Laws? The BLUE PERIL is threatening us. Puritanism has found its recrudescence in the present prohibition movement. INTOLERANCE, bigotry, fanaticism are rampant today as of old. There is no danger that witches will be put to death as a result, but there is danger that our standard of citizenship will be lowered. As one writer truly says:

"Laws that come from the spirit of the BLUE PERIL do not make men better. They make men weaker. They do not make men patriots; they make them hypocrites. Men under such law cease to exercise freedom of the will; lose their sense of responsibility; become no longer independent, responsible, self-controlling men—and without such men what have we."

What have we?—nothing certainly that would make for higher citizenship. No state-wide prohibition in California, in view of present public sentiment, could result in anything but widespread violation of the law and contempt for all law.

Men would merely do clandestinely what they now do openly; and it may be laid down as a social and political axiom that anything which tends to turn men into sneaks is bad for the individual and bad for the State. No "reform" of the liquor traffic or any other traffic can be made effective against the will of the majority; and because a large majority of the people of California today use alcoholic beverages of one sort or another, all prohibitory and other intolerant laws are doomed to utter failure.

The election in November will decide a question much bigger and more important than that of prohibition. It will decide whether or not California is to continue her present progress—moral progress as well as material—or will join the ranks of the unprogressive freak States.

Vote NO Against
Amendments 1 and 2

United California Industries
310 Humboldt Bank Bldg.
San Francisco

hibitionists could have wished for."[55] Simultaneous with the film's release in California in October, voters were considering two Prohibition amendments appearing on the California ballot in 1916. The United California Industries, representing the vineyard interests of the state, endeavored to defeat the amendments through a large-scale advertising campaign in California newspapers. They apparently entered into a mutual agreement with the Griffith company to capitalize on the October screenings of *Intolerance* as they headlined their advertisements in the newspapers of various cities in California where the film was playing, "Intolerance — The Menace," "Intolerance — The Blue Peril," "Intolerance — Tyranny of Laws," "Intolerance — Thou Shalt Not." As part of the joint publicity for the film and their cause, the vineyard interests reproduced *The San Francisco Bulletin* editorial on *Intolerance*, adding:

> See D.W. Griffith's *Intolerance* and learn through the story of the ages how Intolerance and Prohibition have disrupted states, brought suffering to innocent people and invaded the privacy of homes. Learn from this picture how you should vote on Amendments 1 and 2 at the November election.[56]

The joint advertising campaign and the record-breaking attendance at *Intolerance* may have contributed to the defeat of the Prohibition amendments in November.

Statewide efforts to halt Prohibition were futile, however, when the war served as a catalyst for the passage of a Constitutional amendment instituting national Prohibition. Once again, the spirit engendered by the war ran counter to Griffith's interpretation of an important social issue and was reflected in declining box-office attendance. In analyzing the director's miscalculation of "the predilections of his audience," Robert Sklar contends that Griffith thought his audience shared in his condemnation of what "he believed were a small but noisy minority of censors and moral uplifters" and failed to understand that they "backed the reforms that he ridiculed, like Prohibition and the suppression of prostitution."[57] A moralist Progressive like Bryan could accept Griffith's arraignment of war and modern social injustice but would have found his tolerance of saloons and brothels and the scenes of near-nudity in the Babylonian Story objectionable. Although many Progressives did not favor Prohibition, few of them condoned prostitution. In general, Progressive leaders were resolute upholders of public morality; Roosevelt and Wilson were as supportive of

Opposite: One of a series of advertisements appearing in the "San Jose Mercury-Herald," October 1916, as part of a campaign to defeat Prohibition in California. Sponsored by the United California Industries, representing the vineyard interests, these ads were designed to capitalize on the showings of "Intolerance." Other ads were headed, "Intolerance — Thou Shalt Not," "Intolerance — Tyranny of Laws," and "Intolerance — the Menace."

Victorian proprieties as Bryan. Griffith's indictment of modern American society clearly reveals his sympathy for genuine reform, but he opposed the self-righteous views of many Progressives who confused regulation of economic and social inequities with regulation of personal behavior.

The Conservative Backlash

Another reason for the ultimate commercial failure of *Intolerance* was the long-suppressed and smoldering conservative backlash, a contributory factor in the disintegration of the Progressive movement. In spite of Roosevelt, conservatism continued to dominate the Republican Party. The power brokers of the conservative Republican majority and the minority of Democrats following in the tradition of President Grover Cleveland constituted a force oriented towards business and hostile to the attempts to regulate the practices of large corporations. This conservative coalition served to hold the onrushing tide of Progressivism in check. Wall Street also tended to oppose reforms, often reacting with panic when Bryan, Roosevelt, Wilson, La Follette and other Progressive statesmen proposed legislation curbing corporate power.

To these elements, Griffith's titanic film with its powerful denunciation of capitalist brutality toward labor seemed almost subversive. In his final interview in 1947, Griffith, commenting on the HUAC investigations, recalled: "I was called a Communist myself when *Intolerance* was branded radical and dangerous."[58] In spite of Heywood Broun's criticism that the film advocates the "lost cause" of "laissez-faire," measured by Griffith's treatment of private interests, his film affords cold comfort to strict believers in "laissez-faire" capitalism. His depiction of Jenkins calling on the state militia to suppress the strike, using his influence to legislate public morality and establishing a "charitable" foundation to oversee public welfare, symbolizes unregulated capitalism controlling and usurping the state. The "laissez-faire" attitude expressed by Griffith applies, not to an economic system, but to the assertions of the individual over societal controls.

Conservative reviewers articulating big business's uneasiness with the film were quick to take potshots at *Intolerance*. The reactionary *New York Sun*, a fervent supporter of corporate interests whose vitriolic attacks on Progressivism had stirred the ire of Roosevelt and other leaders, said that watching the film was "a real task and the person who tries to find meaning must feel something like dramatic indigestion after seeing the picture." A conservative critic in the *Philadelphia North American* complained the film shows that "the poor are oppressed, and forced into an environment which ruins their lives, and this merely for the purposes of producing additional funds for the wealthy, which the latter uses to advertise themselves as reformers of the poor, who in actuality they repress," and ended by advising that "the interest of the community will be served by our friends staying away from the theaters where *Intolerance* is shown."[59]

Under the pressures of the war and postwar unrest, which hastened the factionalization and disintegration of the reform movement, the conservative backlash of corporate interests, combining with the most repressive aspects of Progressivism in 1917–20, produced a new consensus that supported a viewpoint diametrically opposed to the social-historical vision of *Intolerance*. This new conservative consensus, scarred by racial and religious prejudice and dominating the American scene until the Great Depression, rejected pacifism, supported harsh penal laws including capital punishment and favored moral reforms such as national Prohibition. The activism of small, radical anti-war labor groups, the postwar strikes of organized labor and the fear of revolution emanating from Bolshevik Russia which led to the great Red scare of 1919–20 created a schism between the middle class and labor. With their distrust of the labor movement and rising prosperity, the middle class identified their interests with the corporate structure. Weary of the constant cries for reform, the middle class comprising the film industry's major market for the new feature films followed the advice of the critic of the *Philadelphia North American* and turned their backs on Griffith's "chef d'oeuvre," *Intolerance*.

Further militating against Griffith's type of social criticism were the landslide victories of Warren G. Harding in 1920 and Calvin Coolidge in 1924, indicative of the impressive gains of conservatism in the United States during the early 1920s. The death of Roosevelt and the collapse of Wilson in 1919 had deprived Progressivism of its most outstanding leaders. The nation as a whole, in the words of William Allen White, "was tired of issues, sick at heart of ideals and weary of being noble."[60] The writings of F. Scott Fitzgerald described a "lost generation" of youth, alienated from politics, whether conservative or liberal, and "dedicated more than the last (generation) to the fear of poverty and the worship of success; grown to find all Gods dead, all wars fought, all faiths in man shaken."[61] The liberal intelligentsia, who had grown disillusioned with the dogmatic positions taken by their former heroes, Bryan, Roosevelt and Wilson, during the atmosphere of the war years, accepted H.L. Mencken's scathing criticism of those heroes as fraudulent deceivers of the people. Their faith in liberalism further shaken by the outcome of the Versailles peace settlement, some of the Progressive intellectuals began to look to the Bolshevik Revolution for inspiration. With the return of prosperity, both major political parties in the United States embraced conservatism in 1924, and La Follette, the last defender of the old-time Progressivism, went down to defeat in his third-party campaign for the presidency. Despite his forthright championship of civil liberties and social reform, even La Follette contributed to the conservative mood through his unyielding isolationist opposition to U.S. membership in the League of Nations.[62]

The unraveling of the Progressive consensus and its effect on *Intolerance* foreshadowed the far-reaching impact of the film on Griffith's career. While he continued to produce major artistic triumphs after *Intolerance*, "Anything following [it] ... still the biggest picture ever made, was liable to be anti-climactic."[63] Nevertheless, the primary reason that most of his later films dealing with social, political and historical themes failed to attain the commercial success of *The Birth of a Nation* was Griffith's continuing allegiance to Progressivism, the very quixotism that, in the context of the times, had blunted the popularity of *Intolerance*. As long as he concentrated his creative energies on topical war themes or intimate, lyrical dramas, he was triumphant at the box office. *Hearts of the World* reestablished him as the public's favorite director. *Broken Blossoms* (1919), a poetic story about a Chinese shopkeeper in love with an English waif, and *Way Down East*, a 1920 production about a girl victimized by rural, narrow-minded puritanism, were the greatest critical and popular successes of all his postwar films. Although these films are strong attacks on the racism and self-righteous morality that were part of the emerging conservative consensus, the delicate beauty in Griffith's treatment of the theme of love, their lower production costs, the personal popularity of their stars, Richard Barthelmess and Lillian Gish, and the propitious timing of their release before the conservative coalition was solidified, ensured their commercial success.

Confronted with the challenge of the Bolshevik Revolution abroad and the march of conservatism at home, Griffith reaffirmed the ideals of Progressive democracy as he returned to broader social, political and historical themes in *Orphans of the Storm* (1922), *America* (1924), and *Isn't Life Wonderful?* (1924). *Orphans of the Storm*, an epic of the French Revolution, pictures the injustices of the Bourbon "ancien regime" toward the poor, an apparent analogy to the "Bourbon reactionary" types, as Roosevelt called them, of American capitalism. At the same time, the film condemns the extremism of Robespierre in the Reign of Terror, which Griffith identified with the Bolsheviks. In Griffith's conception, the true hero is the revolutionary leader, Danton, the defender of liberal democracy and "the Abraham Lincoln of France." *America*, a spectacle of the revolutionary sacrifices that created the nation, is Griffith's tribute, in authentic Progressive tradition, to the roots of the American political heritage. Significantly, Bryan was the only major politician to give this film a strong endorsement. *Isn't Life Wonderful?*, a sympathetic look at poverty and inflation in postwar Germany, confirmed Griffith's commitment to Wilsonian internationalism and the League of Nations. Countering the mood of an America wedded to isolationism and Coolidge prosperity, this grimly realistic portrayal of social unrest in a defeated nation brought an end to Griffith's career as an independent producer. While critically acclaimed, these three films were successively less popular with the public as the pattern set by *Intolerance* during the war years repeated itself. *Orphans of the Storm* broke even at the box office, while *America* and *Isn't Life Wonderful?* lost a great deal of money.[64]

Not only did Griffith's continued support of Progressivism result in diminishing box-office receipts, it also ran counter to the conservative Republican values of the majority of the powerful motion picture executives of the 1920s. Louis B. Mayer, for example, in his newsreels supported Herbert Hoover in his 1928 campaign against liberal Democrat Al Smith. To producers like Mayer, Griffith may have seemed politically unreliable with his announced but unfulfilled plan to make a mammoth sequel to *Intolerance* which he asserted would continue the earlier film's indictment of "capitalism, militarism, and all forms of tyranny through the ages."[65]

After the failure of his Mamaroneck studio, Griffith worked for other producers, directing less ambitious entertainment films before returning to Progressive themes in his last two films and only talkies, *Abraham Lincoln* (1930) and *The Struggle* (1931). In the cynical atmosphere of the pre–New Deal early 1930s, these themes were even more out of vogue than in the 1920s. Of all his films, only *The Birth of a Nation* continued to be exhibited in theaters for decades, long after his other works had been withdrawn from commercial distribution. Often patronized by a revived Ku Klux Klan antithetical to Griffith's philosophy, the Civil War–Reconstruction epic was his sole major film to prove acceptable to the conservative consensus.

Foreign Reception

In contrast to the sudden shift in popularity in the United States, *Intolerance* enjoyed a sustained success in foreign countries, continuing to draw large, enthusiastic crowds throughout the 1920s and evoking praise among luminaries from British royalty to Soviet revolutionary leaders. Its foreign reception coincided with the swelling tide of various political and social movements, from parliamentary liberalism to revolutionary radicalism, sweeping across the globe during the first quarter of the twentieth century. Unlike that of the United States, the political mood of most other countries in the throes of change was not sidetracked by a conservative swing during the time the film was being shown abroad.

Intolerance was first presented outside the United States in Montreal, Canada during the Christmas holidays of 1916. Immediately popular, it had lengthy runs in a war-weary Canada. After its initial success in Montreal, *The New York Dramatic Mirror* records capacity houses for its showings in Toronto and London, Ontario in February, 1917. In April, it played to packed houses in Ottawa and St. Catherine's, Ontario, and Regina, Saskatchewan, where it ran for four weeks; in May and June, audiences in Vancouver and Calgary filled the theaters. A return engagement in Toronto in September, 1917, brought large crowds for several weeks. A revival in London, Ontario, in February, 1918, was equally well received.[66]

The European premiere of *Intolerance* in London in April, 1917, was a personal triumph for Griffith and one to which he referred in his later years as his proudest moment.[67] Indeed, Griffith's presentation of *Intolerance* at a command performance for the royal family "helped gain the attention of English society and political figures including the Prime Minister, David Lloyd George."[68] The leading figure in British liberalism for two decades, Lloyd George instituted major social reforms, earning him recognition as the father of the British welfare state. He was impressed with the Progressive theme of *Intolerance* and lavish in his praise, telling Griffith that "he had the greatest power in his hands for the control of men's minds that the world has ever seen"[69] and "it was only a question of time when governments would recognize this and subsidize pictures that would help them nationally and internationally."[70]

H.G. Wells, distinguished novelist, socialist and a leading influence on international progressive thought of the time, regarded Griffith's work so highly that some years later he discussed with him the possibility of collaborating on a film about the League of Nations, a project that was never realized.[71] Other noted Britons who expressed their admiration for the film included Sir James Barrie, Winston Churchill and Lord Beaverbrook.[72] Lady Cynthia Asquith, a favorite in cultured circles and the daughter-in-law of Liberal prime minister Herbert Asquith, recorded in her diary:

> Went ... to the great movie, *Intolerance* which, as the papers say, "leaves the spectator gasping." It is an incredible thing — such a "mélange" — great stories each seen in snippets ... The Babylon pictures were spectacularly marvellous ... I enjoyed it very much ...[73]

Despite the acclaim it received from the British elite, *Intolerance* ran only two months in London, which, when compared to the seven-month London run of *The Birth of a Nation*, made it more of a "succès d'estime" than an overwhelming commercial triumph. In Miss Gish's opinion, "As in the United States, Mr. Griffith's sermon on peace and brotherhood ran counter to the temper of the British people" during World War I.[74] However, Mae Marsh, who played the Dear One, recalls that a later revival of *Intolerance* in London drew "enormous crowds."[75]

The impact of *Intolerance* reached all parts of the globe. It premiered to capacity houses in Australia in February, 1917, and began its lengthy run in Latin America with a presentation in Buenos Aires, Argentina, in May, 1917.[76] A tremendous box-office hit in Japan in 1919, its message coincided with rising public sentiment for democratic reforms. Indeed, it was so popular that Takejiro Otani, a theatrical producer, was inspired to found the Shochiku Film Company, while the work of the early Japanese directors was influenced by Griffith's cinematic techniques.[77]

Successful screenings in the Scandinavian countries beginning in 1918 were reflective of its compatibility with the spirit of the ascendant Social Democratic movement. In 1920, Danish director Carl Dreyer made *Leaves from Satan's Book*, a film modeled after *Intolerance*, in which Satan is portrayed as a constant force throughout history, instigating revolutionary terrorism and other kinds of evil. A reviewer for the Socialist newspaper, *Arbejdet*, called *Leaves from Satan's Book* "one big scream against the hated Reds," and contrasting it with *Intolerance*, wrote: "The American capitalist film company can afford to be open-minded, while the Danish film, as often before, sets a record for spiritual narrow-mindedness and poisonous hatred for the workers."[78]

Intolerance had its greatest impact in Russia, where it ran for ten years and, despite the fact that it was an import, was "the new-born Soviet film industry's first great success — artistically, at the box office, and even politically."[79] Paradoxically, the film made to promote Wilsonian liberalism aided its international ideological rival, Leninist radicalism. There were, in fact, certain basic attitudes that American Progressives and Russian Bolsheviks had in common, explaining the phenomenal success of *Intolerance* in the Soviet Union. The dominant American liberal ideology and the ascendant Russian Marxist ideology both embraced the perfectibility of man; both excoriated the injustices and inequities practiced by capitalists; both abhorred the feudalist and monarchical regimes that still controlled much of the world; and both viewed history as a process of continual movement toward greater social egalitarianism and increased scientific and technical progress. Their greatest difference lay in their means of accomplishing their goals. The Progressives believed that the amelioration of unjust systems could be brought about through reform, while the Bolsheviks maintained that true progress could occur only after violent overthrow by the proletariat of entrenched oppressive systems.

Nevertheless, the disparity over methods does not belie the assumptive similarities between the ideologies. Wilson acknowledged at a Versailles meeting in 1919 that "a certain latent force behind Bolshevism ... attracted sympathy," a manifestation of the widespread opposition to large vested economic and political interests.[80] Lenin initially characterized Wilson's 1918 Fourteen Points Speech as "a tolerant one for a 'class opponent' to write and ... 'a great step ahead' toward worldwide peace."[81] The conversion of several American Progressives from Wilsonism to Leninism in 1919 had a striking counterpart in Russia when Griffith's artistic monument to American Progressivism achieved unsurpassed popular acceptance.

The underground process by which *Intolerance* reached a Russia wracked by civil war is described by Thorold Dickinson:

> By a quirk of history a copy of *Intolerance* reached Berlin in March, 1917 only to be impounded next month as enemy property, when the

> U.S.A. declared war on Germany. After the war the German com-
> munist International Workers' Aid smuggled the film among a
> steady flow of foodstuffs and medical supplies across the blockaded
> frontier into the Soviet Union ...[82]

With some retitling and reediting, including the elimination of the Christian epilogue, *Intolerance* was prepared for Soviet distribution. After
Lenin saw the film, it is said that he "personally arranged to have it shown
throughout Russia."[83] According to a *New York Times* article on Griffith
appearing on April 13, 1924, "hundreds of prints" of *Intolerance* were
made available for its Russian release. "Not only were these shown in the
established picture houses, but auto vans equipped with projecting
paraphernalia were sent out so that the film could make its appeal to the
remoter parts of the country."[84]

The widespread popularity of *Intolerance* with Soviet audiences was
rooted in its relevance to the historic conditions that led to the Russian
Revolution. As Jay Leyda points out, "the alert, embattled Soviet audience
... had never seen such a believable tragedy of American working-class life
[as the Modern Story]—it must have given life to every slogan they had
heard about the sympathies of foreign workers with the revolution in
Russia."[85] Not only did the Russians find the depiction of capitalist oppression in the Modern Story germane to their cause, they also saw
parallels in the other stories to the injustices that had plagued them under
centuries of Tsarism. The Judean Story was in accord with their belief that
the "bandit nations" of the West, professedly Christian, had betrayed
Christ's original doctrines. With the portrayal of the massacre of St. Bartholomew's Day evoking memories of mass killings by the Tsarist government such as the infamous slaughter on "Bloody Sunday" in 1905, the
French Story became to the Russians a trenchant commentary on the institution of autocratic monarchy. The reactionary High Priest of Bel, who
symbolized theocratic despotism in the Babylonian Story, reminded Soviet
audiences of the powerful Eastern Orthodox clergy using their traditional
authority to bolster the Tsarist state. To Americans, the depiction of
repression by monarchical and theocratic regimes seemed remote, but to
the Russians, the stories embodied vital significance, paralleling their recent history under the Romanovs.

Lenin was so impressed with *Intolerance* that he sent several delega-
tions to Griffith, asking him to take charge of the Russian film industry.
Joseph Malkin, one of these emissaries, told Griffith that *Intolerance* "was
a powerful influence ... in cementing the feeling for the new government"
and that "you—unknown to yourself—were one of our biggest agents."[86]
Although other commitments prevented Griffith from accepting the Soviet
offer, his film, convincing Lenin that "of all the arts, for us the cinema is
the most important," became the outstanding inspiration to a generation
of Soviet filmmakers.[87] Sergei M. Eisenstein stated that "all that is best in

the Soviet cinema has its origins in *Intolerance*,"[88] while another great Russian director, V.I. Pudovkin, was so impressed with Griffith's film that, because of it, he abandoned chemistry for the cinema as he recalled in an interview in 1929:

> About that time [1920] I happened to see Griffith's great film, *Intolerance*. In that wonderful work I saw for the first time the possibilities of the epic picture. Yes, Griffith was really my teacher. Later on I saw *Broken Blossoms*, and I fell more and more under the spell of Griffith. My first three pictures, therefore, were really influenced by this great American director.[89]

Through its popularity and influence on Soviet culture and society, *Intolerance* not only recreated, but also shaped history as it helped to determine the course of the cinema as a mass medium capable of directing thought.

The history of the reception of *Intolerance* testifies to the power of its plea for the liberation of the individual from oppressive institutions. In America, the penultimate moment of Progressivism, ensuring the reelection of the liberal champion, Woodrow Wilson, was responsible for the film's initial popularity. However, because of the repressive climate of the war and postwar years, *Intolerance* failed commercially, and Griffith's popularity ultimately suffered as the ascendant conservative ideology supplanted Progressivism.

Other countries caught up in various liberal and radical movements, including Russia, found the message of *Intolerance* highly relevant to their causes. Nevertheless, the film's fate in the United States presaged, not only the fortunes of Griffith's career, but his critical reputation as well. Although well received by the preponderance of critics in 1916, its subsequent reception by the public caused some observers to see its box-office debacle as a vindication of the adverse criticism of Griffith's thematics and narrative structure. Thus, the original critical controversy, inevitably tinged by the turmoil surrounding *The Birth of a Nation*, set the tone for the critical guidelines for *Intolerance* in the following decades. The full significance of the film, therefore, cannot be entirely clear until it is analyzed in relation to Griffith's other works.

7. Criticism and Legacy

In the decades since the films of David Wark Griffith first exploded on the world consciousness in the 1910s, Griffith has been universally recognized by film critics and historians as a central figure in the development of the cinema from its primitive state into an artistic medium. Still, a critic recently wrote that "Griffith's stature as an artist has been the subject of continuous debate among film scholars, and his critical reputation has suffered more fluctuations than that of any other major figure in film history."[1] This inconsistency has never been more apparent than in the critical appraisal of *Intolerance*. While the overwhelming majority of film analysts acknowledge its technical importance, they all too frequently either dismiss or fail to grasp its value as a meaningful work of art conveying a social-historical vision which characterizes his entire "oeuvre." Yet a careful study of *Intolerance* and its relation to his work as a whole, coupled with an understanding of his heritage and his times, reveals a continuity of vision which is rooted in an adherence to Jeffersonian democracy and finds expression in his films in an intertwined allegiance to anti-imperialism, anti-puritanism and the assertion of individuality.

Critical Evaluation

The heritage of critical and retrospective writing about Griffith, which has quadrupled in the past two decades, has produced a bewildering array of contradictions by commentators. He has been described as a racist and an anti-racist, a reactionary supporter of the status quo and an incipient revolutionary, a priggish fundamentalist and an anti-puritanical free-thinker, a sexist and a feminist, a cloudy sentimentalist and a powerful realist. That Griffith excites these extremes of reaction is in itself a tribute to his role as a cinematic pioneer and artist since none of his predecessors, including Méliès, Porter and Hepworth, have aroused this much critical attention and controversy. Nevertheless, the debate surrounding Griffith has tended to obscure not only his vision in *Intolerance*, but also the consistent philosophical beliefs permeating his work.

Many commentators seem to be unwilling to grant *Intolerance* thematic unity, maintaining that the 1916 film is an elaborate attempt to yoke together unrelated stories in an imposed structure. To these critics, *Intolerance* is a hodgepodge devoid of any clear-cut vision. Representative of this critical viewpoint is David A. Cook's commentary on Griffith in the highly acclaimed 1981 book *A History of Narrative Film*. Although the film historian recognizes Griffith as "perhaps the greatest cinematic genius in history" and "unquestionably the seminal genius of the narrative cinema and its first great visionary artist,"[2] he maintains that *Intolerance* has been praised "far beyond its intrinsic worth" due to its influence on the Soviet cinema. Cook rationalizes that Griffith, failing to understand his theme, used "intolerance" as "an omnibus word encapsulating any form of human evil," an opinion that can be traced back to Alexander Woollcott's review in 1916. He further argues that the theme of *Intolerance* "is scarcely germane to either the Babylonian or the Modern sequences."[3]

The flaws in this critique are apparent upon closer scrutiny of the film. Paul O'Dell, in *Griffith and the Rise of Hollywood*, rejects the notion that Griffith simply inserted the word "intolerance" in his subtitles "to replace an element in the film itself." Refuting the claim that "the Modern Story had ... little to do with intolerance," O'Dell maintains that "the central characters' lives are governed by the intolerance of the self-styled reformers," and "to suggest that Griffith recognized a need to bolster up the Modern Story with obvious titles shows a remarkable lack of insight."[4] In analyzing the Babylonian Story, O'Dell contends that Griffith uses the vivid depictions of the battle scenes to set the stage for his "desperate pleas for peace and tolerance" in the concluding sequences.[5] Additionally, by assigning the responsibility for the fall of Babylon to an entrenched theocracy and analogizing the characters of the puritanical Jenkinses with the High Priest of Bel, Griffith not only reinforces his theme but also establishes the historical continuity of intolerance.

Concomitant with the charge of thematic confusion is the claim that Griffith lacked the intellectual capacity to project a historical vision. Leading among these commentators is critic Andrew Sarris, proponent of the "auteur" theory, in which the director is viewed as the author of the film. To Sarris, Griffith, limited by his Southern rural background, was incapable of understanding the forces of history including "social organisms and class structures," relying more "on a theory of character than a theory of history." Sarris contends that Griffith's true genius lay in the lyrical presentation of the small details of domestic life rather than in "cosmic configurations." According to Sarris, "there is more of eternity in one anguished expression of Mae Marsh or Lillian Gish than in all of Griffith's flowery rhetoric on Peace, Brotherhood, and Understanding." Predictably, Sarris dismisses *Intolerance* as consisting of "platitudinous generalities" and fails to see any meaning or philosophical motif in the linking of the four stories.[6]

Like Cook's arguments, Sarris's critique of Griffith's social-historical vision falls apart in the light of the interpretations of other film historians and an objective analysis of *Intolerance* in relation to the director's other films. In contending that Griffith shows the social structure from a simplistic standpoint, emphasizing character over social-historic forces, Sarris ignores the literary milieu that influenced the director's method of presentation and the continuity of vision that characterizes his work. By viewing the tides of history and social change as they affect the individual, Griffith was following in the tradition established by Scott, in which fictional characters are personifications of social and historical forces. Thus, Jenkins represents monopolistic capitalism, the High Priest of Bel embodies religious absolutism and Brown Eyes and Prosper Latour stand for the average Protestants buffeted by the conflicts of the Reformation. Robert M. Henderson counters the view that Griffith lacked the ability to deal effectively with social problems, noting that the director treated them "forcefully" and "managed to show class contrasts sharply through crosscut images." He also asserts that Griffith "was not afraid to take the side of social reform, yet he held the society do-gooder up to scorn."[7]

Sarris, apparently sharing Cook's view that Griffith reduces history to a melodramatic "dime novel" approach in which the "good guys" are pitted against the "bad guys," presents a superficial reading of *Intolerance*. The injustices of the penal system in the Modern Story are not the result of individual malevolence but are rooted in the system. As Griffith himself pointed out, the indictment of legal cruelty is not an attack on individual judges or policemen; the judge, for example, who sentences the Boy to death is not a scheming villain but a personification of legal abstraction. In addition, Griffith does not devise punishments for most of his malefactors including Jenkins, an interpretation which differs from a melodramatic moral vision in which the good are rewarded and the evil are punished.

In limiting Griffith's art to his skill in handling the minutiae of daily life and the presentation of intimate portraits, Sarris distorts the poetics of the director's films. The juxtaposition of the small and the big, the depiction of the individual in relation to the larger events or forces of the time and society, unites the elements in his social-historical epics as well as his intimate films, forming the basis for his film grammar and his art. Sarris's attempt to separate the larger view embodied in Griffith's "flowery rhetoric on Peace, Brotherhood, and Understanding" from the "anguished expressions" of his heroines is an example of the critic's failure to recognize the relationship between the director's didacticism and the experiences of his characters. The "anguished expressions" of the Dear One (Mae Marsh) as she witnesses the strike and her husband's trial are reactions to the social turmoil, underscoring Griffith's belief in the need for justice and harmony. As for the domestic details that Sarris admires, they derive their beauty and poignancy from their contrast with the vast sweep of history and its violent upheavals which inexorably shatter the tranquil lives of Griffith's characters.

Another criticism often leveled at *Intolerance* is that it lacks emotional impact. Critics holding this view claim that the emphasis on spectacle and the attempt to derive a philosophy of history from the intercutting of the four stories detract from the film's emotional qualities. Cook, in articulating this position, asserts that "Emotional appeal was not one of *Intolerance*'s strong points, for Griffith had deliberately subordinated personal involvement with its characters to spectacle and historical process."[8] This criticism, however, is countered by accounts of the film's reception upon its release, when it was recorded that audiences were moved to tears.[9] In his analysis of *Intolerance*, O'Dell praises the film for

> those intimate scenes ... in which he (Griffith) is able to convey an
> emotional intensity worthy of a Goya painting; where it is necessary
> to think twice as to whether or not we metaphorically heard a cry,
> or a scream of terror, or a moan from the soul of humanity.[10]

The tendency of many critics and historians to belittle the vision in *Intolerance* is based not solely on the film's inherent qualities but is part of an overall perception of Griffith's work as pro–Establishment. These commentators, while praising his creative achievements as a technical pioneer, argue that Griffith's inability to adapt to social change brought about his artistic and commercial decline in the postwar era. Describing him as an uncritical advocate of Victorian values, they regard the director as a reactionary both culturally and politically. In *A Short History of the Movies*, Gerald Mast, commenting on *The Birth of a Nation*, characterizes the "general moral system" in Griffith's films as one "in which he viewed all social establishments as good because they are established and all attempts to change the Establishment as bad because they are disruptive, violent, and disorderly."[11] Feminist author Marjorie Rosen in *Popcorn Venus*, her book on the depiction of women in films, finds a conservative bias in Griffith's treatment of women. She argues that the director was a sexist whose heroines were child-women who never grew up and "perverse" projections of his romantic Southern fantasies.[12] That Griffith was a staunch upholder of the white racist views of his time is a common criticism due to the controversy over *The Birth of a Nation* and, more than any other position ascribed to him, has evoked continuing hostile reaction and acerbic comments such as Cook's labeling him "a muddleheaded racial bigot"[13] and Sarris's description of him as a man of "flagrant bigotry."[14]

In contrast to analysts who see the director as a reactionary, the critics contending that Griffith possessed a valid world vision and that he grew as an artist reject the notion that he was a supporter of the Establishment. Marxist critics, for example, laud the social protest contained in his films. Countering the argument that Griffith was anti-revolutionary, Seymour Stern states that "no other American director of the past half-century has put upon the screen so unfavorable, so unsavory, an image of *ruling class*, both as an historic fact and as a species, as Griffith."[15] Georges Sadoul cites the "courageous social criticism" of *Intolerance*[16]; another Marxist film writer, Béla Balász, in his book *Theory of the Film*, describes the 1916 epic as "radically democratic and progressive" and "the most courageous pacifist manifestation of the time" in which, "turning against imperialist chauvinism, he (Griffith) depicted the methods of big business."[17]

The charges that sexism and racism underlie Griffith's vision have also been challenged. Feminist critic Molly Haskell in *From Reverence to Rape*, her book on the history of women in films, points out that Griffith, in his reverence for femininity, "integrates woman into the flow of life.... Griffith's heroines were never passive love objects or martyrs to male authority."[18] J.N. Thomas agrees, noting in *The Berkeley Barb* that Griffith's women "had the virtues of being honestly presented, profoundly felt as characters and most importantly, taken seriously, respected." Thomas also disputes the charge of racism, commenting that Griffith in most of his films "rarely portrays questions of race in terms other than those of tolerance and understanding."[19] Describing a scene of interracial brotherhood in the lost film *The Greatest Thing in Life* (1918), Henderson states:

> The film could be thought of as an unusual one for a Southerner to make if one assumes that Griffith was a doctrinaire Southerner and ignores those films in which he displays a growing liberal and enlightened attitude.[20]

Opposing the claim that Griffith's later films represent a steady artistic decline due to the inherent limitations of his vision is William Cadbury's article in *Film Quarterly*, "Theme, Felt Life and the Last-Minute Rescue in Griffith After *Intolerance*."[21] G. Charles Niemeyer in *Film Heritage* also refutes the critics who "have repeated without knowledge" the myth of Griffith's decline, pointing out that "there is absolutely no evidence whatever to indicate that his artistic skill or judgment deteriorated throughout the 'golden age' of the 1920's."[22]

Although Griffith's defenders present cogent arguments in rebutting the attempts to disparage the content of his films, the intensity and vehemence of adverse criticism has not diminished. Undoubtedly, the continuing strong reaction to *The Birth of a Nation* has played a role in swaying the critical opinion surrounding Griffith's entire work. In the context of an era influenced by the civil rights movement and the revisionist interpretation of Reconstruction, the 1915 epic projects racial attitudes which have been discredited. Contemporary critics, reflecting the changing climate, have often been unrestrained in their condemnation of the film's content. Cook describes it as a work replete with "apocalyptic, gut-churning racism ... second in its manipulative distortion only to" *The Eternal Jew* (1940), the notorious Nazi anti–Semitic propaganda documentary.[23] Sarris, in commenting on what he regards as an "outrageously racist" film, concludes that Griffith's "small-town agrarian vision of the world is intellectually inadequate by any standard."[24]

Paradoxically, commentators like Cook and Sarris who deplore its content consider *The Birth of a Nation* to be Griffith's most significant epic, a view prompting their lengthy analyses of the film. Invariably in their reviews of the Civil War–Reconstruction film, they arrive at generalizations which they apply as yardsticks to measure his entire work. Mast, for example, infers from Griffith's defense of the Old South against the Northern incursion that he was a champion of the established order. Cook, in looking at Griffith's assimilation of Thomas Dixon's melodramatic formulas in the second half of *The Birth of a Nation*, claims that he saw human history in terms of a "dime novel." Sarris views the director as a narrow-minded provincial unable to see the larger picture. Had these analysts evaluated *The Birth of a Nation* within the context of his entire work, recognized *Intolerance* as, in Lillian Gish's words, "his monument, the measure of the man himself," or weighed the influence of his cultural heritage, his personal background and his times in forming his vision, perhaps their assessment of Griffith would have been more sympathetic.[25] Indeed, those commentators who are more favorable toward Griffith show a greater appreciation for his work as a whole.

Griffith's Continuity of Vision

Although there are inevitable contradictions in an "oeuvre" as vast as Griffith's, drawn from diverse literary sources, recurring motifs give a continuity of vision to his work. The great writers of his generation, Frank Norris, Jack London and Theodore Dreiser, reveal in their works tensions between Social Darwinist individualism and their collective concern for the impoverished masses, and a dichotomy between the rival claims of scientific materialism and religious mysticism. In contrast, Griffith, throughout his career, manifested an unwavering philosophic commitment to Jeffersonian democracy. Nurtured by his father's dedication to Jeffersonianism, Griffith expanded and strengthened his understanding of these values through his study of Whitman and nineteenth-century novels glorifying the common man, his commitment to the Bryan and Wilson political movements and his personal experiences as a traveling actor and a laborer. While these influences allowed him to break free from the militaristic and fundamentalist attitudes ascribed to the South, his identity as a Southerner and belief that he was part of an oppressed people became the wellspring of his liberalism, enabling him to empathize with those who suffered injustice.

The spirit of Thomas Jefferson's idealism, which experienced a resurgence under the political leadership of Bryan and Wilson, is based on the exaltation of the ordinary individual to the central role in society, a concept that is crystallized in Griffith's social-historical vision. Manifesting his dedication to the integrity of the individual, Jefferson spoke out against oppression and regimentation in many forms including imperialism, puritanism and aristocracy. He condemned imperialism, declaring, "If there be one principle more deeply written than any other in the mind of every American, it is that we should have nothing to do with conquest."[26] He denounced aristocratic privilege and the established church, bringing him into conflict with the heirs of the New England Puritans who, in turn, excoriated him as an "atheist" and a "Jacobin." He distrusted industrialism, which he believed would lead to despotism and the exploitation of the proletarian masses. Placing his faith in the small farmers, he described them as "the chosen people of God, if ever he had a chosen people, whose breasts he has made his peculiar deposit for substantial and genuine virtue."[27] He envisioned an essentially agrarian republic benefiting the common man that would spurn involvement with the Old World and its incessant imperial wars and its monarchical, aristocratic and theocratic institutions. These values, engrained in Griffith's character at an early age, formed the basis for the director's philosophy, pejoratively characterized by Sarris as a "small-town agrarian vision of the world," but which, in fact, is the heart of American culture.

The turn-of-the-century debate over American imperialism, along with Griffith's commitment to Jeffersonian ideology and identity as a scion of the defeated South, may have provided the stimulus for the anti-imperialist motif that is dominant in all the director's feature-length social-historical films. The U.S. conquest of the Philippines brought together such luminaries as William Jennings Bryan, Samuel Gompers, Mark Twain, David Starr Jordan, Andrew Carnegie, Grover Cleveland and Carl Schurz, who spearheaded an anti-imperialist movement opposed to foreign conquest and military occupation on the grounds that these policies violated the principles upon which the republic was founded. To the anti-imperialists, American actions in the Philippines marked the erosion of traditional American values and threatened to transform the New World into a replica of the Old World with its continuing struggle for hegemony among nation-states. Citing Jefferson to support his position, Bryan articulated the tenets of the anti-imperialist movement when he declared:

> Imperialism might expand the nation's territory but it would contract the nation's purpose. It is not a step forward toward a broader destiny; it is a step backward, toward the narrow view of kings and emperors.[28]

Also prominent in the anti-imperialist movement were a number of Southern politicians. Senator Augustus O. Bacon, who headed the movement in Congress for Philippine independence, decried the new imperial policy. The Georgia senator stated that it signaled an abandonment of the United States' "peaceful career" in favor of a grab for "empire and power" that would extend to "the ends of the earth" in an attempt to "dominate and rule over distant lands and peoples of every race, condition and color." He warned that this new direction could involve the United States in a world war.[29] It was not uncommon in the Congressional debates over imperialism from 1898 to 1902 for anti-imperialist Southerners to compare the occupation of the Philippines with the military occupation of the South during Reconstruction. Senator Edward M. Carmack of Tennessee, for example, dramatized this sentiment when he asked "how anyone could expect gentle or compassionate treatment of the Filipinos at the hands of an American army of occupation, when a similar army had perpetrated such horrors upon its own countrymen during Reconstruction."[30] Other Southern politicians saw a relationship between the new American expansionism and economic imperialism at home. South Carolina's Senator John L. McLaurin pointed to this link as he contended that

> Imperialism means self-building at the expense of others. Its roots are embedded in lust of power and insatiable greed. The trusts and money power, that now hold so many of our people in financial bondage, are crying out for new fields to explore.[31]

The other side of the debate was supported by equally outstanding public figures including Theodore Roosevelt, Senator Albert J. Beveridge of Indiana, Admiral Alfred T. Mahan, Henry Cabot Lodge, Elihu Root and historian Albert Bushnell Hart. Citing the precedence of the conquest of the West resulting from the Mexican War and a series of Indian Wars, the pro-imperialists argued that foreign colonization was a direct continuum of Western expansion. Indeed, Roosevelt said that "Throughout a large part of our national career, our history has been one of expansion."[32] Further, the imperialists believed that foreign expansion was America's destiny, saving it from stasis and decadence. Representative of this philosophy was Admiral Stephen B. Luce, who argued that "War is one of the great agencies by which human progress is made." As he saw it, war was a test of endurance, annealing the character and offering the added benefits of stimulating "national growth" and solving "otherwise insoluble problems of domestic and political economy."[33] Roosevelt also attested to the character-building aspects of war, asserting that "The courage of the soldier ... stands higher than any quality called out merely in time of peace."[34] Equally fervent in his support of the military virtues was Senator Beveridge who declared: "I subscribe to the doctrine of war. It is the divine instrument of progress."[35] Beveridge also envisioned advantages of imperialism to the American economy:

> The trade of the world must and shall be ours ... We will establish
> trading-posts throughout the world as distributing-points for
> American products ... Our institutions will follow our flag on the
> wings of our commerce.[36]

Providing added impetus and moral justification for the imperialist view
was the messianic impulse to spread the blessings of American Christian
civilization to the "backward" and "heathen" peoples of the world. Albert
Bushnell Hart, posing the rhetorical question, "Who can doubt that the
purpose of the American people is not only to make the nation felt as a
world power, but also to spread Western civilization eastward?" revealed
the fundamental missionary and racist motives that underlay the drive to
create an American empire.[37]

Although the imperialist controversy had subsided by the time Griffith
began his directorial career, its repercussions have been felt throughout the
twentieth century in debates on U.S. foreign policy. During the two years
Griffith was filming *Intolerance*, the major issue of the period was the role
the United States should play in the war that was raging in Europe, with
Roosevelt, the most outstanding imperialist spokesman of the 1890s,
heading the interventionist movement, and Bryan, the chief political opponent of the conquest of the Philippines, leading the neutralist cause. The
debate over the war was essentially a restatement of positions which had
fueled the controversy surrounding American expansionist policies of the
1890s. The interventionists held the view that the United States had a moral
obligation as a world power to use its military might to advance the cause
of civilization and democracy. The neutralists, on the other hand, believed
that America should not extend its influence beyond the Western
Hemisphere to become involved in a foreign fray which would weaken the
republic in an attempt to expand the empire.

The war issue ignited Griffith's fervor against imperialism, a sentiment
interwoven in the fabric of *Intolerance*. Not only did the film express his
unmistakable support for the anti-war position, depicting the horrors of
conflict in the battle scenes in the Babylonian Story and underscoring them
with pacifist didacticism in the subtitles, it also allowed him to present a
broader condemnation of imperialism. His portrait of Cyrus as a villain,
an interpretation at odds with Greek and Jewish historiography, is an indictment of conquest reflecting the Jeffersonian tradition in its opposition
to imperial monarchies. Conquest, in Griffith's view, was not an agent for
progress as the imperialists maintained but, on the contrary, could lead to
the destruction of even the most advanced civilization. The Persian invasion of Babylon, for Griffith in part a metaphor for the North's devastation
and occupation of the South, terminated the cultural autonomy of ancient
Mesopotamia as implied in the film. Griffith reinforces his anti-imperialist
message in the other stories, arraigning the use of military force to subor-
dinate the civilian population and simultaneously attacking monarchy,

theocracy and monopolistic capitalism. Implicit in his depictions of Jenkins calling on the uniformed militiamen to suppress the strikers, Catherine de Medici utilizing the soldiers to slaughter the Huguenots and the Roman soldiers leading Christ to Calvary, is the belief that these entrenched systems can only maintain their power through military measures. Additionally, Griffith shows that imperialist oppression must be justified by its perpetrators through an allegedly superior moral or religious system which they impose on the populace. Thus he condemns the kind of rationale that spurred the American turn-of-the-century expansionist movement, a course of action based on assumptions of cultural superiority.

The anti-imperialist theme in *Intolerance* was not new to Griffith but first emerged in his Biograph films when he dramatized the oppression of the American Indians by the whites during the settlement of the West. *The Redman's View*, made in 1909, one of the most powerful of these films, represents a stunning refutation of the imperialists' arguments, including Roosevelt's, that American policy toward the Indians was justified by our need to expand and control the barbarities of the "savages" who they claimed had been treated fairly. Using a dramatic technique that he adapted to subsequent films, Griffith shows the tranquility of the Kiowa Indians disrupted by their conquerors, armed whites bent on taking their lands. The whites, forcing the Indians to leave their peaceful village to march westward on a "long trek," subject them to "relentless persecutions" until the old chief succumbs to the ordeal and the Indian heroine is captured and enslaved by her conquerors.[38] A review in *The New York Dramatic Mirror* characterized the film as "an appeal in pictures on behalf of the Indian," noting that "the injustice that the red race has suffered at the hands of the whites is held up to our eyes in convincing picture language and the conclusion is conveyed that they are now receiving as wards of the nation only scant and belated recognition."[39]

Griffith continued to express his anti-imperialist view in his treatment of Indians in his 1910 film, *Ramona*, adapted from Helen Hunt Jackson's novel. He captures the force of history from the Indian perspective in the first of his panoramic landscapes, showing the Indian hero on a mountain top helplessly looking on as his village is destroyed by white settlers in the valley below. So dramatic was the portrayal with the "burning huts, the hurrying people and the wagons of whites ... clearly visible, though they appear as mere specks in the distance"[40] that it caused a reviewer for *The Moving Picture World* to observe, "one wants to do something to help the unfortunates whose property is destroyed, whose land is taken and who are persecuted and driven even farther into the wilderness."[41]

Judith of Bethulia, his last film for Biograph and his first feature, released in 1914, once again manifests Griffith's aversion to conquest and militarism. Characteristically beginning his film with a peaceful scene, he pictures the Jewish village of Bethulia quietly engaged in its daily pursuits

Anti-imperialism in Griffith's films. Top: Sherman's army devastates the South in "The Birth of a Nation." Bottom: Indian hero rages helplessly as his village is destroyed in "Ramona."

while two young lovers "evolve their own little heart-affair at the city well." The calm is soon interrupted when the mighty army of the Assyrian empire, led by the general Holofernes, descends upon the town "intent upon exploration, battle and glory." Again haunted by the devastation of the Civil War, Griffith depicts the sufferings of the Bethulians as the Assyrian army besieges, massacres and starves the helpless townspeople. The widow Judith, seeking to alleviate the misery of her countrymen, first seduces and then beheads the hot-blooded Assyrian general. Inspired by her action, the Bethulians "arise in a final whirlwind of courage" and the leaderless imperial army flees the town.[42]

As he turned to the Civil War and its aftermath in *The Birth of a Nation*, his most controversial film, Griffith elaborated upon his favorite historical motif, fueling his anti-imperialist statement with a passion born of his heritage. Like the peaceful scenes in his Indian films, *Judith of Bethulia* and the four stories of *Intolerance*, an idyllic picture of the antebellum South where, according to a subtitle, "life runs on in a quaintly way that is to be no more," preludes violence. Personifying the South through the refined, middle-class Cameron family, Griffith portrays a carefree life in which slaves, treated kindly by their master, dwell happily on the Cameron plantation. This "laissez-faire" setting is shattered when the North invades the South and the conquering soldiers burn and pillage anything in their path, including the Cameron home. The destruction peaks with the burning of Atlanta and Sherman's march to the sea. In a scene reminiscent of the plundering of the Indian village in *Ramona*, a Southern family weeps on a hilltop as the Union army ruins the valley.

Griffith continues his attack on imperialism in his presentation of Reconstruction in the second half of the film, picturing the Southern states treated as "conquered provinces" under the leadership of the Northern congressman, Austin Stoneman, a fictionalized version of Thaddeus Stevens. When Northern white carpetbaggers coalesce with black militiamen to impose a military dictatorship on the ravaged South, the Southerners, weary of domination, finally rebel. Disenfranchised by carpetbaggers and Negro troops and responding to the outrages committed by the militia, including the attempted rape and death of the Cameron girl, the Southerners organize the Ku Klux Klan resistance movement. In Griffith's interpretation, the Klan overturns the military rule, restoring white civilian control and saving the remnants of Southern culture from eradication by the imperial North and its Negro agents.

Many critics see racism as the dominant theme in the film. While they often attempt to draw a distinction between the powerful but relatively "benign" first half tracing the course of the Civil War and the second half dominated by racial strife and the Ku Klux Klan, the unity of the work appears to emanate from Griffith's deeply felt opposition to the subjugation of the South by a victorious North intent upon economic and political exploitation. As J.N. Thomas states in *The Berkeley Barb*:

... racism was an unconscious element of the picture, not its *point*. What Griffith was attacking were those "outsiders" who came into the Reconstruction South – in Griffith's view – to mislead innocent, but dangerously ignorant ex-slaves. These "outsiders" were none other than the representatives of Northern industrial capital, which Griffith had attacked as early as 1909 in *A Corner in Wheat*.[43]

Lary May confirms Thomas's contention that Griffith's primary target in *The Birth of a Nation* is Northern economic imperialism: "In its message, the film called for an alliance of the common folk from the formerly warring sections to overthrow a tyranny based on Northern commercial corruption."[44] Indeed, Griffith's ultimate villain is the Northern economic and industrial system which, in its zeal for expansion, introduced slavery to the New World in colonial times and invaded and plundered the South in the nineteenth century.

Griffith states his moral purpose in making the film in his opening subtitle: "If in this work we have conveyed to the mind the ravages of war to the end that *war may be held in abhorrence*, this effort will not have been in vain." In the original release prints, he envisions a peaceful America free from imperialist ambitions as he concludes that "the new nation, the real United States" will have "turned away forever from the blood-lust of war and anticipated with hope the world-millenium in which a brotherhood of love should bind all the nations." Commenting on the power of the cinema to educate the audience, he said in a 1916 article in *The Kine Year Book*: "*The Birth of a Nation* does not profess to be a sermon, but if, incidentally, it does something to show the real character of 'glorious war' it will, I think, have served at least one useful purpose."[45] But the director's noble aims did not impress the militaristic and imperialist Albert Bushnell Hart who, as the only prominent historian of the time to criticize the film, wrote a five-column article in which he accused Griffith of "having made a mockery of the Union victory in our Civil War."[46]

Griffith's return to the subject of the Civil War in *Abraham Lincoln*, his final epic, complements rather than contradicts *The Birth of a Nation* as he again exposes the evils of war and oppression. Tracing the life of the sixteenth president from his birth in a log cabin to his death at Ford's Theatre, Griffith presents slavery and the resulting conflict from Lincoln's perspective, proving that the director could remain true to his historic vision even while shifting his dramatic focus. The prologue in the original release prints contains shots of blacks, lashed and thrown into the sea by brutal traders, as they are being transported to America on slave ships.[47] The original prints also include scenes of "black road-gangs and of slavery auctions ... [with] a lyrical power ... as haunting as anything Griffith had accomplished in his heyday," sequences so moving that they were suppressed by a timid film industry soon after the initial screenings.[48] With these scenes, Griffith sets the tone for Lincoln's intercession to end the imperialist, oppressive institution of slavery. The president thereby preserves the Union and affirms the original ideals of the republic.

Another example of Griffith's attempt to redirect his emphasis in *Abraham Lincoln* is his depiction of the climate that precipitated the war. Unlike *The Birth of a Nation*, in which a peaceful antebellum South is suddenly invaded by the North, the later film shows a restless South on the eve of war, fearful of slave revolts in the wake of John Brown's raid. It is in this mood of apprehension that the South secedes from the Union, beginning the conflict by firing on Fort Sumter, an event Griffith had omitted in the earlier epic.

To avoid diminishing audience sympathy for Lincoln's cause, Griffith does not dramatize the devastation of war through the sufferings of the Southern civilian population as he had done in *The Birth of a Nation*. Instead, he makes his most compelling anti-war statement in a scene in which Lincoln, saving a young deserter from the firing squad, says wearily, "Killing — hanging — blood," as a chorus is heard in the background softly singing "Tenting on the Old Campground." In a parallel scene, a despairing General Robert E. Lee, personifying the nobility and pathos of the South on the verge of defeat, rescinds the orders for a spy's execution, commenting that there will soon be no army left to protect from spies. Without detracting from the president's cause, this quiet sequence indicates Griffith's sympathy with the sufferings of the South and, at the same time, his antipathy to war.

Although Griffith pays tribute to the heroism of the South in the figure of Lee, it is Lincoln who emerges as the man of peace, vowing to take the Southern states back "as though they had never been away." On the other hand, it is the paranoia of the South which produces John Wilkes Booth, the rabid adherent of the Confederate cause, who is introduced in the film on the eve of the war as he pledges to shoot any abolitionist daring to come to Virginia. With dramatic irony, Griffith shows that Booth, embittered by racial hatred and the defeat of the South and obsessed with the idea that Lincoln is planning to make himself the supreme ruler of the land, destroys the only hope the South has to avoid imperialist exploitation when he assassinates the president.

Hearts of the World, Griffith's major film on World War I, gave him the opportunity to comment on war and conquest in a contemporary setting. In many ways, as William K. Everson points out, the film is a remake of *The Birth of a Nation* with "the same family structure, the same separations and reunions, the same editing patterns" and a similar climactic last-minute rescue.[49] Griffith also uses the same motif so effective in *Intolerance, Judith of Bethulia* and the Indian films, opening with a picture of serenity that vanishes abruptly with the onset of turmoil. In *Hearts of the World*, the tranquility of a French village, the adopted home of the two young American protagonists and their families, is destroyed when the invading German army overruns the village, raping, plundering, and enslaving its citizens. The original release prints contain such violent scenes of German soldiers' atrocities that Mrs. Woodrow Wilson protested to the director, a reaction which disturbed Griffith so greatly that he modified and reshot some scenes.[50] Although he was deliberate in his attempt to condemn German aggression, even in his original version he did not abandon his anti-imperialist principles and artistic integrity. Instead, he counterbalanced sequences of German brutality with pacifist preachments in his subtitles and scenes such as the heroine on the battlefield looking for her sweetheart's body and the symbolic image of "a brace of swans, with their cygnets, swimming away from the ripples in their pond caused by falling dirt from a bomb explosion."[51]

Griffith's main problem in making the film seems to have been his ambivalent feelings about the conflict. Like many anti-imperialists of the time, he had a genuine sympathy for the European victims of the mighty German war-machine. On the other hand, he personally rejected the counter-imperialism implicit in the American crusade "to make the world safe for democracy," a Wilsonian maxim at odds with Griffith's loyalty to the Jeffersonian traditions of an insular American republic. His ambivalence is apparent in the reedited version of the film he released after the armistice. In this version, he eliminates or tones down scenes intended to arouse hatred of the Germans. For example, when an enemy soldier is flogging the heroine, another German intervenes, saying "War has made cruel beasts of most of us, but not all of us, thank God."[52] An advertisement for the film in *The New York Dramatic Mirror* of 1919 emphasized Griffith's commitment to pacifism: "A vivid reason for the League of Nations"; "Visualizing the necessity for the cessation of armed strife"; "The horror and futility of war"; "Reasons for avoiding all wars in future."[53]

Despite Griffith's misgivings about the immediate propagandistic function of *Hearts of the World*, his artistry in presenting his vision through believable characters caught up in the path of imperialism enables him to make a classic indictment of war and conquest consistent with his other works. Kevin Brownlow points out that Griffith does not romanticize or glorify war, showing it "mainly as it affects civilians" as he proves once again he was "a man of integrity."[54]

Griffith returned to contemporary Europe for a more subtle indictment of war in *Isn't Life Wonderful?* In this masterpiece of social commentary, he depicts the aftermath of World War I from the German perspective, centering his narrative around the experiences of a Polish refugee family on the outskirts of Berlin struggling to survive in a time of chaos and deprivation. Filmed on location in Germany, it is an intensely personal work, recalling again the director's childhood in a defeated, impoverished region. Mordaunt Hall, reviewing the film for *The New York Times*, observed:

A 1919 advertisement for "Hearts of the World" (the "New York Dramatic
Mirror").

Griffith's picture of poverty. Top: Citizens of postwar Germany stand in line for meat in "Isn't Life Wonderful?" Bottom: The breadlines in "A Corner in Wheat," brought on by capitalist manipulation.

> Through countless deft and effective touches in this simple yet deeply
> stirring narrative, Mr. Griffith again proves himself a brilliant direc-
> tor. He depicts the listlessness and dulled eyes in individuals resulting
> from an ill-nourished condition, the apathy to meals consisting of
> little more than horse turnips ..., the exhilaration of a family over the
> hardly believable sight of a bowl of steaming potatoes ... and the
> boundless joy caused by a feast with liverwurst.[55]

Throughout the film, Griffith vividly illustrates that hunger and rampant inflation are among the bitter fruits of war. In a telling sequence, the
heroine stands in a long line for meat only to find when she reaches the
front of the line that the proprietor of the butcher shop has raised the price
so much that she cannot afford it. The powerfully moving climax shows
the heroine and her German sweetheart attempting to elude the starving
workers who chase them through the woods to steal their cartload of
potatoes. When their pursuers finally overtake them, the couple call the
thieves "beasts" to which a worker responds, "Yes, beasts we are, beasts
they have made us — years of war and strife." Without melodrama, Griffith
thus decries the militarism that breeds want and despair.

In *Orphans of the Storm*, Griffith assails aristocratic privilege and the
monarchy, amplifying his anti-imperialist motif. He gives full rein to his
Jeffersonian beliefs, tracing the history of the Bourbon regime and the
French Revolution through their effect on the heroines, the two sisters or-
phaned by the monarchical system and kept apart by the Reign of Terror.
Hailed by *The New York Times* as "a stirring, gripping picture" which
proved once again Griffith's "mastery over mobs and sweeping panoramic
scenes, and his definiteness in the use of expressive details," the film shows
the conditions that sow the seeds of discontent.[56] While warning of the
dangers inherent in revolutionary extremism, Griffith arraigns the tyranny,
conspicuous consumption and indifference to the poor of the ruling class.
To make his point, he contrasts the feasts of the wealthy, "emphasized by
a slice of cake and the thin cut of a juicy roast," with the poverty of the
masses.[57] In his interpretation, Danton becomes the personification of the
positive aspects of revolution, passionately yearning for justice as he ex-
coriates the venality of the ruling class and leads the uprising against the
royalist government. Griffith builds his case against the "ancien regime" so
compellingly that, by the time the surging crowds are shown storming the
Bastille, they are not merely an unruly mob but a people striving to throw
off the yoke of oppression.

Ineluctably drawn to the intrinsic anti-imperialist message of the
American Revolution, Griffith directed the only definitive film on the col-
onists' resistance to British tyranny. In the scenes in *America* recreating
Paul Revere's ride and the battles of Lexington, Concord Bridge and
Bunker Hill, he avoids portraying chauvinistic tableaux of America's
glories by concentrating on the heroism and sacrifices of the colonial

soldiers fighting against the mighty forces of the empire. As in previous epics, he symbolizes historic forces through his fictional protagonists. The hero serving under George Washington is a representative of the "plain people," a perfect embodiment of Jefferson's beloved farmer class and the source of republican virtue. His sweetheart's father, an aristocrat allied with the Tory cause, exemplifies the link between the privileged colonial class and the Crown. Even the role of the historic Captain Walter Butler reinforces the alliance between the colonial Tory class and the imperial system. The ambitious Butler is shown as the arch-villain who, commanding a force of Redcoats and Indians, engineers the massacre of civilians in the Mohawk Valley. His brutality stems, in Griffith's interpretation, not from a devotion to ideals, but from a desire to build an empire of his own in North America. Griffith was so effective in dramatizing his point of view, infusing his film with a revolutionary dynamism, that *America*, lauded by *The New York World* as "the best picture ever made," was withheld from distribution in Britain for several months because of the government's fear that the film would sway sympathizers with the nationalist movements then challenging British Imperial authority.[58]

Through *Orphans of the Storm* and *America*, Griffith seems to be evoking revolutionary idealism to respond to the economic imperialism of the 1920s. His attacks on monarchical rule and aristocratic privilege appear to represent his criticism of the ascendancy of big business. With the disintegration of Progressivism in World War I, economic expansion replaced social reform as the national goal. The unprecedented growth of large corporations and the public's obsession with the accumulation of wealth represented to Griffith an abandonment of human concerns in favor of materialism and an erosion of the kind of individual enterprise that had characterized his own career. Not only did this new mood eventually undermine his attempts to remain independent from the monopolistic trends of the film industry, it also ran counter to his inherent commitment to Jeffersonianism.

Griffith's condemnation of economic imperialism is obvious in the Modern Story and *A Corner in Wheat*. Jenkins, the ruthless head of Allied Manufacturers in the Modern Story, seeks to extend his control over his workers and the community as a whole. In *A Corner in Wheat*, the capitalist, speculating in wheat, corners the market, impoverishing the farmers and forcing the urban poor to go hungry because they can no longer afford the soaring price of bread. In both instances, Griffith implies that economic conquest, like military conquest, wreaks havoc on society.

Another variation of Griffith's theme appears in *Broken Blossoms* (1919). In this lyrical masterpiece, Griffith assails cultural imperialism, a corollary of military and economic expansionism and the offspring of a belief in moral and religious superiority. The film, unmasking the white man's prejudice toward the Chinese, was unique at a time when popular fiction, including motion pictures, mirrored the racist concept of the

"Yellow Peril," stereotyping the Chinese as wily devils and heathens. These attitudes, which stemmed from hostility to Chinese immigration on the West Coast and were fostered by those attempting to justify Western economic, military and cultural exploitation of China, had existed since the mid-nineteenth century. At the turn of the century, many influential American businessmen, military men and politicans viewed China as a vast market for American products. Among them was Robert T. Hill of the U.S. Geological Survey, who maintained that the Westernization of China presented a golden opportunity for American business interests.[59]

Encouraged and reinforced by economic interests, Christian missionaries launched a massive effort to convert the Chinese to Christianity and Western civilization. The Boxer Rebellion of 1900, which was crushed by the joint forces of the United States and the other great powers, was China's response to Western exploitation and encroachment upon the native civilization. The resistance of the Chinese to Westernization coupled with the fact that they were an easy prey to outside aggressors, including Japan, caused militarists such as Roosevelt and Admiral Luce to perceive China as a decadent, stagnant society lacking in fighting qualities.[60]

Against this backdrop, Griffith, sensitized by growing up in a rural South regarded as backward by an industrial North, approached his subject with extraordinary insight into those who have suffered at the hands of cultural imperialism. The film opens with shots of a city in China where the hero, a young Chinese Buddhist, is preparing to leave for the West to spread the pacific message of Buddhism to "the barbarous Anglo-Saxons, sons of turmoil and strife." His mission unfulfilled in the atmosphere of World War I, he becomes a shopkeeper in London's Limehouse District. There he befriends a young English girl who is repeatedly beaten by her father, a drunken pugilist. The father, hostile to those "who do not come from the same great country as himself," lashes her to death with a whip handle when he learns of her friendship with the Chinese shopkeeper. The grief-stricken hero kills the boxer and then commits suicide.

Griffith enhances his theme through his skillful use of dramatic contrast. By juxtaposing the gentleness of the Chinese hero against the brutality of the English boxer, he challenges the whole assumption of superiority which gave rise to the racist attitude of the West toward the Oriental. In one scene, the shots of the "noble and unassuming face" of the Chinese hero are counterpointed with the close-ups of two Christian missionaries "whose faces exude unctuous hypocrisy" as they hand the Chinese a pamphlet entitled "Hell," and announce they are going to China to convert the "heathen." Siegfried Kracauer points out that "Griffith thus confronts the belief in the white man's superiority with the reality it allegedly covers and through this confrontation denounces it as an unwarranted prejudice."[61] The opening scenes of a Buddhist temple and smiling Chinese women and children, symbolizing a peaceful, civilized society

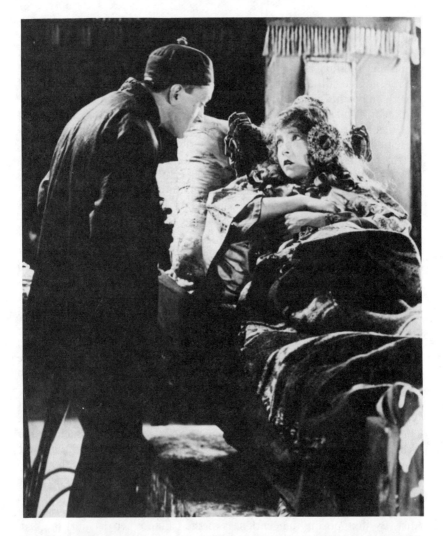

The Chinese shopkeeper befriends the heroine in "Broken Blossoms," Griffith's criticism of Western imperialism.

with noble religious precepts and strong family ties, contrast with Griffith's images of the squalor of London, where anonymity and indifference breed despair and brutality. Through the power of his contrapuntal imagery, Griffith puts forth his message, which, in the words of *The New York Dramatic Mirror*,

> is of special force in this day when nations are struggling for a new order. It is the message that, perhaps, the Orient is a more fertile field

for the idea of universal peace and brotherhood of man than the nations of the West.[62]

In Griffith's interpretation, imperialism is closely allied with puritanism. He views a kind of moral imperialism emanating from puritanical ideologies as the motivating force behind military, economic and cultural imperialism. By implying that the full realization of American democracy was impeded by the Puritan tradition, he was responding to the same set of stimuli in the Progressive Era that produced the anti–Puritan historians of the 1920s. Progressive scholars James Truslow Adams, Vernon L. Parrington and Thomas J. Wertenbaker saw "American history in terms of conflict — as a continuous struggle between the forces of liberalism and conservatism, aristocracy and democracy, and the rich and the poor," a dominant motif in many of Griffith's films. While departing from the traditional exaltation of the New England Puritans in American historiography,

> these historians pictured the Puritans as reactionary rather than progressive, authoritarian rather than democratic, bigoted rather than broad-minded, and pious hypocrites rather than sincere and devout religionists.[63]

These scholars perceived the Puritan movement, not merely as a phenomenon limited to the colonial period, but as the continuing source of the repressive elements embedded in the American psyche. Adams maintained that the reactionary New England religious leaders sought to regulate every detail of the private lives of individuals to conform to their absolutist ideology, using their beliefs as a rationale for subjecting the lower classes to their middle-class rule. Parrington refuted the theory that the Puritans had aided the rise of democracy in the New World, tracing, instead, the mainstream of American liberal thought to Jeffersonianism and the origin of American conservatism to Puritanism.[64] Wertenbaker agreed, pointing out that Thomas Jefferson and his followers broke the power of the Puritan elite in New England. Nevertheless, "the Puritan code of morals ... (has) left an imprint on life in many parts of the United States which has not yet been entirely erased."[65] In denouncing Prohibition and censorship, social critic H.L. Mencken also saw a link between conservative trends in modern America and Puritanism, which he characterized as "the haunting fear that someone, somewhere, may be happy."[66]

Like Mencken, Griffith places puritanism in a contemporary context. In the Modern Story, Jenkins is identified with a puritanical ideology, a depiction confirmed by Matthew Josephson's description of the American capitalists at the turn of the century as "puritanical and pious ... discreet, sober, well-controlled, their strongest lust being the pecuniary appetite."[67]

Two victims of intolerance. Left: the kindly Chinese hero of "Broken Blossoms."
Right: the innocent country girl of "Way Down East."

Jenkins aligns himself with the moral reformers, providing financial support to bring about a puritanization of their community in much the same
way the ministers and magistrates of the Massachusetts Bay Colony sought
to purify their society. Public amusements are curtailed and laws are made
to control citizens' behavior. These measures accomplish more, however,
than regulating personal conduct and eliminating pleasures. They ensure
the bourgeoisie supremacy over the working class just as the repressive
regime of the Puritans intensified class divisions in colonial New England.

Although the religious denomination of the Jenkinses is not specified,
they are presented as piously adhering to a value system issuing from a narrow interpretation of the Protestant ethic, while the working-class hero
and heroine are clearly identified as Catholics. In indicating these sectarian
differences, Griffith is not attempting to suggest religious persecution but
seems rather to be underscoring his belief that a dogmatic elite is able to
impose its creed upon a pluralistic society as the Puritan hierarchy had
done in Massachusetts in colonial times.

Griffith seeks to prove that puritanism, like imperialism, is a historical constant as he links the Pharisees and the High Priest of Bel with the moral reformers in the Modern Story. Acting upon a strict interpretation of Mosiac law, the Pharisees exercise tyrannical control over the daily lives of the citizens of Judea, enforcing a rigid moral code. Like the seventeenth-century practitioners of the Puritan faith, they claim the authority of God and do not tolerate heresy or transgression. Thus, at the Pharisees' behest, Christ is crucified as a heretic and the adulteress is stoned. In the Babylonian Story, the High Priest of Bel also maintains a closed system, forcing his dogma on the entire populace. Griffith ties the High Priest to an austere puritanical ethic in a scene in which he reacts with disgust at the sight of a naked statuette of Ishtar. When his authority is challenged by the reform movement centered around the cult of Ishtar, he joins forces with Cyrus to restore his power, demonstrating that this priest of the ancient Middle East is as intolerant of pluralism as the New World Puritans were in banishing rival denominations.

Griffith anticipated his attacks on puritanism in *Intolerance* in earlier films. *Rose O' Salem-Town*, the only film in which he openly assails the bigotry of historic New England Puritans, was made for Biograph in 1910. Set at the time of the Salem witch-hunts in 1692, it opens with scenes of the spritelike heroine and her mother living happily on the New England seacoast. The girl's happiness is complete when she falls in love with a trapper. This Edenic state of bliss is swept away when the deacon, representing the Puritan hierarchy, tries to seduce the girl. Angered by her rebuff, the hypocritical cleric incites the other churchmen against the girl and her mother, accusing them of being witches. The churchmen, convinced by the mother's reputation as a healer and fortune teller, order their execution. The mother is burned at the stake, but the heroine is saved by her sweetheart and his Mohawk Indian friends when they overpower the Puritans in a last-minute rescue. For Griffith, this confrontation pitting the trapper and the Indians against the Puritans symbolizes the clash between the uncorrupted New World with its promise of freedom and the hierarchical, theocratic despotism of the Old World.

The Reformers, or the Lost Art of Minding One's Business, produced for Biograph in 1913, is a direct forerunner of Griffith's criticism of puritanism in the Modern Story. In this film, a candidate for mayor campaigns on a promise to rid the city of vice. Assisted by the sanctimonious League of Civic Purity, he shuts down bars, brothels and vaudeville houses while his children, whom he neglects in his zeal to clean up the city, become alcoholics. Griffith thus intimates that if this well-to-do bourgeoisie, a latter-day Puritan, had been minding his own business instead of attempting to control the working class by imposing a strict moral standard, he would not have been responsible for the downfall of his own family.

Griffith's anti-puritanical theme appears again in *Way Down East* (1920), the greatest of his rural films. He derived his story from an old stage melodrama which he chose, in the face of industry skepticism, to attack

the puritanism that was still prevalent in small-town America. At the same time, he sought to recapture a rural life that was rapidly disappearing in the postwar era. Set in New England, the plot revolves around an innocent country girl who is seduced by a ne'er-do-well from the city. He arranges a fake marriage ceremony, then abandons her when he finds she is pregnant. After her baby dies at birth, the heroine moves to another community, where she becomes a hired girl with a prosperous farming family. The self-righteous squire, the patriarch of the family, adheres to a rigid moral code following the tradition of his Puritan ancestors, while his son, a sensitive farm boy who falls in love with the girl, is another of Griffith's personifications of the Jeffersonian ideal. When the girl's past is revealed, she falls victim to the bigotry of the entire community, including the squire, who orders her out of his house into a raging storm. The hero, defying his father, rescues his sweetheart from near-death on the ice floes. She is welcomed back by the community when it is learned that she was deceived by her lover.

Although often described as "Victorian," this film is an excellent example of Griffith's ability, like Dickens's, to combine Victorian sentiment with a condemnation of a hypocritical Victorian morality rooted in puritanism. As Everson points out:

> *Way Down East* is very much an anti-Victorian film. The reformers and the self-righteous are condemned. The God-fearing but bigoted New Englanders are forced to admit that they are wrong.[68]

Indeed, it is a tribute to the power of Griffith's direction that he is able to transform a hackneyed melodrama into a valid commentary on the persistence of puritanism in American society, with even the harsh winter landscape in the climax echoing the austere moral code that prevailed in New England.

In *The White Rose*, made in 1923, Griffith continues to expose the bigotry of rural America, this time in his native South. In this story, the heroine, a lowly cigar-stand girl, is seduced, then abandoned by a wealthy minister who fathers her illegitimate child. When the community learns of her predicament, she loses her job and, turned out of her lodgings, wanders aimlessly, sick and near suicide, until she and her baby find refuge with Negroes living near the minister's plantation. Her life is saved by the blacks who befriend her and alert the minister of her condition. In contrasting the actions of the blacks with the response of the small-town bourgeoisie to the plight of the heroine and her baby, Griffith finds that true Christianity issues from a spontaneous sense of compassion rather than a strict adherence to a puritanical code.[69]

Opposite: From "Way Down East": the Squire orders the heroine out of his house when he learns that she gave birth to a child out of wedlock.

Griffith's opposition to revolutionary extremism in *Orphans of the Storm* is based in part on his anti-puritanism. He denounces the Jacobinism of Robespierre for its puritanical fervor as it attempts to regulate the private lives of individuals, establishing a new conservative orthodoxy at odds with the original democratic goals that inspired the Revolution. Following the historical record, he portrays Robespierre as "a highly moral man" who hates those who do not think as he does. He defines the Jacobin leader's goal in the subtitle: "France must be purged of all vice." Contrary to the warmhearted Danton concerned for individual rights, Robespierre appears remote and calculating, looking upon people as so many objects to be manipulated to attain the "Republic of Virtue." He is willing, for example, to order the execution of the heroine who is charged with sedition, not so much because of her alleged crime, but because he "doubts her moral character."[70]

Griffith's depiction of entrenched imperialist and puritanical systems acknowledges the need for, indeed, the inevitability of, revolutionary action to throw off the yoke of oppression and restore the natural order. Although supporting the right to rebel against tyranny, he is also cognizant of the dangers inherent in the emergence of a new despotism, such as Robespierre's moralist regime, which simply perpetuates the old absolutism in a new guise. For this reason, he rejects any ideology that subordinates the individual, who, he believes, is the key to genuine social transformation.

The integrity of the individual is the heart of Griffith's social and historical vision. Griffith's work finds its hope, its optimism, in the belief that the love and compassion of human beings for each other can illuminate the dark violence of history and defeat the racial and religious antagonisms that have plagued humanity throughout the centuries. Without the redemptive possibility of love that springs from the individual heart, history would be to Griffith, as to Stephen Dedalus in James Joyce's *Ulysses*, "a nightmare from which I am trying to awake," and the millenial epilogue of *Intolerance* merely, as Gerald Mast argues, "an interpolated wish rather than a consequence of the film's action."[71]

Throughout his work, Griffith demonstrates his faith in the individual to transcend even the most chaotic or devastating situations through individual acts of kindness and love for one another. Like Whitman, he believed that "Adhesiveness or love ... fuses, ties and aggregates, making the races comrades and fraternizing all."[72] Again and again, he affirms this conviction in his films: in *The Redman and the Child*, made at the beginning of his career in 1908, a Sioux Indian befriends a small white boy, saving him from a gang of thieves; in *The Zulu's Heart*, also made in 1908, a black Zulu chieftain, bereft of his daughter, finds a common humanity in a white Boer child and her family, whom he rescues from the other tribesmen; in *The Redman's View*, the kindness of one white man who assists the Indians relieves the stark picture of genocide; in *The Greatest*

Thing in Life, a prejudiced Southern white officer learns the meaning of love and equality through his comradeship with a dying Negro soldier; in *Broken Blossoms*, the horror of the pugilist's cruelty toward his daughter is alleviated by the love of the Chinese hero for the girl; in *Orphans of the Storm*, Danton's respect for the divinity of the individual and his commitment to a humanistic revolution is manifested in his last-minute rescue of the heroine from the guillotine; in *Isn't Life Wonderful?*, the devastation and poverty of postwar Germany is illuminated by the love and concern of the hero and heroine for each other; and, in a deleted sequence in *Abraham Lincoln*, Lincoln's opposition to slavery is symbolized by his intervention in preventing a master from beating his slave.

So, too, in *Intolerance*, Griffith's faith in the individual holds out hope in the face of despair and upheaval: the love and endurance of the heroine in the Modern Story; the kindly policeman who tries to help the Dear One and her husband after his conviction for murder; the Friendless One who confesses to save the Boy's life; the courageous Mountain Girl fighting in defense of her prince and her civilization in the Babylonian Story; a Catholic priest saving a Protestant child from the massacre of the Huguenots in the French Story; and Christ preventing a self-righteous mob from stoning the adulteress in the Judean Story.

Underlying these examples in *Intolerance* is the implication that, despite the persistence of brutality and intolerance, "the same today as yesterday," the spread of progressive democracy grounded in respect for the individual may yet lead to a more just society. Griffith's optimism partakes of the impulses of Progressivism, which sought, in an increasingly impersonalized industrial age, to make Jefferson's ideal of a community of free cooperative citizens a reality by recognizing, in Roosevelt's words, "the individual's worth or lack of worth as the chief basis of action" for "shaping our whole conduct and especially our political conduct."[73] A legatee of Whitman, Griffith's faith is also a reflection of the reaffirmation of Jeffersonianism embodied in the poet's concept of "spiritual democracy" as expressed in "By Blue Ontario's Shore":

> I swear that nothing is good to me now that ignores individuals,
> The American compact is altogether with individuals,
> The only government is that which makes minute of individuals.[74]

The simple and profound truths of Griffith's social and historical vision in *Intolerance* are scarcely original—they are as old as civilization. Like all great artists, Griffith's originality lies, not in the novelty of his ideas, but in the power and conviction with which he expresses them. As Delacroix stated: "What makes men of genius or rather what they make, is not new ideas; it is the idea—which possesses them completely—that what has been said has still not been said enough."[75] It is Griffith's passionate yet gentle assertion of the dignity and worth of the individual against the backdrop of war and oppression that becomes in *Intolerance*, as in Picasso's painting of *Guernica*, an artistic commentary on man's inhumanity to man. Using the techniques of a new art in four intercut stories, Griffith created, as O'Dell observes, "one continuous philosophical argument made by touching humanities, by forceful and harrowing scenes of mass murder, and always by his ability to return again to the simplest of statements, pure and approachable by adults and children alike, for the preservation of peace and tolerance."[76]

In a world in which the individual has been increasingly degraded to be part of an unthinking mob, in a world threatened by cataclysmic self-destruction during a century scarred by wars and brutal ideologies slaughtering millions who "do not think as I think," Griffith's defense of the individual as the most significant force in history is a relevant insight and a priceless legacy.

Credits for *Intolerance*

(Also known under the titles *The Mother and the Law, A Sun-Play of the Ages,* and *Love's Struggle Throughout the Ages*)

Directed by David Wark Griffith. Produced and distributed by the Wark Producing Corporation. Associate producer: Harry E. Aitken. Written for the screen by D.W. Griffith. Titles by Griffith, assisted by Anita Loos and Frank E. Woods. Edited by Griffith with James and Rose Smith. Photography by G.W. "Billy" Bitzer. Assistant cameraman: Karl Brown. Set design by Frank Wortman and Walter L. Hall. Assistant directors: George Siegmann, W.S. Van Dyke, Erich von Stroheim, Edward Dillon, Tod Browning, Joseph Henabery, Allan Dwan, Monte Blue, Elmer Clifton, Mike Siebert. Research assistants: R. Ellis Wales, Joseph Henabery and Lillian Gish. Advisors to the Judean Story: Rabbi Myers and Father Dodd. Dances staged by Ruth St. Denis. Costumes by the Western Costume Company. Musical score arranged by Joseph Carl Breil and Griffith. Filmed at the Fine Arts Studio, Hollywood, California, and various locations in Southern California from 1914 to 1916. Previewed at Riverside, California, on August 6, 1916. Opened for its world premiere on September 5, 1916 at the Liberty Theatre in New York City. Original length: 14 reels (13,700 ft.); later cut to 13 reels (11,811 ft.) Original running time approximately 3 hours, 30 minutes; present running time of most prints is 2 hours, 50 minutes (at 16 f.p.s.). Cost of production has been estimated to have been from $386,000 to $2,000,000.

The Cast:

Linking the Stories: *The Woman Who Rocks the Cradle* Lillian Gish

The Modern Story (1914 A.D.): *The Dear One* Mae Marsh *The Boy* Robert Harron *The Girl's Father* Fred Turner *Jenkins* Sam de Grasse *Mary T. Jenkins* Vera Lewis *The Friendless One* Miriam Cooper *The Musketeer of the Slums* Walter Long *The Kindly Policeman* Tom Wilson *The Governor* Ralph Lewis *Judge of the Court* Lloyd Ingraham *Attorney for the Boy* Barney Bernard *Father Farley* Rev. A.W. McClure *Prison Guard* J.P. McCarthy *The Friendly Neighbor* Max Davidson *Strike Leader* Monte

Blue *Debutante* Marguerite Marsh *Owner of Car* Tod Browning *Chief Detective* Edward Dillon *Bartender* Billy Quirk *Jenkins's Secretary* Clyde Hopkins *The Warden* William A. Brown *Wife of the Neighbor* Alberta Lee *Uplifters and Reformers* Mary Alden, Eleanor Washington, Pearl Elmore, Lucille Brown, Luray Huntley, Mrs. Arthur Mackley

The Judean Story (A.D. 27): *The Nazarene* Howard Gaye *Mary the Mother* Lillian Langdon *Mary Magdalene* Olga Grey *First Pharisee* Gunther von Ritzau *Second Pharisee* Erich von Stroheim *Bride of Cana* Bessie Love *Bridegroom* George Walsh *The Bride's Father* William H. Brown *A Wedding Guest* W.S. Van Dyke

The French Story (A.D. 1572): *Brown Eyes* Margery Wilson *Prosper Latour* Eugene Pallette *Brown Eyes' Father* Spottiswoode Aitken *Her Mother* Ruth Handford *The Foreign Mercenary* A.D. Sears *Charles IX* Frank Bennett *Henri, duc d'Anjou* Maxfield Stanley *Catherine de Medici* Josephine Crowell *Marguerite de Valois* Georgia Pearce (Constance Talmadge) *Henri of Navarre* W.E. Lawrence *Admiral Coligny* Joseph Henabery *A Page* Chandler House *Catholic Priest* Louis Romaine *Duc de Guise* Morris Levy *Cardinal Lorraine* Howard Gaye

The Babylonian Story (539 B.C.): *The Mountain Girl* Constance Talmadge *The Rhapsode* Elmer Clifton *Prince Belshazzar* Alfred Paget *Attarea, the Princess Beloved* Seena Owen *King Nabonidus* Carl Stockdale *The High Priest of Bel* Tully Marshall *Cyrus the Persian* George Siegmann *The Mighty Man of Valor* Elmo Lincoln *The Runner* Gino Corrado *A Boy Killed in the Fighting* Wallace Reid *Captain of the Gate* Ted Duncan *Bodyguard to the Princess* Felix Modjeska *Judges* Lawrence Lawlor, George Fawcett *Old Woman* Kate Bruce *Solo Dancer* Ruth St. Denis *Slave* Loyola O'Connor *Charioteer* James Curley *Babylonian Dandy* Howard Scott *Auctioneer* Martin Landry *Brother of the Mountain Girl* Arthur Meyer *Gobryas, Lieutenant of Cyrus* Charles Van Cortland *Chief Eunuch* Jack Cosgrove *Girls of the Marriage Market* Alma Rubens, Mme. Sul-te-Wan, Ruth Darling, Margaret Mooney *Favorites of the Harem* Mildred Harris, Pauline Starke, Carmel Myers, Winifred Westover, Jewel Carmen, Eve Southern, Natalie Talmadge, Carol Dempster, Ethel Grey Terry, Daisy Robinson, Anna Mae Walthall *Extras* Owen Moore, Wilfred Lucas, Douglas Fairbanks, Sr., Sir Herbert Beerbohm Tree, Frank Campeau, DeWolfe Hopper, Nigel de Brulier, Donald Crisp, Tammany Young *Dancers* The Denishawn Dancers

Notes

Introduction

1. Quoted in Hanson, 498.
2. Quoted in Gish, *Movies*, 183.

1. The Man and the Art

1. May, 67–68.
2. Henderson, *Life*, 25–28.
3. Griffith and Hart, 35–37.
4. Ibid.
5. Henderson, *Life*, 57.
6. Merritt, "Rescued," 5.
7. Ibid.
8. Gish, *Movies*, 51.
9. Ramsaye, 453–58.
10. Ibid., 414–24.
11. Sklar, 18.
12. Merritt, "Nickelodeon Theaters," 60.
13. Ramsaye, 379–88.
14. Ibid., 532–41.
15. Robinson, 49–50.
16. Ibid.
17. Henderson, *Life*, 108.
18. Sklar, 54.
19. Ibid.
20. Ibid., 57.
21. Henderson, *Life*, 129.
22. Ibid.
23. Smith, "Comment and Suggestion," 19.
24. Henderson, *Life*, 131–32.
25. Ibid., 138.
26. Geduld, 32.
27. Silva, 118.
28. Ramsaye, 643.
29. Moore, 5–6, 16.
30. Raymond A. Cook, 49, 66, 101.
31. *The Cambridge History of American Literature*, s.v., drama.
32. Ramsaye, 643.

33. Editorial, *The Indianapolis Freeman*, 13 November, 1915.
34. Geduld, 101.
35. Silva, 98.
36. Griffith, 23.
37. O'Dell, 46.
38. Henderson, *Life*, 148, 156.
39. Barry, Bowser, 49.
40. Ibid., 50.
41. Griffith and Hart, xii.
42. Robinson, 77–90.
43. Ibid., 145–52.
44. Ramsaye, 761–776.
45. Ibid., 714.
46. Everson, 178.
47. Goodman, 4.

2. *Narrative Structure of* Intolerance

1. Quoted in O'Dell, 85.
2. Baudry, *Cahiers du Cinéma*, No. 241, 32.
3. Dettling, 82.
4. Allen, *Biography*, 561.
5. Dettling, 88.
6. Ibid., 82.
7. Ramsaye, 157.
8. Ibid., 154–55, 157.
9. Ibid., 157.
10. Ibid., 155–57.
11. Barry and Bowser, 26.
12. Wells, 271.
13. Stern, "Birth," 18.
14. O'Dell, 75.
15. Ibid., 49.
16. Ibid., 52.
17. Smith, Review, 22.
18. O'Dell, 62.
19. Ibid., 82.
20. Ibid., 70.
21. Ibid.,57.
22. Ibid., 63.
23. Ibid., 50.
24. May, 84.
25. Ibid.
26. Lindsay, "Photoplay Progress."

3. *Historical Sources*

1. Stern, "Birth," 34.
2. Ibid.

3. Gish, *Movies*, 168.
4. Karl Brown, 135.
5. Brownlow, *Parade's*, 55.
6. Ibid., 61.
7. Ibid.
8. Brownlow, *Hollywood*, 70.
9. O'Dell, 44.
10. Ibid.
11. *The New York Times*, 22 April, 1914.
12. Brownlow, *Parade's*, 55.
13. Ibid., 56.
14. Karl Brown, 115–20.
15. Ibid., 121–22.
16. Löwith, 186.
17. O'Dell, 47.
18. Hanson, 498.
19. Brownlow, *Parade's*, 57–58.
20. Hanson, 498.
21. Karl Brown, 135.
22. Ibid., 136–37.
23. Ibid., 130.
24. Noguères, 24.
25. Guizot, 566.
26. Noguères, 104.
27. Guizot, 546.
28. Ibid., 572.
29. Noguères, 104.
30. Guizot, 588.
31. Davidson, 68.
32. Guizot, 588.
33. Noguères, 104.
34. Gish, *Movies*, 168.
35. Hanson, 498.
36. Karl Brown, 135.
37. Fagan, 41–82.
38. Jastrow, *Aspects*, 295.
39. Rogers, 72–73.
40. Sayce, 89.
41. Mitry, 173.
42. Jastrow, *Aspects*, 59.
43. Oates, 135.
44. Ibid., 134.
45. Dougherty, 169–70.
46. Herodotus, 117–18.
47. Dougherty, 179.
48. Ibid., 183.
49. Oates, 135.
50. Dougherty, 179.
51. Ibid., 172.
52. Letter in *The New York Times*, 22 October, 1916.
53. *The New York Times*, 27 November, 1922.

54. Letter in *The New York Times*, 22 October, 1916.
55. Dougherty, 167.
56. Oates, 136.
57. Herodotus, 121.
58. Sandars, 45.
59. Fagan, 14.
60. Oates, 133.
61. Silva, 17.
62. Everson, 95.
63. Sayce, 46.
64. Jastrow, *Aspects*, 275.
65. Ibid., 137–38.
66. Sayce, 266.
67. Sandars, 26.
68. Jastrow, *Aspects*, 138.
69. Sayce, 266.
70. Ibid., 231.
71. Jastrow, *Aspects*, 134.
72. Pritchard, 108.
73. Jastrow, *Aspects*, 409.
74. Ibid.
75. Pritchard, 103.
76. Jastrow, *Aspects*, 410.
77. Oates, 67.
78. Herodotus, 120–21.
79. Sayce, 87.
80. Oates, 136.
81. Dougherty, 181.
82. Ibid., 184, 198.
83. Review in *The New York Herald*, 6 September, 1916.
84. Layard, 115.
85. Ibid., 115–18.
86. Ibid., 118–20.
87. Karl Brown, 148.
88. Hanson, 504.
89. Mitry, 174.
90. Hanson, 503.
91. Oates, 150.
92. Brownlow, *Parade's*, 61.
93. Gish, *Movies*, 170.
94. Hanson, 504.
95. Herodotus, 120.
96. Gish, *Movies*, 172.
97. Hanson, 504.
98. Johnson, 77–81.
99. Hanson, 498, 502.

4. *Artistic Influences*

1. Gish, *Movies*, 152.

2. Ibid.
3. Fulton, 103.
4. Ibid., 114.
5. Karl Brown, 168.
6. Review in *The San Francisco Chronicle*, 10 October, 1916.
7. Ramsaye, 755.
8. Hanson, 511.
9. Fulton, 110.
10. Stern, "Birth," 88.
11. O'Dell, 55.
12. Fulton, 110.
13. Ibid., 109.
14. Geduld, 105.
15. Fulton, 111.
16. Geduld, 105.
17. Karl Brown, 121–23.
18. Scott and Bullard, 129.
19. Ibid., 133.
20. Ibid., 99.
21. Ibid., 100.
22. Mras, 130.
23. Hanson, 504–06.
24. Ibid., 506–08.
25. Ibid.
26. Ibid., 508–11.
27. Vardac, 250–51.
28. Ibid., 65.
29. Ibid., 22–23.
30. Ibid., 25–27.
31. Ibid., 74.
32. Ibid., 76–81.
33. Ibid., 94–101.
34. Ibid., 138.
35. Ibid., 146–50.
36. Geduld, 33.
37. Ibid., 34.
38. Ibid., 28.
39. Slide, "The Other Griffith Actors," 481.
40. Vardac, 130.
41. Ibid., 131.
42. Slide, "The Other Griffith Actors," 481.
43. Vardac, 131–32.
44. Ibid., 133.
45. Merritt, "Rescued," 9.
46. Ibid., 10.
47. O'Dell, 91.
48. Merritt, "Rescued," 10.
49. Sadoul, *Films*, 16.
50. Brownlow, *Hollywood*, 71.
51. Hanson, 500.
52. Brownlow, *Parade's*, 590.

53. Geduld, 62.
54. Tennyson, 6.
55. Ibid.
56. Joseph, 45.
57. Tennyson, 6–7.
58. Joseph, 6.
59. Tennyson, 133.
60. Joseph, 4.
61. Tennyson, 855–58.
62. Joseph, 25.
63. Tennyson, 9–11.
64. Ibid.
65. Gish, *Movies*, 47, 167.
66. Griffith, Hart, 161.
67. Allen, *Biography*, 212.
68. Ibid., 52.
69. Whitman, 380.
70. Allen, *Biography*, 51–52.
71. Whitman, 74.
72. Ibid., 344.
73. O'Dell, 84.
74. Crawley, 73–74.
75. Ibid., 75.
76. Whitman, 233.
77. Ibid., 104.
78. Allen, *Biography*, 122.
79. Ibid., 154–55.
80. Whitman, 150–53.
81. Allen, *Guide*, 204–07.
82. Whitman, 150–53.
83. Karl Brown, 171.
84. Whitman, 88.
85. Ibid., 232.
86. Ibid., 318.
87. Crawley, 102.
88. Stern, "Birth," 31.
89. Whitman, 124.
90. Crawley, 140.
91. Allen, *Biography*, 236.
92. Whitman, 237–38.
93. Ellis, 60.
94. Pratt, 111.
95. Geduld, 53.
96. David Brown, 27.
97. Stanley J. Solomon, 13.
98. Jeffares, 118.
99. Geduld, 104.
100. Barry and Bowser, 23.
101. Cooper, *Deerslayer*, 511.
102. Axelrad, 8.
103. May, 73.

104. Petrie, 187–88.
105. Eisenstein, 195–255.
106. O'Dell, 90.
107. Eisenstein, 195–255.
108. Henderson, *Biograph*, 175.
109. Norris, *Octopus*, 458.
110. Norris, *Criticism*, xiv.
111. Ibid., xv.
112. Ibid.
113. Ibid., 97–98.
114. Griffith, 14, 21, 23, 24

5. *Influence of the Progressive Movement*

1. May, 94.
2. Ibid.
3. Harbaugh, 136.
4. May, 61.
5. Hofstadter, 180.
6. May, 69.
7. Koenig, 456–57.
8. Ibid., 11.
9. Collin, 27, 29
10. Ibid., 154.
11. Hofstadter, 170.
12. Brownlow, *War*, xv.
13. Anderson, 117.
14. Harbaugh, 325–26.
15. May, 61.
16. Wilson, 32: 310–11.
17. May, 84.
18. Geduld, 28.
19. Anderson, 117.
20. Ibid.
21. May, 93.
22. Hofstadter, 170.
23. Ekirch, 239.
24. Gish, *Movies*, 182.
25. Hofstadter, 5.
26. Ekirch, 60.
27. Griffith, 22.
28. Gish, *Movies*, 316.
29. Ibid., 183.
30. May, 61.
31. Hofstadter, 2.
32. Ekirch, 92.
33. Ibid., 71.
34. Hofstadter, 74–77.
35. Koenig, 359.
36. Ibid., 403–05.

37. Everson, 96.
38. Hofstadter, 74–77.
39. Ibid.
40. Ekirch, 54–55.
41. Ibid.
42. Hofstadter, 80.
43. Geduld, 47.
44. Hofstadter, 80.

6. *Impact of* Intolerance

1. Brownlow, *Hollywood*, 72.
2. *The Dramatic Mirror*, September, 1916–May, 1917.
3. Editorial, *The San Francisco Bulletin*, 19 October, 1916.
4. *The Dramatic Mirror*, May–June, 1917.
5. Gish, *Movies*, 180.
6. *The San Francisco Examiner*, 10 October, 1916.
7. Brownlow, *Hollywood*, 72.
8. Johnson, 71–81.
9. *The Dramatic Mirror*, September, 1917.
10. Wagenknecht, 81.
11. *The Dramatic Mirror*, 1918.
12. Brownlow, *Hollywood*, 72.
13. Smith, Review, 22.
14. *The Dramatic Mirror*, 1916.
15. *The New York Evening Post*, 6 September, 1916.
16. *The New York Journal*, 6 September, 1916.
17. Anthony, *The San Francisco Chronicle*, 10 October, 1916.
18. *The New York Herald*, 6 September, 1916.
19. *The San Francisco Call-Post*, 10 October, 1916.
20. Carr, *The Los Angeles Times*, 18 October, 1916.
21. Soule, *The New Republic*, 30 September, 1916.
22. Broun, *The New York Tribune*, 7 September, 1916.
23. Woollcott, *The New York Times*, 10 September, 1916.
24. Smith, "Comment and Suggestion," 19.
25. Stevens, *The Chicago Examiner*, 3 December, 1916.
26. Dell, *The Masses*, November, 1916.
27. Editorial, *The San Francisco Bulletin*, 19 October, 1916.
28. Ekirch, 54–55.
29. Silva, 103.
30. Brownlow, *War*, 30–38, 69–77.
31. Brownlow, *Hollywood*, 80.
32. Wilson, 34: 426–27.
33. Brownlow, *Hollywood*, 80.
34. Karl Brown, 177.
35. O'Dell, 60, 86.
36. Silva, 98.
37. Rochester, 16, 18.
38. Ibid., 16.
39. Ibid., 22.

40. *The Dramatic Mirror*, January 27, 1917.
41. Brownlow, *War*, 153.
42. Eastman, 147.
43. Brownlow, *Hollywood*, 80.
44. Sellin, 118.
45. *The Dramatic Mirror*, 1915–17.
46. Sellin, 124–31.
47. Griffith, 20.
48. Fulton, 109.
49. Geduld, 46.
50. Sklar, 64.
51. Brownlow, *Hollywood*, 111.
52. Silva, 97.
53. Slide in *Magill's Survey* 4: 1645.
54. *The London Times*, 29 June, 1922.
55. Carr, *The Los Angeles Times*, 18 October, 1916.
56. *The San Jose Mercury-Herald*, 21 October, 1916.
57. Sklar, 64.
58. Goodman, 10.
59. May, 86.
60. White, 597.
61. Fitzgerald, 282.
62. Rochester, 150.
63. Brownlow, *Parade's*, 106.
64. Robinson, 53–54.
65. Stern, "Griffith and Movies," 308.
66. *The Dramatic Mirror*, December, 1916–February, 1918.
67. Griffith, Hart, 121–23.
68. Henderson, *Life*, 182.
69. Gish, *Movies*, 186.
70. *The New York Times*, 13 April, 1924.
71. Brownlow, *Parade's*, 106.
72. Gish, *Movies*, 186.
73. Asquith, 294.
74. Gish, *Movies*, 186.
75. Rosenberg and Silverstein, 212.
76. *The Dramatic Mirror*, 1917.
77. Sadoul, *Filmmakers*, 190.
78. Bordwell, 207.
79. Leyda, 142.
80. Walworth, 2: 264.
81. Ibid., 2: 152.
82. Dickinson, 22–23.
83. Leyda, 142.
84. *The New York Times*, 13 April, 1924.
85. Leyda, 143.
86. *The New York Times*, 13 April, 1924.
87. Leyda, 161.
88. Barna, 74.
89. *The New York Times*, 12 May, 1929.

7. *Criticism and Legacy*

1. David A. Cook, 59.
2. Ibid., 59, 106.
3. Ibid., 96–98.
4. O'Dell, 59–60.
5. Ibid.
6. Silva, 107–08.
7. Henderson, *Biograph*, 172.
8. David A. Cook, 98.
9. *The San Francisco Bulletin*, 19 October, 1916.
10. O'Dell, 89.
11. Mast, 81.
12. Rosen, 37–58.
13. David A. Cook, 59.
14. *The New York Times*, 19 January, 1975.
15. Stern, "Birth," 24.
16. Sadoul, *Films*, 158.
17. Balász, 51–52.
18. Haskell, 35, 54.
19. Thomas, *The Berkeley Barb*, 7–13 November, 1975, 13.
20. Henderson, *Life*, 194.
21. Cadbury, "Theme," *Film Quarterly*, 1, 28, 39.
22. Geduld, 140.
23. David A. Cook, 60.
24. Silva, 106, 110.
25. Gish, *Movies*, 179.
26. Bryan, 41.
27. Grob and Billias, 328.
28. Bryan, 27.
29. Bryan, 537.
30. Healy, 241.
31. Bryan, 591.
32. Healy, 34.
33. Ibid., 102–03.
34. Ibid., 118.
35. Ibid., 104.
36. Ibid., 170–71.
37. Ibid., 128.
38. *Biograph Bulletins*, 149.
39. *The Dramatic Mirror*, 25 December, 1909, 15.
40. Ibid., 4 June, 1910, 16.
41. Brownlow, *War*, 330.
42. Lindsay, *Art*, 90–92.
43. Thomas, *Berkeley Barb*, 7–13 November, 1975, 13.
44. May, 81–82.
45. O'Dell, 13.
46. Gish, *Movies*, 158.
47. Klotman, 5.
48. Hirsch, 79.
49. Everson, 98.

50. Brownlow, *War*, 153.
51. Everson, 81.
52. Brownlow, *War*, 152.
53. *The Dramatic Mirror*, August, 1919.
54. Brownlow, *War*, 155.
55. *The New York Times*, 1 December, 1924.
56. *The New York Times*, 4 January, 1922.
57. Ibid.
58. *The New York World*, 22 February, 1924.
59. Healy, 166.
60. Ibid., 103.
61. Kracauer, 307.
62. Review, *The Dramatic Mirror*, 27 May, 1919.
63. Grob and Bilias, 74.
64. Ibid., 76–77.
65. Ibid., 92.
66. Ibid., 74.
67. Matthiessen, 131.
68. Everson, 158.
69. Klotman, 577.
70. *The New York Times*, 4 January, 1922.
71. Mast, 92.
72. Crawley, 102.
73. Collin, 183.
74. Whitman, 318.
75. Roger-Marx and Cotte, 83.
76. O'Dell, 92.

Bibliography

Newspapers and Periodicals

The Indianapolis Freeman, 1915–17.
The London Times, 1915–30.
The Los Angeles Times, 1910–32.
The Masses, 1914–17.
Motion Picture Classic, 1914–22.
Motion Picture Magazine, 1914–22.
The New York Dramatic Mirror, 1908–22.
The New York Evening Post, 1915–17.
The New York Journal American, 1914–26.
The New York Times, 1909–32.
The New York World, 1914–24.
Photoplay Magazine, 1914–34.
Picture Play, 1914–22.
The San Francisco Bulletin, 1914–20.
The San Francisco Call-Post, 1914–20.
The San Francisco Chronicle, 1911–31.
The San Francisco Examiner, 1912–30.
The San Jose Mercury-Herald, 1913–30.
The Theatre Magazine, 1913–30.

Books, Articles and Pamphlets

Agee, James. *Agee on Film:* Volume 1. New York: Grosset & Dunlap, 1958.
Allen, Gay Wilson. *The Solitary Singer: A Critical Biography of Walt Whitman*. New York: New York University Press, 1967.
————. *A Reader's Guide to Walt Whitman*. New York: Octagon Books. 1971.
Anderson, David D. *Woodrow Wilson*. Boston: G.K. Hall, 1978.
Anthony, Walter. Review of *Intolerance*. *The San Francisco Chronicle*, 10 October 1916.
Asquith, Lady Cynthia. *Diaries 1915–18*. New York: Alfred A. Knopf, 1969.
Axelrad, Allan M. *History and Utopia: A Study of the World View of James Fenimore Cooper*. Norwood, PA: Norwood Editions, 1978.
Balász, Béla. *Theory of the Film: Character and Growth of a New Art*. New York: Dover Publications, 1970.
Barna, Yon. *Eisenstein*. Bloomington: Indiana University Press, 1973.
Barry, Iris, and Eileen Bowser. *D.W. Griffith: American Film Master*. Garden City, NY: Doubleday, 1965.

Baudry, Pierre. "Les Adventures de l'Idée: *Intolerance.*" *Cahiers du Cinéma.* July–August, 1972 (No. 240), September–October, 1972 (No. 241).

Biograph Bulletins: 1908–1912. Ed. Eileen Bowser. New York: Farrar, Straus and Giroux, 1973.

Bitzer, Billy. *Billy Bitzer: His Story.* New York: Farrar, Straus and Giroux, 1973.

Blum, Daniel. *A Pictorial History of the Silent Screen.* New York: Grosset & Dunlap, 1953.

Bordwell, David. *The Films of Carl-Theodor Dreyer.* Berkeley: The University of California Press, 1981.

Bravermann, Barnet. "David Wark Griffith: Creator of Film Form." *Theater Arts* 29 (April 1945).

Broun, Heywood. Review of *Intolerance. The New York Tribune,* 7 September 1916.

Brown, David. *Walter Scott and the Historical Imagination.* London: Routledge & Kegan Paul, 1979.

Brown, Karl. *Adventures with D.W. Griffith.* New York: Farrar, Straus and Giroux, 1973.

Brownlow, Kevin. *The Parade's Gone By.* New York: Alfred A. Knopf, 1968.

————. *The War, the West, and the Wilderness.* New York: Alfred A. Knopf, 1979.

————, and John Kobal. *Hollywood: The Pioneers.* New York: Alfred A. Knopf, 1979.

Bryan, William Jennings, et al. *Republic or Empire? The Philippine Question.* Chicago: The Independence Company, 1899.

Cadbury, William, "Theme, Felt Life, and the Last-Minute Rescue in Griffith after *Intolerance.*" *Film Quarterly* 28, No. 1 (Fall 1974).

Carr, Harry. Review of *Intolerance. The Los Angeles Times,* 18 October 1916.

Collin, Richard H., ed. *Theodore Roosevelt and Reform Politics.* Lexington, MA: D.C. Heath and Company, 1972.

Cook, David A. *A History of Narrative Film.* New York: W.W. Norton, 1981.

Cook, Raymond A. *Thomas Dixon.* New York: Twayne Publishers, 1974.

Cooper, James Fenimore. *The Leatherstocking Tales.* 5 vols. Garden City, NY: Doubleday.

Cooper, Miriam, with Bonnie Herndon. *Dark Lady of the Silents.* Indianapolis: Bobbs-Merrill, 1973.

Crawley, Thomas Edward. *The Structure of* Leaves of Grass. Austin: University of Texas Press, 1970.

Davidson, Marshall B. *The Horizon Concise History of France.* New York: McGraw-Hill, 1971.

Dell, Floyd. Review of *Intolerance. The Masses* 9, no. 1, issue no. 65 (November 1916).

DeMille, Cecil B. *The Autobiography of Cecil B. DeMille.* Englewood Cliffs, NJ: Prentice-Hall, 1959.

Dettling, J. Ray. "Time Travel: The Ultimate Trip." *Science Digest* (September 1982).

Dickens, Charles. *Works.* New York: Dodd, Mead & Company.

Dickinson, Thorold. *A Discovery of Cinema.* London: Oxford University Press, 1971.

Dixon, Thomas, Jr. *The Clansman: An Historical Romance of the Ku Klux Klan.* Phoenix, AZ: Associated Professional Services, 1965.

Dorris, George E. "Griffith in Retrospect." In *Man and the Movies*, edited by W.R. Robinson. Baltimore: Penguin Books, 1967.

Dougherty, Raymond Philip. *Nabonidus and Belshazzar: A Study of the Closing Events of the Neo-Babylonian Empire*. New Haven, CT: Yale University Press, 1929.

Eastman, Max. *Love and Revolution: My Journey Through an Epoch*. New York: Random House, 1964.

Eisenstein, Sergei M. *Film Form*. London: Dennis Dobson, 1951.

Ekirch, Arthur A., Jr. *Progressivism in America: A Study of the Era from Theodore Roosevelt to Woodrow Wilson*. New York: New Viewpoints, 1974.

Ellis, Jack C. *A History of Film*. Englewood Cliffs, NJ: Prentice-Hall, 1979.

Everson, William K. *American Silent Film*. New York: Oxford University Press, 1978.

Fagan, Brian M. *Return to Babylon: Travelers, Archaeologists, and Monuments in Mesopotamia*. Boston: Little, Brown, 1979.

Films in Review: The David Wark Griffith Centennial Issue. Vol. 26, no. 8. (October 1975).

Fitzgerald, F. Scott. *This Side of Paradise*. New York: Charles Scribner's Sons, 1960.

Franklin, Joe. *Classics of the Silent Screen*. New York: Citadel Press, 1959.

Fulton, A.R. *Motion Pictures: The Development of an Art from Silent Films to the Age of Television*. Norman: The University of Oklahoma Press, 1960.

Geduld, Harry M., ed. *Focus on D.W. Griffith*. Englewood Cliffs, NJ: Prentice-Hall, 1970.

Gish, Lillian. *Dorothy and Lillian Gish*. New York: Charles Scribner's Sons, 1973.

————, with Ann Pinchot. *The Movies, Mr. Griffith and Me*. Englewood Cliffs, NJ: Prentice-Hall, 1969.

Goodman, Ezra. *The Fifty-Year Decline and Fall of Hollywood*. New York: Simon and Schuster, 1961.

Gordon, Henry Stephen. "The Story of David Wark Griffith." *Photoplay Magazine* (June–November 1916).

Griffith, D.W. *The Rise and Fall of Free Speech in America*. Hollywood: Larry Edmunds Book Shop, 1967.

————, and James Hart. *The Man Who Invented Hollywood*. Louisville, KY: Touchstone Publishing Company, 1972.

Griffith, Linda Arvidson. *When the Movies Were Young*. New York: Dover Publications, 1969.

Griffith, Richard, and Arthur Mayer. *The Movies*. New York: Simon and Schuster, 1957.

Grob, Gerald N., and George Athan Bilias., eds. *Interpretations of American History: Patterns and Perspectives*. V.1, *To 1877*. New York: Macmillan, 1967.

Guizot, M. *The History of France*, Volume III. Boston and New York: Fourth Estate Press.

Hanson, Bernard, "D.W. Griffith: Some Sources." *The Art Bulletin* 54, no. 4 (December 1972).

Harbaugh, William Henry. *The Life and Times of Theodore Roosevelt*. New York: Macmillan, 1966.

Haskell, Molly. *From Reverence to Rape: The Treatment of Women in the Movies*. New York: Holt, Rinehart and Winston, 1974.

Healy, David. *US Expansionism: The Imperialist Urge in the 1890s*. Madison: The University of Wisconsin Press, 1970.

Henderson, Robert M. *D.W. Griffith: The Years at Biograph.* New York: Farrar, Straus and Giroux, 1970.

_____. *D.W. Griffith: His Life and Work.* New York: Oxford University Press, 1972.

Herodutus. *The Histories.* Tr. Aubrey de Sélincourt. Suffolk: Penguin Books, 1980.

Hirsch, Foster. *The Hollywood Epic.* New York: A.S. Barnes, 1979.

Hofstadter, Richard, ed. *The Progressive Movement: 1900–1915.* Englewood Cliffs, NJ: Prentice-Hall, 1963.

Huff, Theodore. *A Shot Analysis of D.W. Griffith's* The Birth of a Nation. New York: The Museum of Modern Art, 1966.

_____. Intolerance: *The Film by David Wark Griffith: Shot-by-Shot Analysis.* New York: The Museum of Modern Art, 1966.

Jackson, Helen Hunt. *Ramona.* New York: Grosset and Dunlap.

Jacobs, Lewis. *The Rise of the American Film: A Critical History.* New York: Teachers College Press, 1967.

Jastrow, Morris, Jr. *Aspects of Religious Belief and Practice in Babylonia and Assyria.* New York: Benjamin Blom, 1971.

_____. *The Civilization of Babylonia and Assyria.* Philadelphia and London: J.B. Lippincott Company, 1915.

Jeffares, A. Norman, ed. *Scott's Mind and Art.* Edinburgh: Oliver and Boyd, 1969.

Johnson, Julian. "The Shadow Stage." *Photoplay Magazine* 2, no. 1 (December 1916).

Joseph, Gerhard. *Tennysonian Love: The Strange Diagonal.* Minneapolis: The University of Minnesota Press, 1969.

Kael, Pauline. "The Current Cinema." *The New Yorker* 44, no. 1 (24 February 1968).

Klotman, Phyllis Rauch. *Frame by Frame: A Black Filmography.* Bloomington: Indiana University Press, 1979.

Koenig, Louis W. *Bryan: A Political Biography of William Jennings Bryan.* New York: G.P. Putnam's Sons, 1971.

Kracauer, Siegfried. *Theory of Film: The Redemption of Physical Reality.* New York: Oxford University Press, 1965.

Lardeau, Yann. "Retrospective David Wark Griffith: King David." *Cahiers du Cinema* no. 346 (April 1983).

Layard, Sir Austen Henry. *Digging in Assyria.* Ed. Shirley Glubok. New York: Macmillan, 1970.

Lennig, Arthur. *The Silent Voice: A Text.* Troy, NY: Walter Snyder, 1969.

Leyda, Jay. *Kino: A History of the Russian and Soviet Film.* New York: Macmillan, 1960.

Lindsay, Vachel. *The Art of the Moving Picture.* New York: Liveright Publishing Corp., 1970.

_____. "Photoplay Progress." *The New Republic* 10, no. 120 (17 February 1917).

Loos, Anita. *A Girl Like I.* New York: The Viking Press, 1966.

Love, Bessie. *From Hollywood with Love.* London: Elm Tree Books, 1977.

Löwith, Karl. *Meaning in History.* Chicago: The University of Chicago Press, 1949.

Mast, Gerald. *A Short History of the Movies.* New York: Bobbs-Merrill, 1971.

Matthiessen, F.O. *Theodore Dreiser.* New York: William Sloane Associates, 1951.

May, Lary. *Screening Out the Past: The Birth of Mass Culture and the Motion Picture Industry.* New York: Oxford University Press, 1980.

Merritt, Russell. "Nickelodeon Theaters 1905–1914: Building an Audience for the Movies." In *The American Film Industry*, edited by Tino Balio. Madison: The University of Wisconsin Press, 1976.

————. "Rescued from a Perilous Nest: D.W. Griffith's Escape from Theatre into Film." *Cinema Journal* 21, no. 1 (Fall 1981).

Mitry, Jean. *Histoire du Cinéma: Art et Industrie*. Vol. 2, *1915–1925*. Paris: Editions Universitaires, 1969.

Moore, R. Laurence. "Flawed Fraternity—American Socialist Response to the Negro, 1901–1912." *The Historian* 32, no. 1 (November 1969).

Moses, Montrose J. In *The Cambridge History of American Literature*. Vol. 3, *Later National Literature: Parts II and III*. New York: Macmillan, 1933.

Mras, George P. *Eugene Delacroix's Theory of Art*. Princeton, NJ: Princeton University Press, 1966.

Nash, Alanna. "Remembering D.W. Griffith." *Take One* 4, no. 7 (December 1974).

Niver, Kemp R. *Motion Pictures from the Library of Congress Paper Print Collection, 1894–1912*. Berkeley: University of California Press, 1968.

————. *D.W. Griffith: His Biograph Films in Perspective*. Los Angeles: Historical Films, 1974.

Noguères, Henri. *The Massacre of Saint Bartholomew*. New York: Macmillan, 1961.

Norris, Frank. *The Octopus: A Story of California*. New York: The New American Library of World Literature, Inc., 1964.

————. *The Literary Criticism of Frank Norris*. Ed. Donald Pizer. Austin: University of Texas Press, 1964.

Oates, Joan. *Babylon*. London: Thames and Hudson, 1979.

O'Dell, Paul. *Griffith and the Rise of Hollywood*. New York: A.S. Barnes, 1970.

Paine, Albert Bigelow. *Life and Lillian Gish*. New York: Macmillan, 1932.

Petrie, Graham. "Dickens, Godard, and the Film Today." *The Yale Review* 64, no. 2 (December, 1974).

Pickford, Mary. *Sunshine and Shadow*. Garden City, NY: Doubleday, 1955.

Pratt, George C. *Spellbound in Darkness: A History of the Silent Film*. Greenwich, CT: New York Graphic Society, 1973.

Pritchard, James B., ed. *The Ancient Near East*. Vol. 2, *A New Anthology of Texts and Pictures*. Princeton, NJ: Princeton University Press, 1975.

Pudovkin, V.I. *Film Technique and Film Acting*. New York: Lear, 1954.

Ramsaye, Terry. *A Million and One Nights: A History of the Motion Picture*. New York: Simon and Schuster, 1964.

Richie, Donald, and Joseph L. Anderson. *The Japanese Film: Art and Industry*. Rutland, VT: Charles E. Tuttle, 1959.

Robinson, David. *Hollywood in the Twenties*. London: A. Zwemmer, 1968.

Rochester, Stuart I. *American Liberal Disillusionment in the Wake of World War I*. University Park and London: Pennsylvania State University Press, 1977.

Roger-Marx, Claude, and Sabine Cotte. *Delacroix: The Great Draughtsman*. New York: George Braziller, 1971.

Rogers, Robert William. *The Religion of Babylonia and Assyria Especially in Its Relations to Israel*. New York: Eaton & Mains, 1908.

Rosen, Marjorie. *Popcorn Venus*. New York: Avon Books, 1973.

Rosenberg, Bernard, and Harry Silverstein. *The Real Tinsel*. New York: Macmillan, 1970.

Sadoul, Georges. *Dictionary of Filmmakers*. Berkeley: The University of California Press, 1972.

_____. *Dictionary of Films*. Berkeley: The University of California Press, 1972.

The San Francisco Bulletin. Editorial on *Intolerance*. 19 October 1916.

Sandars, N.K. *The Epic of Gilgamesh*. Middlesex: Penguin Books, 1972.

Sarris, Andrew. Article on D.W. Griffith. *The New York Times*, 19 January 1975.

Sayce, Archibald Henry. *Lectures on the Origin and Growth of Religion as Illustrated by the Religion of the Ancient Babylonians*. London: Williams and Norgate, 1888.

Scott, David W., and E. John Bullard. *John Sloan 1871–1951: His Life and Paintings, His Graphics*. Boston: Boston Book & Art, 1971.

Scott, Sir Walter. *The Waverley Novels*. New York: P.F. Collier & Son.

Sellin, Thorsten, ed. *Capital Punishment*. New York: Harper & Row, 1967.

Silva, Fred, ed. *Focus on* The Birth of a Nation. Englewood Cliffs, NJ: Prentice-Hall, 1971.

Sklar, Robert. *Movie-Made America: A Cultural History of American Movies*. New York: Random House, 1975.

Slide, Anthony. *The Griffith Actresses*. New York: A.S. Barnes, 1973.

_____. Review of *The Struggle*. In *Magill's Survey of Cinema: English Language Films*. Vol. 4. Englewood Cliffs, NJ: Salem Press, 1980.

Smith, Frederick James. Review of *Intolerance*. *The New York Dramatic Mirror* 76, no. 1969 (16 September 1916).

_____. "Comment and Suggestion," "Motion Pictures." *The New York Dramatic Mirror* 76, no. 1970 (23 September 1916).

Solomon, Jon. *The Ancient World in the Cinema*. New York: A.S. Barnes, 1979.

Solomon, Stanley J., ed. *The Classic Cinema: Essays in Criticism*. New York: Harcourt Brace Jovanovich, 1973.

Soule, George. Review of *Intolerance*. *The New Republic* (30 September 1916).

Stern, Seymour. "An Index to the Creative Work of D.W. Griffith." *Index Series*. London: The British Film Institute, Nos. 2, 4, 7, 8, 10 (1944–47).

_____. "D.W. Griffith and the Movies." *The American Mercury* 68, no. 303 (March 1949).

_____. "*The Birth of a Nation*." *Film Culture*, no. 36 (Spring–Summer 1965).

Stevens, Ashton. Review of *Intolerance*. *The Chicago Examiner*, 3 December 1916.

Tennyson, Alfred, Lord. *The Works of Tennyson*. New York: Macmillan, 1932.

Thomas, J.N. "D.W. Griffith Rediscovered." *The Berkeley Barb*, issue no. 534 (7–13 November 1975).

Tucker, Jean E. "Voices from the Silents." *The Quarterly Journal of the Library of Congress* 37, nos. 3–4 (Summer–Fall 1980).

Vardac, A. Nicholas. *Stage to Screen: Theatrical Method from Garrick to Griffith*. Cambridge: Harvard University Press, 1949.

Vidor, King. *A Tree is a Tree*. New York: Harcourt, Brace, 1953.

_____. *King Vidor on Filmmaking*. New York: David McKay, 1972.

Wagenknecht, Edward. *The Movies in the Age of Innocence*. Norman: The University of Oklahoma Press, 1962.

_____, and Anthony Slide. *The Films of D.W. Griffith*. New York: Crown, 1975.

Walworth, Arthur. *Woodrow Wilson*. Vol. 1: *American Prophet*, Vol. 2: *World Prophet*. New York: Longmans, Green and Company, 1958.

Wells, H.G. *The War of the Worlds, The Time Machine, and Selected Short Stories*. New York: Platt & Munk, 1963.

White, William Allen. *The Autobiography of William Allen White.* New York: Macmillan, 1946.

Whitman, Walt. *The Complete Poetry and Prose of Walt Whitman.* Garden City, NY: Garden City Books, 1954.

Williams, Martin. *Griffith: First Artist of the Movies.* New York: Oxford University Press, 1980.

Wilson, Woodrow. *The Papers of Woodrow Wilson.* Vol. 32, *January 1–April 16, 1915.* Vol. 34, *July 21–September 30, 1915.* Princeton, NJ: Princeton University Press, 1980.

Woollcott, Alexander. "Second Thoughts on First Nights." *The New York Times*, 10 September 1916.

Zimmerman, Paul D. "Griffith: Film's Old Master." *Newsweek* 77, no. 10 (8 March 1971).

Index

191

Hicksville Public Library
169 Jerusalem Avenue
Hicksville, New York
Telephone Wells 1-1417

Please Do Not Remove
Card From Pocket

HI